ORDNANCE SURVEY
Illustrated
ATLAS
of
VICTORIAN & EDWARDIAN
BRITAIN

AA | OS

ORDNANCE SURVEY
Illustrated
ATLAS
of
VICTORIAN & EDWARDIAN
BRITAIN

Produced by The Automobile Association
Fanum House, Basingstoke, Hampshire RG21 2EA

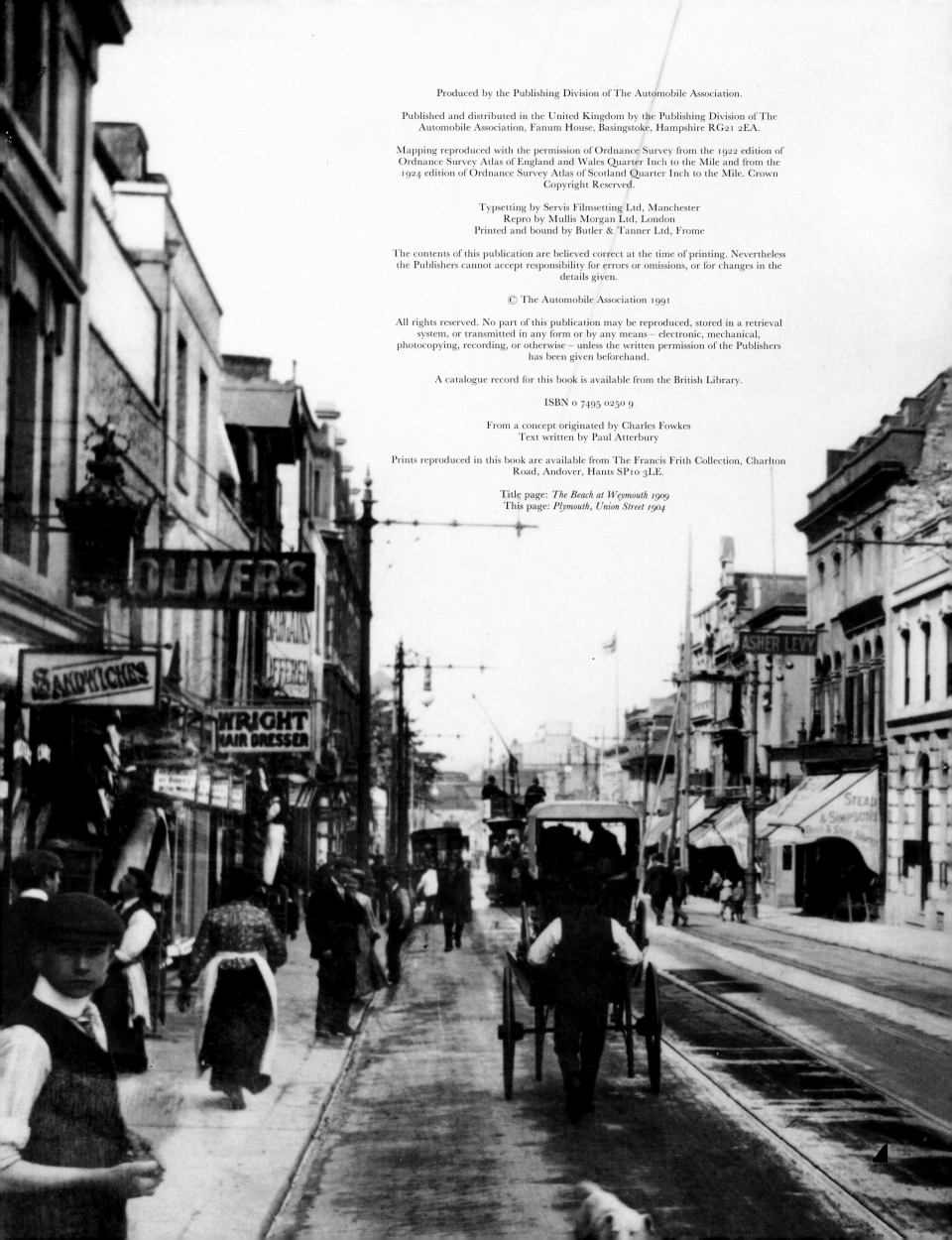

Produced by the Publishing Division of The Automobile Association.

Published and distributed in the United Kingdom by the Publishing Division of The Automobile Association, Fanum House, Basingstoke, Hampshire RG21 2EA.

Mapping reproduced with the permission of Ordnance Survey from the 1922 edition of Ordnance Survey Atlas of England and Wales Quarter Inch to the Mile and from the 1924 edition of Ordnance Survey Atlas of Scotland Quarter Inch to the Mile. Crown Copyright Reserved.

Typsetting by Servis Filmsetting Ltd, Manchester
Repro by Mullis Morgan Ltd, London
Printed and bound by Butler & Tanner Ltd, Frome

From a concept originated by Charles Fowkes
Text written by Paul Atterbury

Prints reproduced in this book are available from The Francis Frith Collection, Charlton Road, Andover, Hants SP10 3LE.

Title page: *The Beach at Weymouth 1909*
This page: *Plymouth, Union Street 1904*

TWO HUNDRED YEARS OF ORDNANCE SURVEY

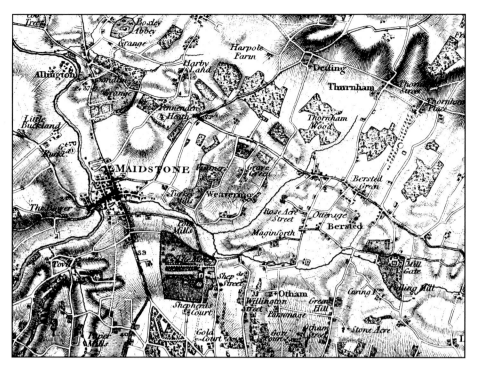

ORDNANCE SURVEY takes its name from the Board of Ordnance which, in the late 18th century, was the department of state responsible for the defence of the realm. In 1791 the Board initiated a national mapping programme although the need for this was recognised much earlier; indeed the formation of Ordnance Survey owes a great deal to the advocacy of Major-General William Roy. He was a renowned surveyor, engineer and archaeologist who, as a young man, was responsible for the production of a military map of Scotland. This map was a consequence of the Jacobite Rebellion in 1745 when Charles Stuart (Bonnie Prince Charlie) was defeated at the Battle of Culloden. In 'pacifying the Highlands', as the victorious Duke of Cumberland described it, the inadequacies of the mapping then available to the army were glaringly obvious. Roy's map (at a scale of one inch to 1,000 yards) clearly showed routes of communication and the necessary details of the terrain. It is now held in the British Library.

In 1791 the French were threatening to invade Britain. The British Army needed detailed, accurate mapping of the south coast of England at a scale of one inch to one mile; the Board of Ordnance undertook the survey and so Ordnance Survey was born. The threat of invasion receded but it became apparent that there were a number of civilian uses for the mapping. The Industrial Revolution was underway and as towns and communication networks expanded rapidly politicians, administrators, planners and industrialists quickly recognised the value of accurate mapping. Gradually the survey was extended to cover other areas of the country and further surveys were also undertaken at a scale of six inches to one mile in order to provide information of even greater detail. There were scientific projects too and so, by the mid 19th century, Ordnance Survey had assumed its modern role as provider of a national survey for scientific, military, government and public use. The authority for many of its activities is the Ordnance Survey Act of 1841.

As urban and industrial development continued, the demand for more detailed large-scale maps increased. The one-inch map was not suitable for the detailed requirements of the tithe surveys, nor for engineers laying out routes of new railways, nor for defining the exact position of boundaries. Indeed, the six-inch map was inadequate for use in the implementation of sanitary reform, land registration and Poor Law legislation. The survey of London, begun in 1848 to meet the needs of this legislation, was in fact carried out at a scale of sixty inches to one mile.

The controversy surrounding the selection of the most appropriate scales of mapping to be adopted by the Ordnance Survey (known as 'The Battle of

An extract from the first Ordnance Survey one-inch map of Kent, published in 1801.

An extract from the Ordnance Survey one-inch New Series, published from 1872.

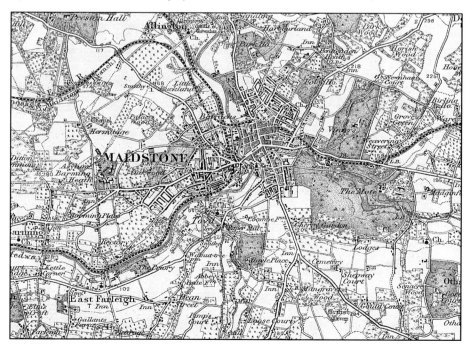

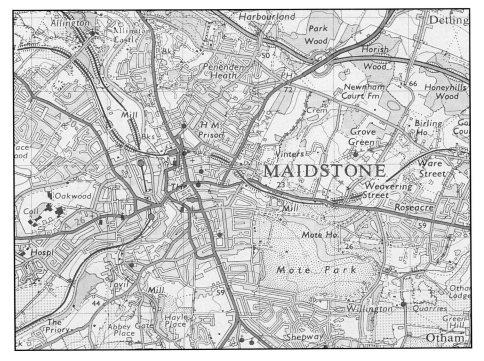

An extract from the Ordnance Survey 1:50 000 First Series, published from 1974.

An extract from the Ordnance Survey Motoring Atlas 1991, graphic output from 1:250 000 digital map data.

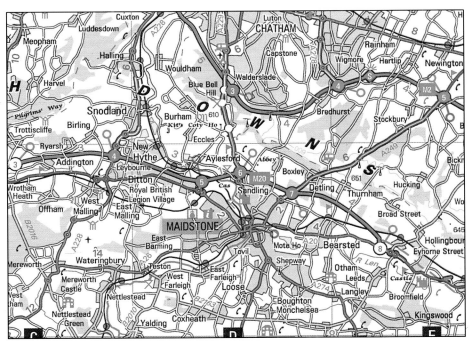

the Scales') continued until 1863. It was then decided to adopt the one-inch scale for a general topographical map series of the whole country, the six-inch scale for mountainous and moorland areas, a twenty-five inches to one mile map series for cultivated areas, and large-scale mapping of ten feet to one mile for built-up areas with a population of 4,000 or more.

In the latter half of the 19th century, smaller-scale maps were produced from the more detailed, larger-scale maps. These included a series of maps at a scale of four miles to one inch (1:250 000). Work for this national series, which ran to a total of forty two sheets, began in 1859 and was completed in 1888. By 1912 a second edition incorporating new sheet lines had been launched and in the next decade a third series was begun, specifically designed with the motorist in mind. The twenty one sheets contained Ministry of Transport road numbers and also directions at sheet edges. It is this

third series that has been used as the basis for the Atlas reproduced in this publication.

By the end of the 19th century much of the mapping – especially of urban areas – was out of date and the problem of revision had to be addressed. The Dorrington Committee was accordingly set up in 1892 and recommended a cyclic revision system for the one-inch series.

The Depression after World War I ensured that economies in map production were imperative and so cutbacks were necessary. These cuts unfortunately coincided with a new wave of social legislation including land registration (1925), town planning (1925), land drainage (1926), slum clearance (1930) and land valuation (1931), all of which required accurate mapping. By the early 1930s it became clear that Ordnance Survey had been left ill-equipped to supply sufficiently accurate and up-to-date maps. A Departmental Committee under the chairmanship of Sir JC (later Lord) Davidson was therefore set up in 1934 to consider how to restore the effectiveness of the national survey.

Although published in 1938, the Davidson report could not be implemented until after World War II. Nevertheless, it formed the operational framework for today's Ordnance Survey. The major recommendations of the Davidson Report included the introduction of a metric National Grid as a reference system for all large- and small-scale maps; the recasting of the twenty-five inches to one mile (1:2 500) scale map series on national instead of individual county lines; the introduction of a system of continuous revision for large-scale maps; and the testing of a fifty inches to one mile (1:1 250) scale survey for densely populated urban areas.

Today, Ordnance Survey is a government agency with its headquarters in Southampton and a network of small local survey offices throughout the country. The main tasks identified by the Davidson Report and initiated after World War II, as well as the conversion from imperial to metric scale, begun in 1969, have all been completed. The emphasis now is on the revision and maintenance of this huge archive of survey information, to keep it up-to-date and to meet customer needs. New technology has been harnessed to positive effect in many areas of production; large-scale maps at 1:1 250 and 1:2 500 scales are now produced using automated cartographic techniques and the projected date for completion of a digital database of the whole country at these scales is now the year 2000. Digital databases of smaller-scale mapping for the whole country are already available.

Ordnance Survey mapping at four miles to one inch (1:250 000), first published in the Victorian age to the specification reproduced in this atlas, has developed through the years to meet users' changing requirements and is even now being adapted to meet the needs of the 21st century.

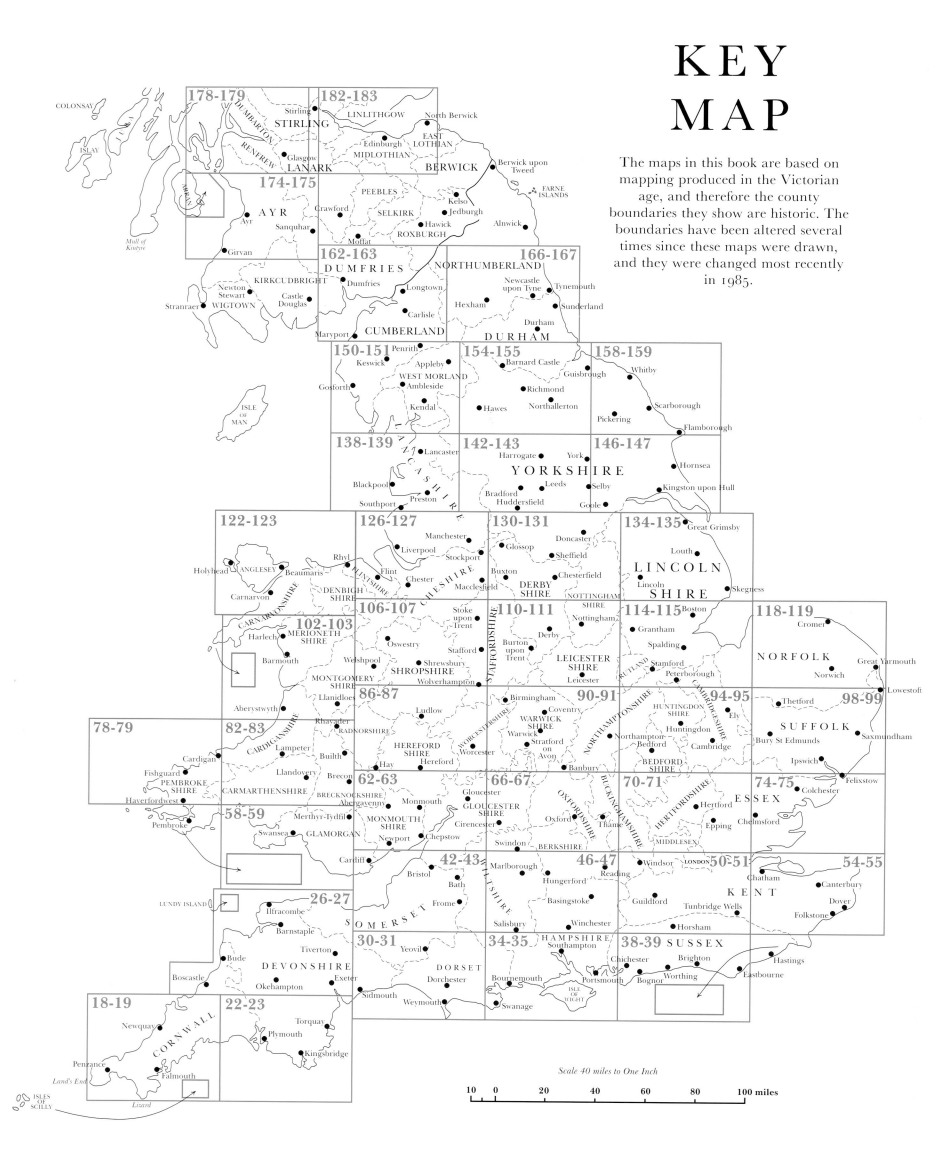

KEY MAP

The maps in this book are based on mapping produced in the Victorian age, and therefore the county boundaries they show are historic. The boundaries have been altered several times since these maps were drawn, and they were changed most recently in 1985.

Scale 40 miles to One Inch

10 0   20   40   60   80   100 miles

CONTENTS

THE

FRANCIS FRITH

COLLECTION

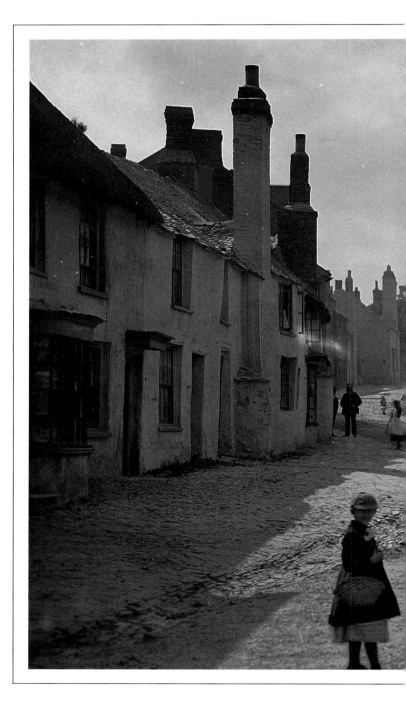

IN 1860 FRANCIS FRITH set out to make a photographic record of the whole of the British Isles, a gargantuan task that was to keep him and his assistants fully occupied for many decades. When Frith died in 1897 the task was far from complete, but what he had achieved in the intervening thirty seven years was a remarkable record of late Victorian Britain – a kind of visual Domesday Book that documents many aspects of Britain and the British at a time of dramatic social and economic change.

So ambitious a project reveals much about the character of Francis Frith and the age in which he lived. Independent, strong-willed, morally secure and supremely confident in his determination to succeed, Frith was every inch the Victorian entrepreneur, the self-made man whose success was based on enterprise and hard work. Born in 1822, he was the only son of a Derbyshire Quaker family. His father, a successful cooper, instilled in his son the conventional Victorian virtues, with the additional support of a strong religious faith that was to stay with Francis throughout his life. A childhood spent in Chesterfield was followed by education at a Quaker school in Birmingham, and at the age of sixteen Francis was apprenticed to a local manufacturer, his family having moved to Birmingham in the meantime. Despite finding his work unrewarding, he completed the apprenticeship in 1843, having developed in his spare time interests in art and science. Two years later he moved to Liverpool to start, with a partner, a wholesale grocery business. This grew rapidly over the next six years in that expanding city, giving Francis his first taste of wealth and success. In 1851 he sold his share, and used the money to start a printing business. This enjoyed even greater success, rising quickly to become one of the two leading printing firms in Liverpool, with a turnover of £200,000 per year. In 1856 he sold out again and found himself, at the age of thirty four, a gentleman of leisure with time and money to spare. However, this role was to be short-lived, for Francis Frith had already planned his next venture.

Interested in the new science of photography at least since the mid 1840s, Frith had been a founder member of the Liverpool Photographic Society in 1853, and had exhibited his work on a number of occasions. Of particular interest were the links between photography and printing, and he had kept abreast of the latest developments in photogravure and photomechanical reproduction, pioneered from 1850 by Firmin Gillot in France and William Fox-Talbot in England. He had certainly been aware of the setting up by Paul Pretsch in 1854 of Britain's first photomechanical press. As a practising photographer, Frith had firm views about the status of this new technology, regarding it

as an art. At the same time, he was greatly attracted by its commercial implications, and it was this above all that decided him to sell his printing business and devote himself to the pursuit of photography.

At this point, practical photography was still less than twenty years old, experiments in several countries having come to a head in 1839 with three related but independent developments. In that year Louis Daguerre produced a permanent photographic image via the light-sensitive qualities of silver iodide, Fox-Talbot developed the calotype process which involved the printing of a photographic negative on to sensitised paper and the astronomer Sir John Herschel demonstrated the technique of exposing an image on to a glass plate treated with silver carbonate. When brought together the discoveries made by Fox-Talbot and Herschel resulted in the wet collodion process, the quickest and most efficient form of photography yet known, and the basis upon which most subsequent

INSTOW, NORTHAM VILLAGE 1900
There can be few better illustrations of the Frith style of photographic composition than this view of a north Devon village at the turn of the century. What is apparently a carelessly captured moment in time on a quiet summer's day is actually a masterly exercise in structure, with every element carefully arranged by the photographer. At the same time, it is a record of the particular qualities of English village life that were about to be changed for ever by the motor car.

developments have been built. In this, a glass plate covered with a chemical preparation was exposed to light while still wet, and then quickly developed and fixed in a darkroom, a method that allowed photographs to be taken in minutes. Hitherto, exposures of an hour or more had been commonplace.

It was this new method that Francis Frith used, and its speed made his ambitious schemes a practicality. At the same time, it was still a very demanding technique, for cameras were large and cumbersome and a photographer had to travel with a fully-equipped mobile darkroom in which the wet plates could first be prepared, and then developed after exposure. Piles of brass- and leather-bound mahogany cases were the natural impediments of any travelling photographer in the mid-Victorian period, some of which required two men to carry them. Despite these physical difficulties, photography developed at an astonishing rate during this period, and its potential was quickly grasped by scientists, artists, journalists, travellers and the general public, the last-named keen to enjoy the accurate images of people and scenes that could be purchased relatively cheaply.

Of particular interest at this time were photographs taken by visitors to hitherto inaccessible, and thus unknown, countries and continents, many of which were now being published in book form. These illustrated visions of other worlds played an important role in fostering the growth of popular tourism, and were studied with enthusiasm by both armchair and actual travellers. Here was a field that would combine Frith's interest in photography with his sound commercial sense, and so he decided to make a photographic tour of Egypt and the Holy Land, a decision in which his religious convictions also played a part. Over the next four years he was to make three trips to Egypt, Palestine and Syria, visits that were followed by exhibitions, lectures and the publication of his first book, *Egypt and Palestine Photographed and Described*, which was issued in twenty five parts at ten shillings each. The success of this book confirmed his belief in the commercial potential of photography.

Having experienced the extreme difficulties and torturous conditions faced by the travelling photographer, Frith now turned his attentions nearer to home. In 1860 he married, and settled with his wife in Reigate, in Surrey, where he was to remain for the rest of his life. Over the next few years the couple were to have eight children, and Frith entered with vigour into another new role, that of the Victorian paterfamilias. Devoted to his family, he now concentrated on his photographic record of the British Isles, beginning the pattern of continuous travel that was to be the characteristic feature of the rest of his life. Frequently he took his family with him on his photographic tours and so the Frith

THE WISHING WELL 1909 A quiet Surrey lane in summer, with a thatched cottage, bosky hedgerows, the old well and the little girl – all in white – who is opening the gate, captures completely the sentimental vision of rural England so popular with photographers and painters at the end of the Victorian period.

party, with its domestic servants, assistants and piles of baggage, became a familiar spectacle on the railway stations of Britain. The new railway network, which continued to expand throughout the latter part of the 19th century, was the vital key in his plans, and by the 1880s the combination of the train and local horse-drawn transport had opened up practically every corner of England and Wales.

Initially Frith concentrated on the proven book market and his British publications include *The Book of the Thames* and *Dovedale*. However, he was quick to realise that this market was limited both by expense and exclusivity. His real ambition was to reach the far wider and more popular market that was directly dependent upon the growth in tourism and travel. This was the period when the foundations of modern patterns of leisure and holidays were being laid down, inspired both by Acts of Parliament and changes in commercial and industrial practice. Helped by the railways and the burgeoning new seaside and inland resorts, tourism

AYSGARTH FALLS 1889
The discovery and appreciation of the wilder parts of Britain's landscape was a phenomenon of the late Victorian period, with travel made easier by the railway network and the increase in leisure time. Particularly popular was North Yorkshire, with its dramatic coastline, hill and moorland scenery and the river valleys of the Dales. Typical was Aysgarth in Wensleydale, where the Ure tumbles down a series of rock steps.

was fast becoming a regular part of the British way of life. Manufacturers in many fields had been quick to realise that tourists want souvenirs, and it was this market that Frith was keen to exploit. He was certain that visitors would prefer to take home a photograph rather than the traditional engravings, and so he trained a team of assistants and set up a network of sales representatives to sell Frith's Souvenir Views. By the end of the century his photographs were being sold in 2,000 shops all over Britain. The success of this venture brought him a second fortune, which was augmented by commissions and studio work, framing services and even lessons in photography, but most significant of all was Frith's role in the development of the picture postcard.

In 1870 the Post Office had introduced the plain postcard which could be sent at half the letter rate, and this was an immediate success despite considerable limitations affecting any message. Non-official cards were charged at the full rate, while picture cards had to be virtually message-free, for nothing other than the address was permitted on the address side. Frith's photographs, with or without a message, had, therefore, to be sent in an envelope, at the full rate. These restrictions did not seriously limit the growth of business but it did mean that the picture postcard could not exist in its present form until 1897, when all limitations were finally removed. From that date the picture postcard became a major business, and a universally popular hobby, with Francis Frith's photographs making a significant contribution. Frith himself lived just long enough to see this part of his ambition fulfilled, even though his photographic coverage of the British Isles was still far from complete.

After his death in 1898 two of his sons continued to run the business and his trained assistants maintained the Frith tradition, covering new areas and re-photographing those that needed bringing up to date. By this time the technology of photography was constantly changing. Roll and sheet film negatives were gradually replacing the original collodion process and exposures were now a matter of seconds. Development, processing and printing no longer had to be immediate, and so the portable darkroom became a thing of the past. As a result, the photographer was better able to record rather than arrange actuality. In the 1860s Francis Frith had generally had to work with a forty-second exposure, and with far longer ones for interior shots. Long exposures encouraged the taking of care and time with the composition and every effort was made to ensure that the printed result underlined photography's status as an art form. Particularly striking in this respect is the way Frith controlled the placing of the people in his photographs, with carefully arranged groups of individuals balancing the composition and generally all facing the camera. The blur of accidental movement does

occur, especially in busy street scenes, but Frith obviously went to great lengths to construct and control the image. From the 1860s he travelled regularly the length and breadth of Britain, and made a number of visits to the continent, photographic forays on which he was frequently accompanied by his assistants and his family. It is therefore not surprising that he often used them as models, relying on their experience to guide the local inhabitants in the art of posing for the camera. The results are often dramatic and intimate, with the carefully arranged figures maintaining the illusion of a moment frozen in time, when the reality must sometimes have meant hours of careful preparation.

Frith was particularly masterly in his use of children, both his own and other people's found on the scene, exploiting the kind of sentimentality that

appealed to a number of Victorian photographers, such as Lewis Carroll, as well as to the public as a whole. At the same time, Frith's images have a powerful sense of reality, and they are full of reminders of the major social and economic changes underway at the end of the 19th century.

Later, after his death, and even more so after World War I when most of the assistants actually trained by Frith were no longer active, attitudes changed. The photographer became a recorder of actuality rather than an artist, with less emphasis given to composition and the arrangement of the components of the scene. Effects were achieved increasingly in the darkroom, often by retouching. Despite these changes, Frith's photographic views and postcards maintained their popularity through a period of steadily increasing leisure, and the company remained in business until 1971.

However, it is Francis Frith the photographer of Victorian life that is primarily remembered today. There is no doubt that the heyday of his business was during his lifetime, in the last decades of the Victorian era, and in the Edwardian years that preceded World War I, when his influence was still dominant, and the 60,000 glass negatives that survive from this time are his most valuable legacy. It is from this library that the images included in this book have been selected, and the aim has been to give an insight today into the vision of England and Wales in the 19th and early 20th centuries so faithfully recorded by Francis Frith and his assistants. Linked to Ordnance Survey maps of a similar period, this survey explores in detail many aspects of the agricultural, rural, urban industrial, commercial and domestic life of the time, from the western tip of Cornwall to the Scottish Borders.

DANCING BEAR 1895
Frith's photographs are, above all, records of social change and none more so than the views of street life. In a period when horses, trams and bicycles were dominant, and electric lighting still quite rare, street life was very different, and more leisurely than today. A group of photographs depict street sellers and performers, the most unusual of which is this view of a dancing bear with its bugler attendant in a suburban road in south London. Commonplace enough at the time to arouse only limited attention from passers-by, this is a vision of Victorian life that has, quite rightly, been consigned to the history books.

15

Traditional crafts, customs and industries are shown, but what is particularly striking are the social changes that were affecting all classes of society at the turn of the century. Much is revealed by the photographs, notably the emergence of the modern leisure industry and other elements that were to dominate life in Britain in the later decades of the 20th century.

The Selection

The principles of selection have been to give the broadest possible view of each region, with a careful balance between images of town and country, and industry and leisure. Naturally there are gaps, but these are generally gaps left by Frith himself. His personal view of Britain led him to record some areas in great detail while ignoring others completely, and the selection in this book has had to follow

MORECAMBE ESPLANADE 1899
One of the major developments of the Victorian period was the seaside holiday, and the astonishing popularity of this new form of entertainment can be seen in this view of a famous Lancashire resort. Until the railway arrived in 1848, Morecambe was little more than a fishing village, but its rapid growth over the next fifty years is reflected by this view of the town, with its hotels, horse-drawn trams, piers and beaches, and esplanade thronged with smartly-dressed visitors.

in his footsteps. Each region included, defined by the related section of map, has a short introduction that discusses a particular feature of Victorian life relevant to that region. The photographs that follow the map pages in each section have been described in detail, to underline changes that have taken place in the century or so since they were taken.

Today, the primary appeal of Frith's vision of Britain, buried beneath a hundred years of change, may seem to be nostalgic. However, it is important to look beyond the surface, to see Frith's breadth of vision and his remarkable eye for detail in order to appreciate to the full this unique visual and documentary record of Britain in the Victorian and Edwardian eras.

LOOE HARBOUR 1912
Edwardian Looe still boasted a busy harbour filled with fishing boats and coastal trading vessels, many of which were kept employed by the coal trade. At the same time, the increasing popularity of Cornwall was giving these little towns a new lease of life. New villas can be seen spreading up the hills that surround the harbour, artists are at work recording the scene and, in the foreground, a young visitor is enjoying the bustle and activity.

THE GRAND PUMP ROOM, BATH 1901
Though a much quieter, more genteel town than in the heady days of 'Beau' Nash, Bath was still a popular centre for visitors at the turn of the century. This timeless view of the majestic Pump Room, deserted except for one shadowy figure, is one of the few interior photographs in Frith's collection. At the time this photograph was taken visitors could still bathe in the Roman baths next door.

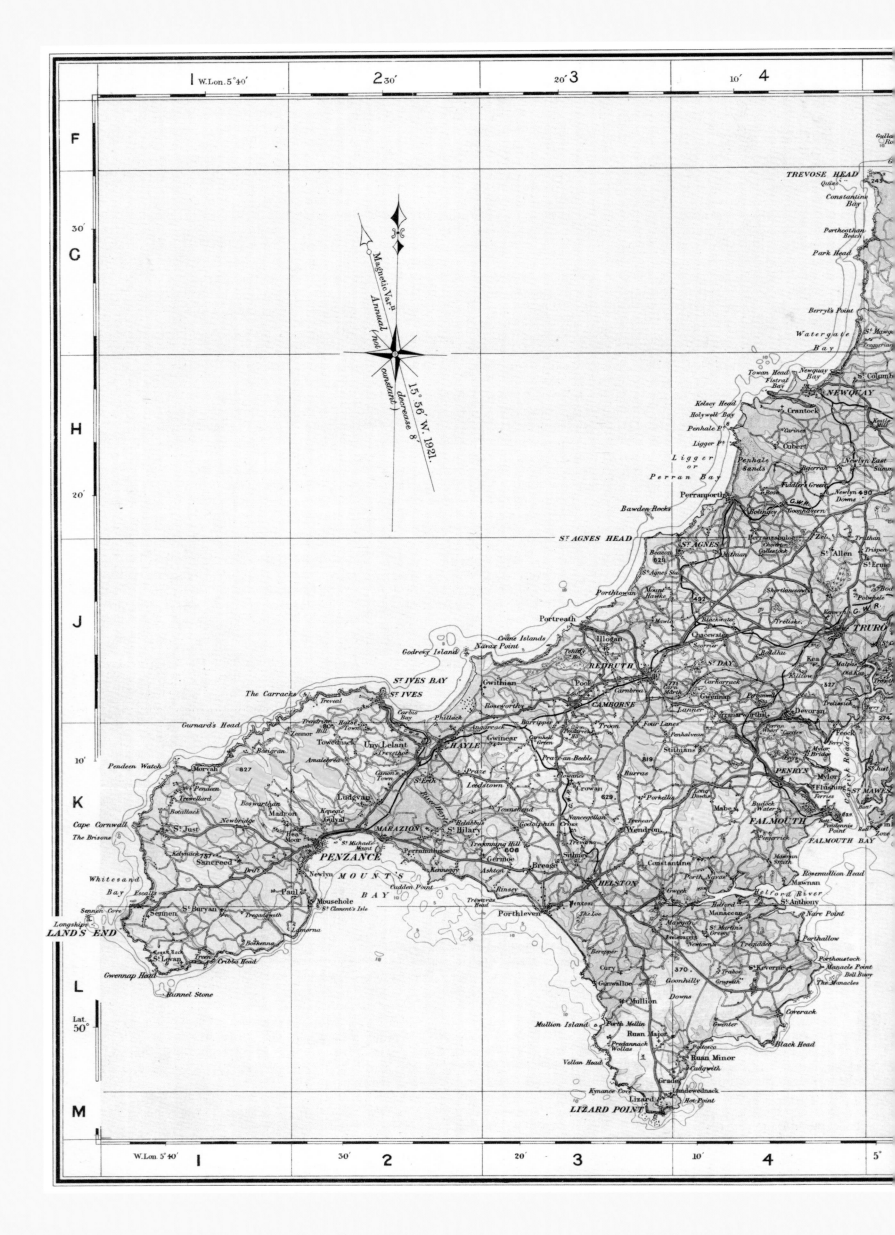

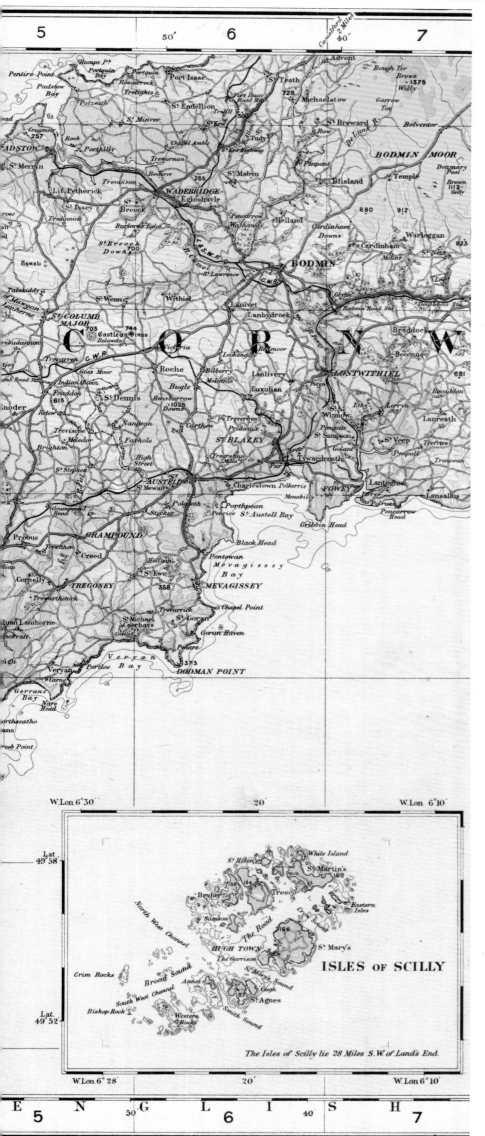

VICTORIAN CORNWALL WAS very different from the county so popular with holiday-makers today. The region's landscape, coastline, history and traditions were naturally those which attract so many visitors a century later, but in the 19th century these were overshadowed by industry. In the context of Cornwall today, industry to most people will mean fishing, agriculture in the form of spring vegetables and flowers, and tourism. Fishing and agriculture were certainly a major part of the economy of Victorian Cornwall, but far more significant were the heavy industries of engineering and mining.

Cornwall's huge deposits of tin and copper had been exploited since Roman times, but it was in the late 18th century that the extraction and smelting of these metals became a major industry, bringing untold wealth into the region and turning Cornwall into one of the most inventive cradles of Britain's Industrial Revolution. Steam engines and railways were pioneered in the county, developments related directly to the needs of the mining industry, and by the middle of the 19th century up to 1,000 massive beam engines were in use, pumping water from mines driven up to 3,000 feet below ground, and powering machinery for crushing and refining the ore. Many of these machines were made locally, and the name of Harvey's of Hayle became famous in mines all over the world.

The tin and copper mines were at their most productive in the early Victorian period, when over 30,000 people were employed in the industry. From then on the discovery of huge deposits in South America, Australia and Malaya gradually drove the Cornish mines out of business, causing thousands of miners to emigrate. In 1870 300 mines were still in operation, but most of these had closed by World War I. The legacy of this massive industry can be seen in the old engine-houses and mining debris that litter the landscape of west and north Cornwall and in the old ports and former industrial towns, much of which has now been given by time a kind of romantic appeal that actually draws visitors to the county. Indeed, it was the collapse of the mining industry that prompted Victorian railway companies to develop the Cornish holiday business.

Cornwall's other major industry in the 19th century was the china clay trade. The huge china clay deposits in the granite uplands north of St Austell were first exploited commercially at the end of the 18th century and then grew progressively through the Victorian period, prompting the development of ports such as Par, Fowey and Charlestown from which the fine clay was shipped all over the world. Unlike the metal mines, this industry has continued to flourish and expand.

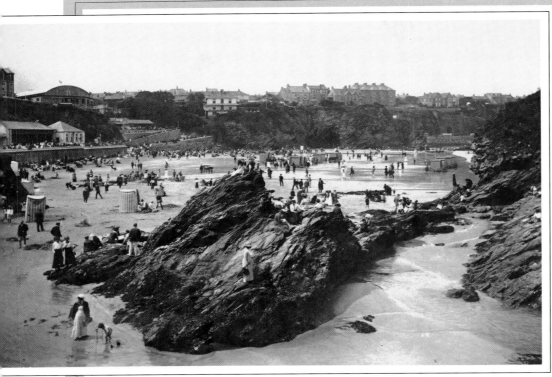

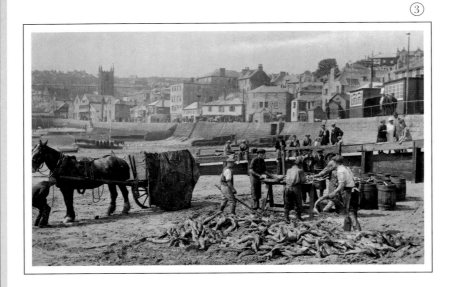

⑤

⑥

1 NEWQUAY *Towan Beach 1912*
The development of Cornwall's coastal resorts was a Victorian phenomenon, helped both by the expanding railway network and the increased leisure time. That the holiday habit was well established can be seen in this view of Newquay's fine beach, crowded with private tents, bathing-machines and smartly-dressed holiday-makers.

2 HELSTON *Meneage Street 1913*
This market town was popular with visitors who used it as a convenient base for visits to the Lizard, the port of Porthleven and the Helford River. Fashionable shops and street lighting show how Cornwall benefited directly from tourism.

3 ST IVES HARBOUR
Cleaning Fish c.1910
In the early years of this century fishing was still the staple industry in small ports like St Ives, with much of the catch being sent to London and other cities by special trains. At the same time, St Ives was one of the first of the pictur-esque ports to develop its tourist industry, helped by its reputation as an artists' colony which had been established in the Victorian era by painters from Newlyn.

**4 CHARLESTOWN
HARBOUR** *St Austell 1912*
Completed in 1801 to the designs of the engineer John Rennie, Charlestown harbour was built specifically for the import of coal and the export of china clay from the newly-developed quarries around St Austell. Busy through-out the 19th century, the little

harbour cut into the steep cliffs was also popular with visitors who came to watch the trading schooners loading and unloading.

5 CARN BRAE *Redruth 1906*
The capital of the Cornish mining industry, Redruth was hardly a tourist centre in the Victorian era. Yet, even in those days, the great rocky hill of Carn Brae which dominates the town attracted visit-ors as it does today.

6 LOSTWITHIEL
The Restormel Road 1906
Away from the popular coastal resorts and the mining regions, Victorian Cornwall had a rural tranquillity unchanged for cent-uries. Typical is this view of the road north from Lostwithiel to the ruined Norman castle at Restormel, overlooking the Fowey.

BOATING AND SAILING

were, in the Victorian period, an even greater feature of east Cornwall and south Devon than today, and the progressive development of the rivers of the region for leisure purposes was a contemporary phenomenon. The main impetus came from the railway companies, eager to capture a share of the new holiday business, and during this period branch lines were opened to existing ports and potential resorts such as Looe, Salcombe, Kingswear (for Dartmouth), Brixham, Torquay and Exmouth. Much of the expanding railway network either followed or made accessible the famous boating rivers that drew visitors to the region – the Tamar and the Tavy, the Yealm, the Kingsbridge estuary, the Dart and the Teign.

By the end of the 19th century pleasure craft had begun to dominate these waters, but Victorian visitors would still have seen plenty of commercial traffic on the rivers and estuaries. Inland towns such as Calstock, Kingsbridge, Totnes and Newton Abbot still had active ports that were visited by coastal trading schooners carrying a wide range of industrial, agricultural and domestic cargoes. Even the inland town of Liskeard had for years been connected to the sea at Looe by a small canal, but this was closed by the building of the railway. At this time many different craft were to be seen on the rivers and in the ports of the region: Plymouth Sound was always busy with naval traffic sailing to and from the dockyards at Devonport, and training vessels were regular visitors to the Dart. Also widespread were the fishing boats, and notably the fleets of distinctive sailing trawlers based at Brixham.

Today, the rivers of south Devon are a mecca for sailing and pleasure-boating, and even in the Victorian period these waters were popular among both British and European holiday-makers. The Dartmouth regatta was already a well-established event in the annual sailing calendar, and many local fishermen were finding it as profitable during the season to take visitors for trips as to go fishing. In the high summer the upper reaches of the main rivers were crowded with sailing dinghies, skiffs, canoes and steam launches, and through the middle of this busy traffic the ferries and pleasure steamers plied to and fro. There were regular services up the Tamar and Tavy from Plymouth, along the Dart and the Teign, as well as between ports and resorts along the coast. In the Edwardian era Torquay was one of the West's most fashionable resorts, and an essential component of every holiday were the healthy steamer trips across Babbacombe and Tor Bays, and round Berry Head and Start Point to Salcombe.

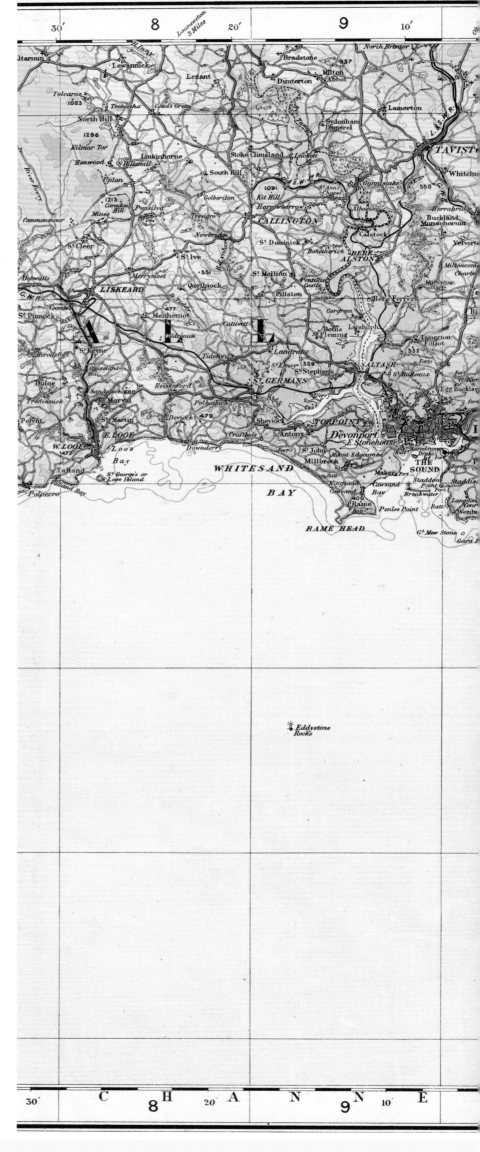

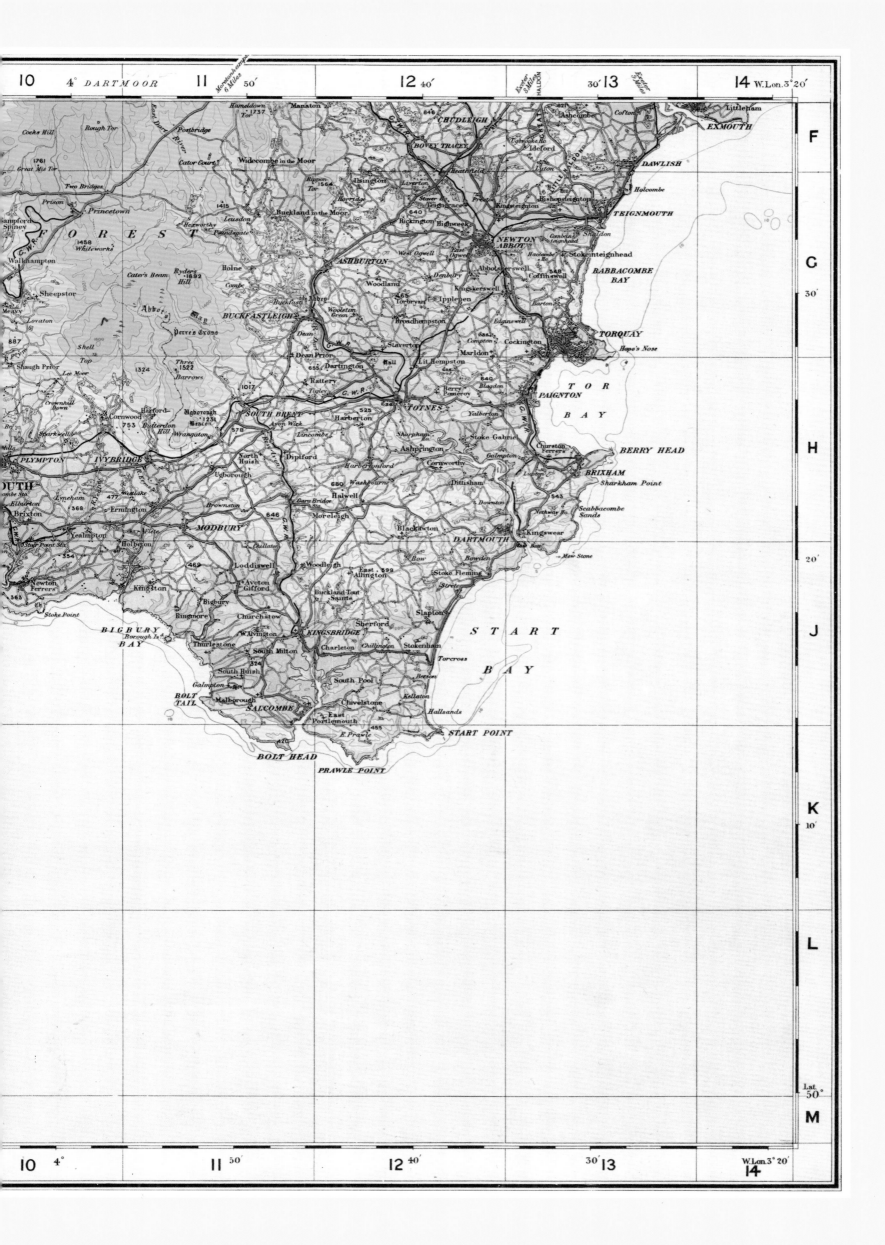

1 PLYMOUTH *Union Street 1904*
Long established as a major naval town with a busy harbour, Plymouth grew rapidly during the 19th century to become the major shopping centre and market for much of south Devon. This view shows the wide range of shops available by the turn of the century.

2 TAVISTOCK
Abbey and Guildhall 1893
Tavistock's handsome main square, laid out by the Dukes of Bedford, owners of the town until 1911, was a Victorian creation. The decorative Gothic style of the 1848 guildhall, incorporating the remains of the abbey, reflects the great wealth from copper that changed the face of this town.

3 BRIXHAM *Harbour 1891*
This view of Brixham's harbour, overlooked by the characteristic terraces of cottages on the steep hillside, has changed little in the intervening century. The statue of William of Orange, commemorating his landing here in 1688, still dominates the waterfront.

4 DARTMOUTH *Regatta 1889*
Dartmouth's regatta, a highpoint of the West Country's sailing season for well over a century, has always been marked by the lines of

⑤

⑥

moored yachts and boats that flank the wide estuary of the Dart. This view shows hills above Teignmouth and the railway that runs along the river's eastern shore.

5 TORQUAY *1888*
The major development of Torquay and the resort beaches of Babbacombe Bay took place in the late 19th century, but it was not until well into this century that the area became known as the English Riviera. Fishing and pleasure-boating, as seen in this view, were important elements of the Devon holiday in late Victorian England.

6 HOPE *Cottages 1890*
The picturesque qualities of Hope's thatched cottages, so typical of rural Devon, were being appreciated for the first time at the end of the 19th century, with more adventurous visitors seeking out the rocky coves of Bigbury Bay.

7 SALTASH *The Ferry c.1910*
The completion of Brunel's great bridge across the Tamar at Saltash in 1859 was the last link in the main railway line from London to Cornwall, opening the region up for tourism. The ferries continued to carry vehicles and passengers across the river until 1961, when the graceful suspension bridge that carries the A38 was opened.

⑦

It was, above all, the landscape, coastal scenery, market towns and beaches of north Devon that attracted late Victorian visitors to the region. In those days the train was the only practical means of long-distance travel, and it was the railway that made Exeter and Barnstable the gateways to this part of the country. There were lines from Exeter radiating out in seven directions, and from Barnstable in five, and it was these train journeys that made the landscape both accessible, and enjoyable.

At this time the qualities of moorland scenery, and the distinctive wildlife associated with them, were being properly appreciated for the first time, and the study of the ponies, deer, otters, birds and unusual insects and flora of Dartmoor and Exmoor was becoming a major Victorian pastime. At the same time, otter- and deer-hunting were still considered a normal part of country life, and so modern attitudes to wildlife conservation were either non-existent, or in their infancy.

Still popular was the now-disgraced hobby of egg collecting, while looking for shells and flower pressing were common family activities. The characteristic animals and birds of the area were, of course, still to be seen in considerable numbers, for the most destructive 20th-century predators, the motor car, the agri-chemical industry, and tourism, were yet to make a serious impact on the countryside.

Particularly attractive to Victorian visitors were the sandy beaches and dramatic cliffs of the coastline, along with the traditional fishing villages such as Clovelly which were all still relatively inaccessible. Local transport from the railway station was by horse-drawn vehicle or bicycle, and this protected much of the landscape and its remote villages from all but the most dedicated tourist.

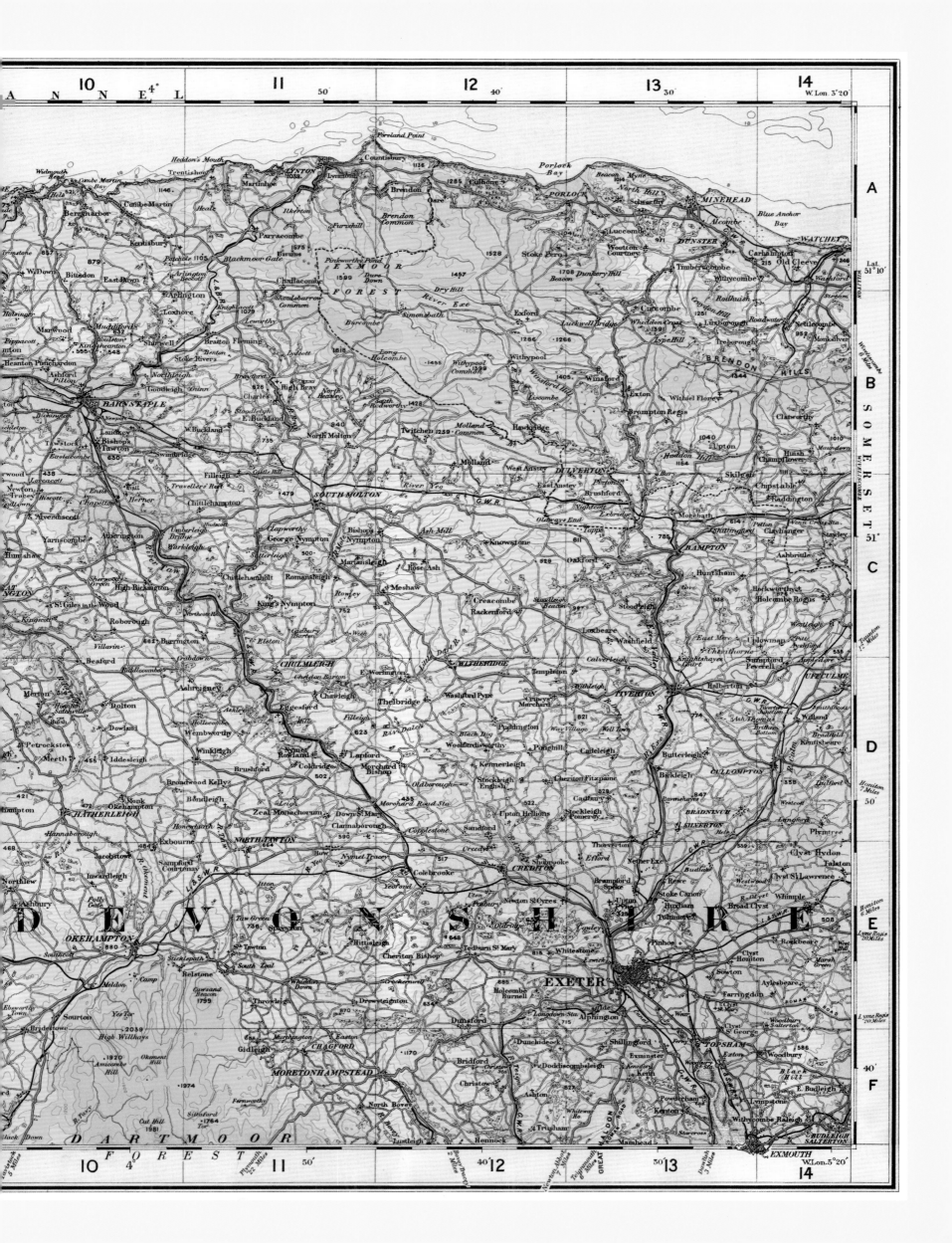

①

②

④

1 LYNMOUTH
Pier and Beach 1890
The poet Shelley was one of the first to discover the delights of the fishing village of Lynmouth, whose qualities remained unchanged throughout the 19th century. This view shows the pier and the original Rhenish tower (a salt-water store) that were destroyed by the floods of 1952.

2 EXETER *High Street 1900*
Exeter's busy commercial heart has traditionally been its High Street, flanked by medieval and later buildings. Delivery vehicles line the pavements, while signs of the new century are the electric street lights and the public telephone office.

3 CHAGFORD *Market Place 1906*
The octagonal market cross, originally an open structure, has long been the centre of this small town set high above the River Teign. The gentle pace of life in the pre-car era is underlined by this view, with an elegant baby carriage the only vehicle in sight.

4 ILFRACOMBE
Capstone Hill and Parade 1911
Famous as a port since the Middle Ages, Ilfracombe was not known as a resort until the railway arrived in 1874. Its popularity then grew rapidly – the beaches and rocky coastline making it a fashionable Edwardian holiday centre. The smart holiday-makers of that era are very different from their modern equivalent.

③

⑤

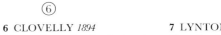

⑥

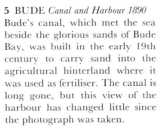

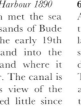

5 BUDE *Canal and Harbour 1890*
Bude's canal, which met the sea beside the glorious sands of Bude Bay, was built in the early 19th century to carry sand into the agricultural hinterland where it was used as fertiliser. The canal is long gone, but this view of the harbour has changed little since the photograph was taken.

6 CLOVELLY *1894*
Also unchanged today is the picturesque north Devon fishing village of Clovelly, where donkeys still carry their burdens up and down the steep cobbled streets. The village, with its tiny harbour and narrow streets set into a cleft in the cliffs, was first discovered by tourists in the 19th century.

7 LYNTON *1911*
The simple stone tower of St Mary's Church dominates this view of an elegant little resort town made both fashionable and accessible by the arrival of the Light Railway from Barnstable in 1898. Horse-drawn carriages were still the most popular way to visit local landmarks such as the Valley of the Rocks and Contisbury Hill.

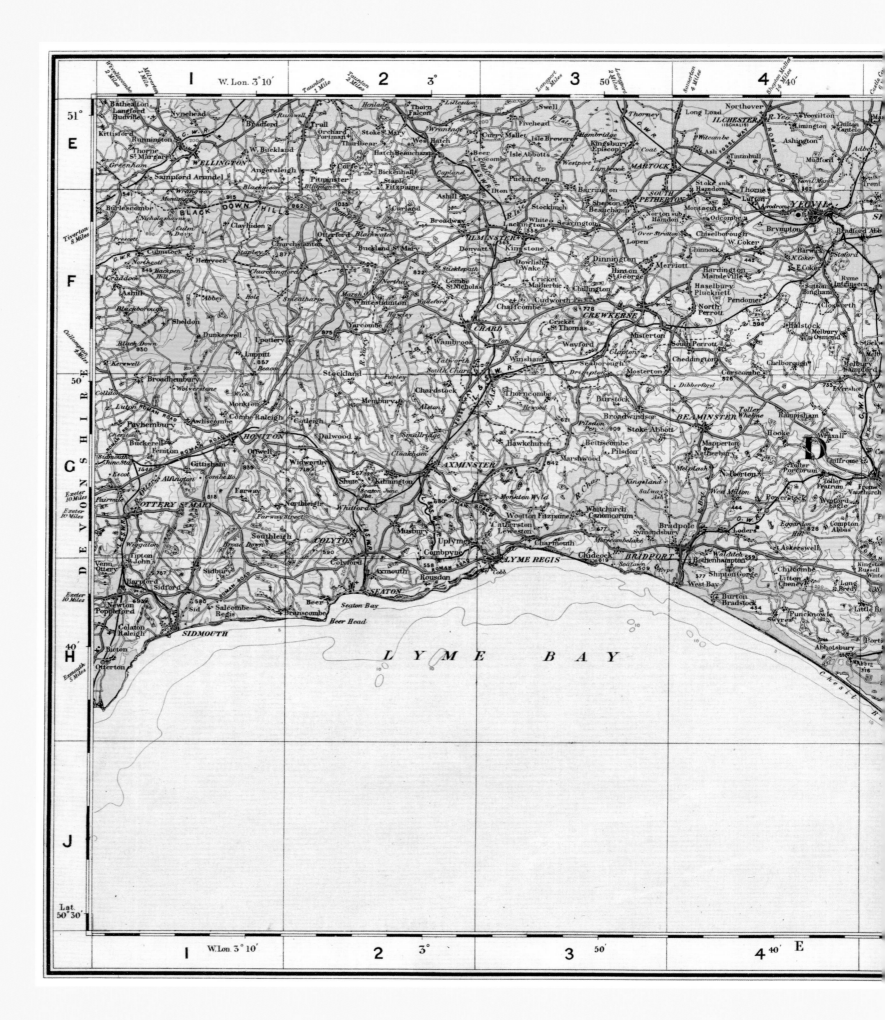

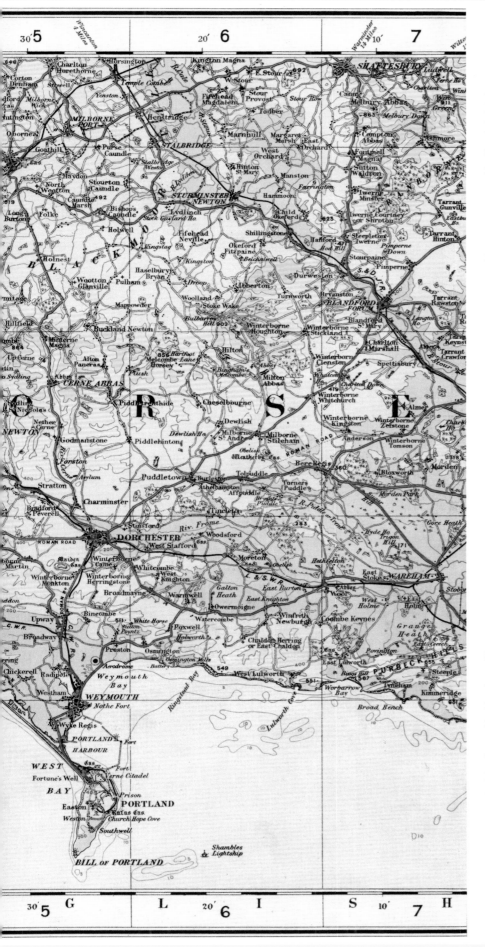

At a time when thomas Hardy was constructing his portraits of rural Dorset life – upon which all subsequent visions of the region have tended to be based – east Devon and south Dorset were actually areas of considerable industrial activity, albeit on a localised scale. Since the Middle Ages the region had been famous for its textiles, and many of these old industries were still active in the Victorian era.

The making of lace was a major cottage industry in Honiton and its surrounding villages throughout the 19th century, even though the new machine-made lace was undermining the industry's traditional craft base. It was at this time that the former wool town of Chard began to specialise in the making of the fine mesh net upon which machine-made lace was woven. Today, Honiton lace survives only in museums and small craft workshops, but at nearby Axminster carpet-weaving is still a major industry, as it was in the Victorian period. Ropes have been made at Bridport for centuries, but the Victorian rope walks where the long flax strands were twisted into shape have been replaced by machines that spin and weave all kinds of nets and ropes from plastics. Bridport ropes were a mainstay of both the navy and the merchant marine in the days of sail, and many of the sails themselves were made at Crewkerne. This traditional industry was dying in the Victorian period, but in their heyday the Crewkerne craftsmen had shaped the sails for Nelson's *Victory*.

Much of Dorset's hilly landscape has always been given over to sheep-farming, and so many towns in the region were traditional centres for the wool, weaving and leather industries. Victorian Yeovil, for example, was famous for its gloves, and this industry is still active today.

Dorset's other great industry in the 19th century was stone-quarrying. In the north of the county and into Somerset, the golden Ham stone has given its characteristic colour to the towns and villages of the area since the Middle Ages. Better-known on a national basis was Portland's hard white limestone, the traditional building material used for many of London's grand structures.

①

②　④

③

⑥

⑦

1 SHERBORNE *Old Castle 1904*
The decayed ruins of Sherborne's 12th-century castle, destroyed during the Civil War, have long attracted visitors.

2 LULWORTH COVE *1894*
The particular appeal of Lulworth Cove, where the stone cliffs almost enclose the small bay, was well known to the Victorians. A century of tourism has inevitably brought changes to Lulworth, but development of the surrounding downland has been limited by the long presence of the army in the region.

3 LYME REGIS *The Smithy 1909*
Until the proliferation of motor transport after World War I, the smithy was a feature of practically every town and village in Britain. Thousands were kept employed shoeing horses and mending agricultural machinery.

4 DORCHESTER
West Street 1891
The handsome main street of Dorset's county town, and Hardy's Casterbridge, still looks much the same today. In the distance are the tower of St Peter's Church and the clock-tower on the town hall.

5 HONITON *Lace Worker 1907*
Honiton has been famous for centuries as the centre of a lace-making region. At her wedding in 1761 Queen Charlotte wore a dress of Honiton lace, and in the Edwardian era it was still a major local industry.

6 WEYMOUTH
The Harbour 1904
Weymouth's harbour, still busy with fishing and pleasure boats, has changed little since this photograph was taken. The bridge was rebuilt in the 1930s and the convict ship, a tourist attraction of the day, has long since disappeared.

7 WEYMOUTH *Sands 1904*
George III made the first of his regular visits to Weymouth in 1789, and the town's popularity as a resort dates from that period. When this view was taken the only interruption in the Georgian façades of the esplanade was the pompous Royal Hotel, completed just five years before.

⑧

8 CHESIL BEACH *1890*
This view, taken from the heights of Portland, looks across the village of Fortuneswell towards the long expanse of Chesil Beach.

THE DEVELOPMENT OF THE Isle of Wight was largely a 19th-century phenomenon, and even today visitors can still enjoy the island's distinctly old-fashioned atmosphere. The Victorians took the Isle of Wight very much to their hearts, for it represented, in miniature, all that they had come to appreciate about England. Conveniently condensed, the island offered its Victorian visitors a varied pastoral landscape, dramatic coastal scenery and fine beaches, picturesque villages and a respectable historical past in the form of the major castle at Carisbrooke. It also offered a good choice of healthy resorts for bathing and boating, all of which were of their own creation. Ryde was the first, its population rising quickly from about 500 at the end of the 18th century to over 3,000 by the 1820s.

Next to be developed were Ventnor, Shanklin and Sandown, and by the 1870s most of the island's resorts were well established. Sailing was another favourite activity, with Cowes having its first regatta in 1814 and building its yacht club a year later. Other particular features of the island, such as the coloured sands of Alum Bay, were also quickly exploited by the Victorians.

Much of the impetus came from Queen Victoria. She had first visited the island in 1831 and quickly acquired the habit, returning regularly before and after her marriage. Prince Albert shared her enthusiasm and in 1845 construction of their great mansion at Osborne started. Another influential local resident was the poet, Lord Tennyson.

Easily reached from the mainland, the Isle of Wight also offered the Victorian visitor easy travel within its shores, thanks to its comprehensive network of railways. The first line, from Ryde to Shanklin, opened in the early 1860s, and by the 1880s the island enjoyed a system that linked all major towns and villages. Nowhere on the island was more than a few miles from a station, and there were even plans to connect the network with the mainland via a tunnel under the Solent. The railways of the Isle of Wight, long since driven into virtual extinction by the car, fulfilled the Victorian dream of a comprehensive system of public transport that was cheap and accessible to everyone.

1 SWANAGE *1897*
This view of Swanage from the pier was taken when the town was at its peak as a popular resort, helped both by the coming of the railway in 1885 and the extensive building of hotels by George Burt, a local speculator and enthusiastic collector.

2 BOURNEMOUTH
The Swanage Boat 1908
Bournemouth's development was entirely a Victorian phenomenon and by 1900 the town had a population of nearly 60,000. Regular paddle-steamer services from the 1880 pier to other resorts such as Swanage were a popular feature of the town's holiday activities.

3 PORTSMOUTH
The Harbour 1898
In the late 19th century Portsmouth's busy harbour was dominated by Nelson's *Victory*, at that time still afloat, whose great wooden walls towered above more modern warships. In the foreground is a Gosport ferry from the fleet of vessels that then, as now, plyed their way continuously across the harbour.

4 SOUTHAMPTON
Bargate, North Front 1908
One of Britain's finest medieval town gates, Southampton's Bargate, was restored in the 1860s. At the time this photograph was taken it must have seemed strange to see trams plunging through the early 15th-century façade.

5 RINGWOOD *1900*
At the end of the 19th century Ringwood was still a small market town, with old thatched cottages in West Street running from the market square to the River Avon. In this peaceful scene the thatcher is at work while a pony cools its feet in the water.

6 CORFE CASTLE
From the Church 1897
Little has changed at Corfe Castle since this photograph was taken nearly a century ago, but how quiet it must have seemed before the busy A351 came through the town. In the distance is the railway to Swanage, opened in 1885, which brought tourism to the Isle of Purbeck.

7 CHRISTCHURCH
Wick Ferry 1900
This view of the ferry across the Avon shows how popular it was with cyclists using Christchurch as a base for explorations of the New Forest and the Hampshire coast during the Edwardian era.

8 RYDE *Union Street 1904*
Ryde was one of the first of the Isle of Wight towns to be developed as a resort, with its origins in the Regency period. This view down Union Street towards the pier with, in the distance, a train making its way to the Pierhead station, captures the island's restful atmosphere in the pre-car period.

⑥

⑦

9 SHANKLIN *Old Village 1897*
Picturesque thatched coattages
with decorative barge-boarding
were popular survivors from the
1850s – Shanklin's first period of
development before the arrival of
the railway in the early 1860s.

Extensive growth of the town
during the next thirty years gave
them an appealing quaintness.

10 VENTNOR
From East Cliff 1899
Fishing boats and bathing-

machines, still strictly segregated
on grounds of sex, give Ventnor's
beach a delightful period charm,
but already the villas are spreading up the side of the east cliff,
giving a clear indication of things
to come.

⑧

⑨

⑩

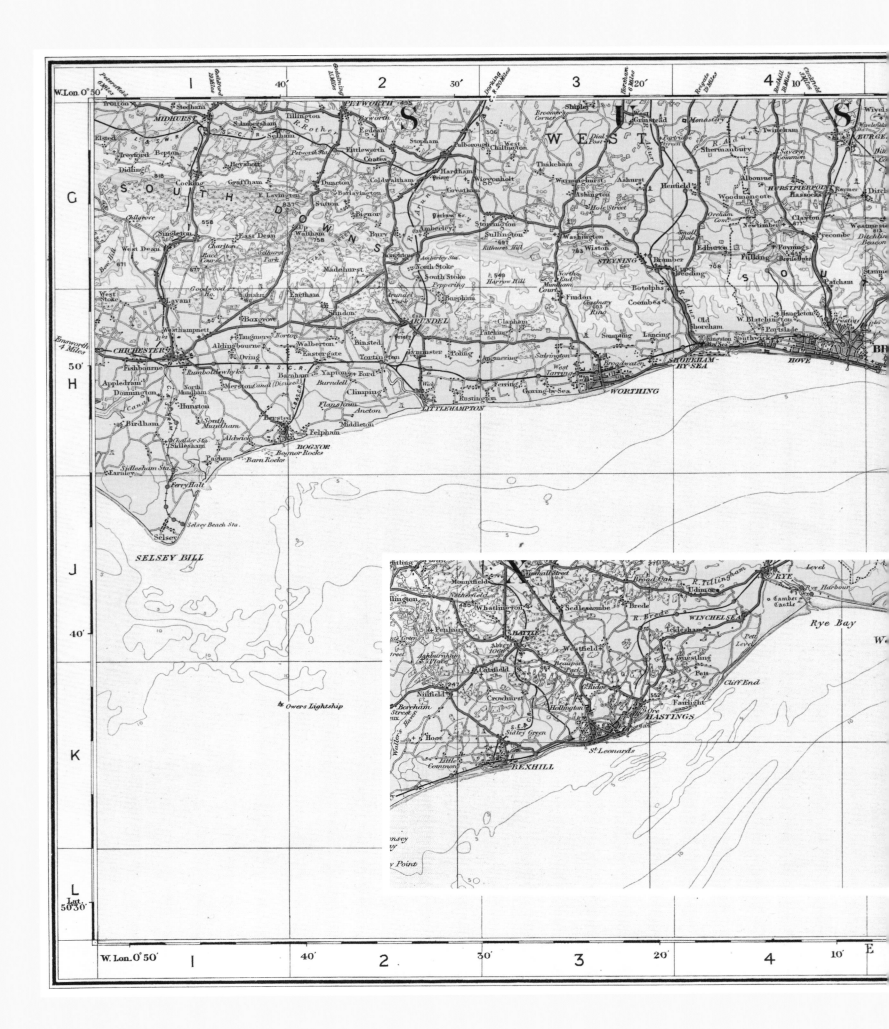

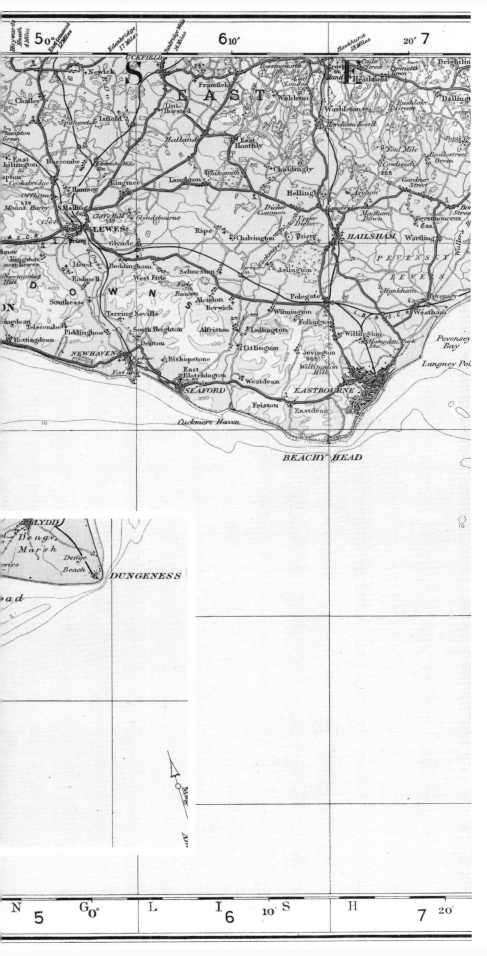

UNTIL THE LATTER YEARS of the 18th century most of the south coast resorts that are household names today were little more than fishing villages. Some were just a few hovels or cottages clustered by a beach or inlet, remote and unknown to the country as a whole. In the 1780s sea bathing became fashionable, for reasons of health rather than pleasure, and from that moment on development occurred steadily along the south coast, stimulated particularly by the activities of the Prince Regent and his circle in Brighton.

However, expansion was rapid until the early Victorian period when it was encouraged first by the railways who made the south coast easily accessible, and second by the increasing appeal of the seaside for leisure and entertainment. The railways made possible quick visits for both business and pleasure. By the 1850s towns like Brighton were only about an hour from London, and so the habit of commuting to work in the city soon became a feature of Victorian commercial and domestic life. At the same time, day and weekend visits to the sea were a common social habit from the 1870s onwards, and for more and more people the annual week's holiday by the sea was becoming a reality.

Despite this rapid growth, the south coast resorts were able to retain much of their village atmosphere throughout the 19th century. The massive expansion of coastal conurbations did not really occur until after World War I, and so even in the last years of the Edwardian era resorts such as Bognor, Littlehampton, Newhaven and Seaford were all still small towns catering for the specific tastes of fashionable and generally well-connected visitors. Today, coastal development spreads almost without interruption from Worthing eastwards to Hastings, but a look at the map shows how, at the time, Worthing, Shoreham, Brighton, Bexhill and Hastings were all separate and distinct resort towns, with open countryside in between, and ample opportunities for the enjoyment of the striking scenery of the cliffs.

①

②

④

③

⑤

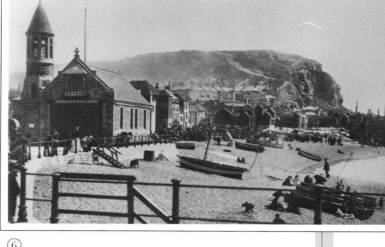

⑥

⑦

1 BRIGHTON *Beach and Pier 1889*
By the late 19th century Brighton was already established as the premier south coast resort, with thousands using the frequent train service from London for day visits and longer stays. This view, looking towards the 1866 West Pier – still Brighton's only pier in 1889 – contains many components of the typical Victorian holiday scene: the fishing boats and bathing-machines, beach photographers and entertainers and the well-dressed crowds.

2 LEWES *High Street 1903*
This view of Lewes's steep High Street, looking towards the Downs from where the war memorial now stands, reveals the extraordinary diversity of shops in even quite a small town in the Edwardian period. Notable are the American Teeth Institute, the Bible Society's depot, and a shop selling mangles, baby carriages and organs.

3 CHICHESTER
Market Cross 1903
Relatively unchanged is this view of Chichester's remarkable market cross with, in the background, the cathedral's dramatic spire. Built in 1501, the octagonal cross was, if anything, looking more battered in 1903 than now.

4 SEAFORD
Seven Sisters Rocks 1891
One of the classic coastal views of Britain is the sight of the Seven Sisters striding away from Cuckmere Haven towards Beachy Head. Taken from Seaford Head, this photograph shows how empty downland and the splendid landscape of the cliffs appealed just as much to the Victorians as it does to visitors today.

5 PETWORTH
Lombard Street 1900
The tile-hung cottages of Lombard Street were picturesque a century ago and they remain so in a town that is a delightful mixture of buildings of all periods. This photograph shows St Mary's Church with the spindly 1827 spire which was removed in 1947 to be replaced with the present tower cap.

6 HASTINGS
Life Boat Station 1890
The most characteristic and attractive parts of Hastings, the Old Town and the black, tarred net stores on the beach around the fish market, are clearly seen in this view. It underlines the relative simplicity of this seaside town in the late Victorian period compared to some of the smarter and more popular resorts further west.

7 RYE AND RIVER ROTHER
1901
The distinctive skyline of Rye, dominated by the castle and the church, has not changed much in the century since this photograph was taken. However, the handsome sailing trawlers in the foreground have now become a part of history – one of the many classes of British coastal sailing vessels now virtually extinct.

8 ARUNDEL *Castle 1902*
The best way to approach Arundel has long been to walk up to the town from the station, crossing the Arun valley and enjoying the view of the castle from the river. Not much has changed over the years, except that there are now fewer trees, exposing more of this predominantly Victorian town, and the bridge was rebuilt in 1935.

⑧

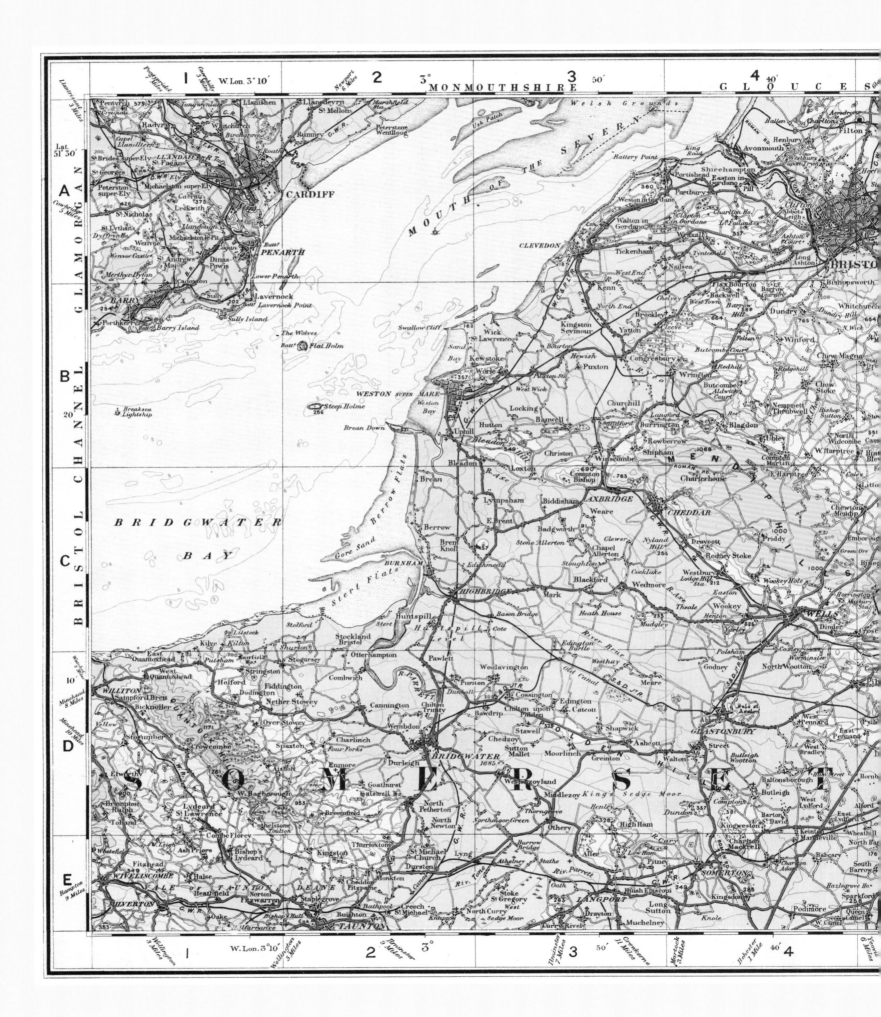

VICTORIAN SOMERSET WAS dominated by two industries, shipping and coal. Throughout the 19th century the mouth of the Severn was the gateway to some of Britain's busiest ports, attacting a wide variety of both domestic and international vessels ranging from small coastal traders to large clippers, barques and steamships. On the Welsh side both Cardiff and Barry had dock complexes developed by the Victorians, while those on the English side were considerably older.

Bridgwater's old quays on the Parrett were given a new lease of life by a set of enclosed docks and this inland port remained in use throughout the Victorian period, although increasingly restricted by size and the tidal river. Bristol, on the other hand, having been one of Britain's premier ports throughout the 18th century, was given increased importance by the creation of the floating harbour during the first decades of the 19th century. This attracted trade from all over the world, maintained Bristol's important position in the wine and spirit trade, and gave a boost to the city's ship-building industry.

One of the major cargoes shipped from the Severn ports in both the 18th and 19th centuries was coal. Barry and Cardiff naturally served the south Wales pits, but the English ports were kept busy by the pits of the Somerset coalfield, to the south of Bristol and Bath. Centred around Radstock and connected to the ports initially by canal, and later by an extensive railway network, the coalfield was active throughout the Victorian period and into this century.

Today, both these industries are little more than historical memories. The Welsh ports survive, much reduced, Bridgwater is long closed and Avonmouth has completely eclipsed Bristol, whose vast acreage of docks is now given over to museums and leisure activities. Of the Somerset coalfield nothing remains save some old buildings, old waste tips now reverted to nature, and the overgrown tracks of the railways – all of which had been obliterated by the 1960s.

①

②

③

④

⑤

1 WELLS *Market Place 1890*
This delightfully empty view of the market place at Wells, with the tower of the cathedral in the background, is in sharp contrast to today's busy scene. Many of the characteristic bay windows on the buildings flanking the market place still survive, along with the 1793 Gothic-style fountain, but the cannon apparently threatening the gateway into the Close has gone.

2 CASTLE COMBE *1907*
This well-known stone village was famous for its prettiness even in the Edwardian era, when decorative, unspoilt villages were far more common than they are today. Delightfully set on a hillside by the river, Castle Combe's traditional stone buildings have a universal appeal. In the distance is the chunky market cross.

3 CORSHAM
Worked Stone Co 1907
In the 19th century the pretty village of Corsham was still one of the centres for the production of Bath's famous honey-coloured stone. New building projects, and the restoration work on historical structures dating from the Middle Ages to the 18th century, kept masons' yards such as this busily employed well into the 20th century.

4 TAUNTON *Market Place 1902*
Taunton's market place has been the town's civic centre for decades, and this view, taken from the 18th-century market house and looking along North Street towards the River Tone, underlines this. The busy market, domestic rather than agricultural, is a scene once commonplace, but now virtually unknown in most English towns of Taunton's size.

5 BRADFORD-ON-AVON
Old Tythe Barn 1900
The 14th-century tithe barn at Barton Farm, on the Frome Road, is one of the largest in England. This handsome stone structure, 168 feet long, is now carefully cared for, but in 1900 it was attractively dilapidated and still in agricultural use – as the wandering chickens reveal.

6 CARDIFF *St Mary Street 1893*
The Victorian wealth of Cardiff is reflected by the extravagant Italianate buildings that line St Mary Street. When this photograph was taken some of these were no more than twenty years old. They underline the kind of civic pride that made Victorian towns so decorative. In the distance is Cardiff Castle, rebuilt in the 1870s by William Burges for the Marquis of Bute.

7 BRISTOL
St Augustine's Bridge 1901
This photograph of St Augustine's Bridge and Parade, the city's commercial centre, shows how much was lost during World War II bombing. Gone are practically all the buildings that flank the quay's eastern side, along with much of St Nicholas's Church, whose fine 18th-century Gothic-style tower can be clearly seen. Open-topped trams were, by 1901, a common feature in many English towns and cities.

8 BARRY ISLAND
Cold Knapp Beach Bay 1899
The coal trade was the main reason for Barry's development as a major port from the 1880s, but less familiar today is the regions other face, as a popular seaside resort. The beaches of Barry Island, and the relatively undeveloped nature of the coastline, enjoyed a widespread popularity in the late 19th and early 20th centuries.

9 BRIDGWATER *1897*
The quays of the River Parrett in Bridgwater are now quiet places, but throughout the 19th century they and the enclosed dock were still busy with coastal sailing vessels loading and unloading. Later, the tides and the port's small size combined to bring about its demise, but in this view there is still plenty of activity and the handsome warehouses are still full.

10 BATH *The Circus 1911*
In the Victorian period the classical formality and elegance of Bath's stone terraces were not appreciated as they are today. Too refined for more exuberant Victorian tastes, they quietly decayed until the end of the century when there was a change of taste that brought classicism back into favour. In this view of the famous Circus, still delightfully free of traffic, a single car hints at changes to come.

⑥ ⑦ ⑧ ⑨ ⑩

45

TODAY, THE PART OF southern England that stretches westwards from the Surrey/Hampshire borders and into Wiltshire is firmly marked by the presence of the military. Garrisons, camps, airfields and other government installations are scattered across the map and play a major part in the life of the region. In the Victorian period the army was still centred around Aldershot, having barely begun the great expansion westwards that was inspired initially by the demands of World War I. Garrisons at Tidworth and Bulford were not established until the early years of this century, and now-famous names such as Boscombe, Porton and the Wallops were no more than small villages.

Although recent, the military colonisation of the region follows strong historical precedents. There is probably no part of England so rich in visible traces of prehistoric civilisations, and camps, barrows, ditches and other earthworks cover the Victorian map in a much more dominant way than today. At the centre is Stonehenge, as much a mystery in the 19th century as now. Since 1900, many of the sites that would have been familiar to the Victorians have been altered or obliterated by the activities of farmers, the military, road-builders and others, and so the 19th-century vision of prehistoric life was actually more complete than it is now. This was also an important region in the Roman period, but their sites have generally been treated with greater respect by the 20th century.

Studying the past was a favourite Victorian activity and knowledge was both considerable and widespread, even if the methods used were less scientific than those practised today. Typical was the fascination with pre-medieval kings such as Arthur and Alfred, and the Victorians were quick to turn Winchester into the centre of this cult. The city was not only Alfred's capital, but also contained Arthur's Round Table, a relic whose authenticity was then rarely questioned. The final expression of this cult was the placing of Alfred's great statue at the bottom of the High Street in 1901, and it is still a prominent landmark.

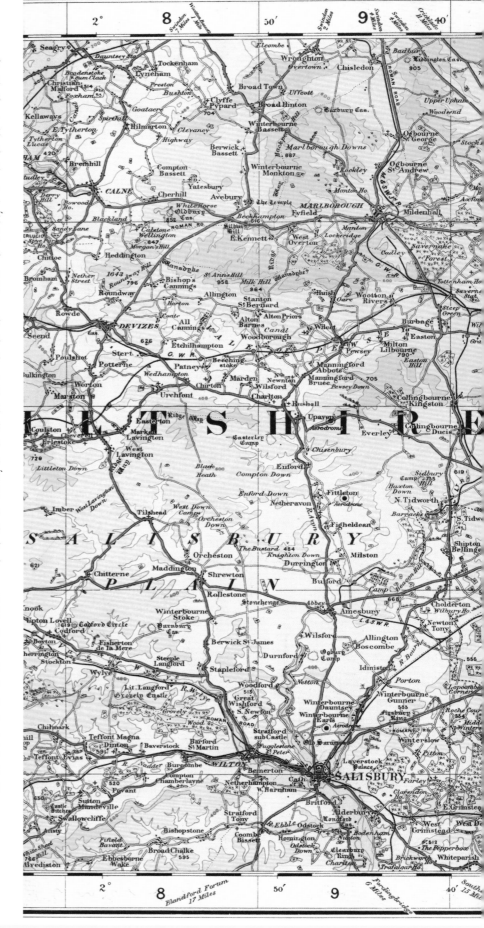

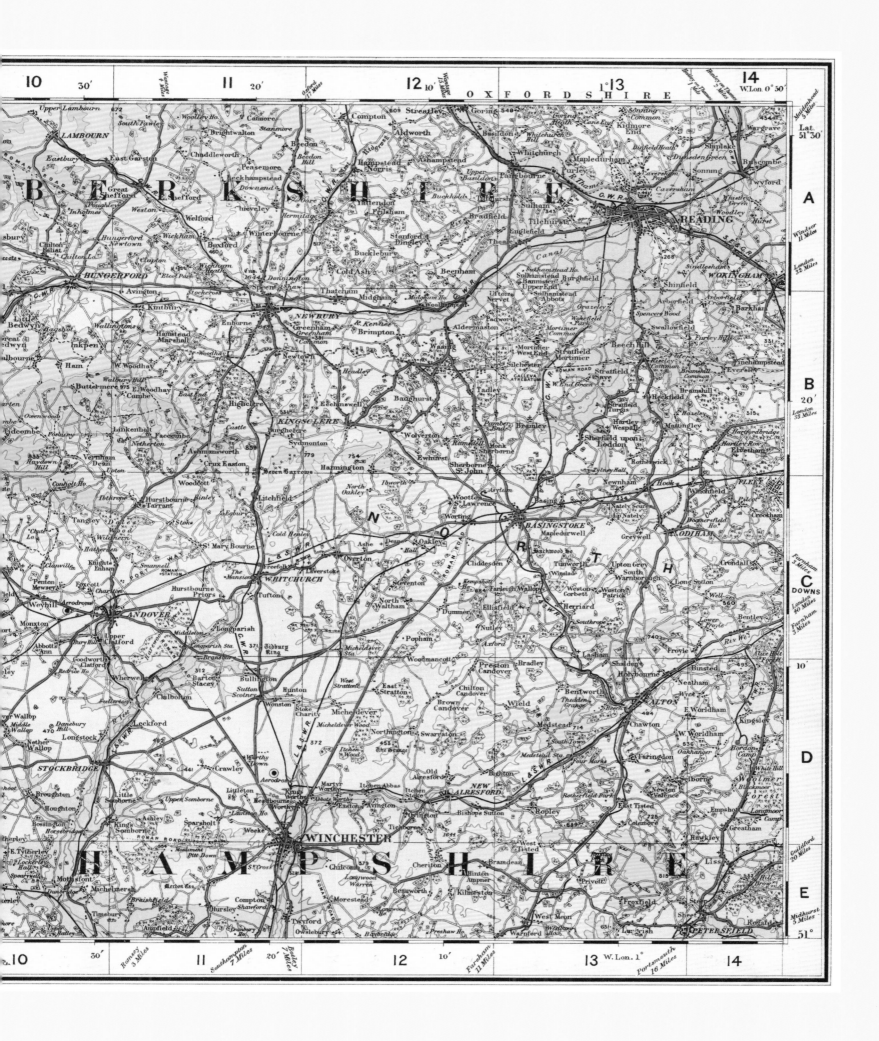

①

⑥

②

④

③

⑤

⑦

⑧

⑨

1 ANDOVER
Town Railway 1901
This view of a typical late Victorian railway station, complete with elegant footbridge and ornamental gas lamp, shows the London & South Western's Andover Town station on the line from Andover Junction south to Southampton via Stockbridge and Romsey. Closed in the 1960s, much of the line is now the route of the Test Way footpath.

2 STONEHENGE *1887*
In the Victorian period Stonehenge was already considered one of the wonders of Britain and people came from far and near to examine the stone circle. In those days visitors were allowed right up to the stones and could even, as this photograph shows, have a leisurely picnic among them.

3 WINCHESTER
High Street 1896
This view of Winchester's main shopping thoroughfare, with its famous clock, shows how pleasant a street it was in the pre-car era, while the distant hills reveal how well contained the city was by the Itchen valley. Today the High Street is a pedestrian zone and so some of this atmosphere has been recaptured.

4 SALISBURY
Cathedral 1887
This classic view of Salisbury's cathedral across the water-meadows of the Avon is virtually as Constable painted it about sixty years earlier.

5 MARLBOROUGH
High Street 1907
The lack of modern traffic is particularly noticeable in this view westwards along Marlborough's wide High Street. Traffic apart, this scene still looks much the same today, although long gone are the big hats worn by the ladies and the straw boaters sported by the boys from Marlborough School.

6 BASINGSTOKE
Hackwood Road 1904
This rural scene of thatched cottages on the road leading from Basingstoke towards Hackwood Park, the seat of the Dukes of Bolton, has completely disappeared. It is a vision of a way of life all but obliterated by the motor car.

7 MAPLEDURHAM
The Mill 1890
The photographer has chosen to show this picturesque, weather-boarded mill much as Constable might have painted it, complete with horse and cart cooling off in the pond. Perhaps rather unexpectedly, this Thames-side mill still looks much the same today.

8 STREATLEY
Swan Hotel 1899
A popular late Victorian occupation was exploring the villages and hotels of the upper Thames, epitomised by Jerome K Jerome's *Three Men in a Boat*. The Swan at Streatley, typically timber-framed and tile-hung, was a particular favourite.

9 PANGBOURNE *1910*
This view of one of the main streets of this Thames-side village, where the only traffic is a bicycle and a baby carriage, shows an interesting blend of traditional old cottages with new Arts and Crafts villas – the latter underlining the increasing popularity of scenic villages that could be easily reached from London.

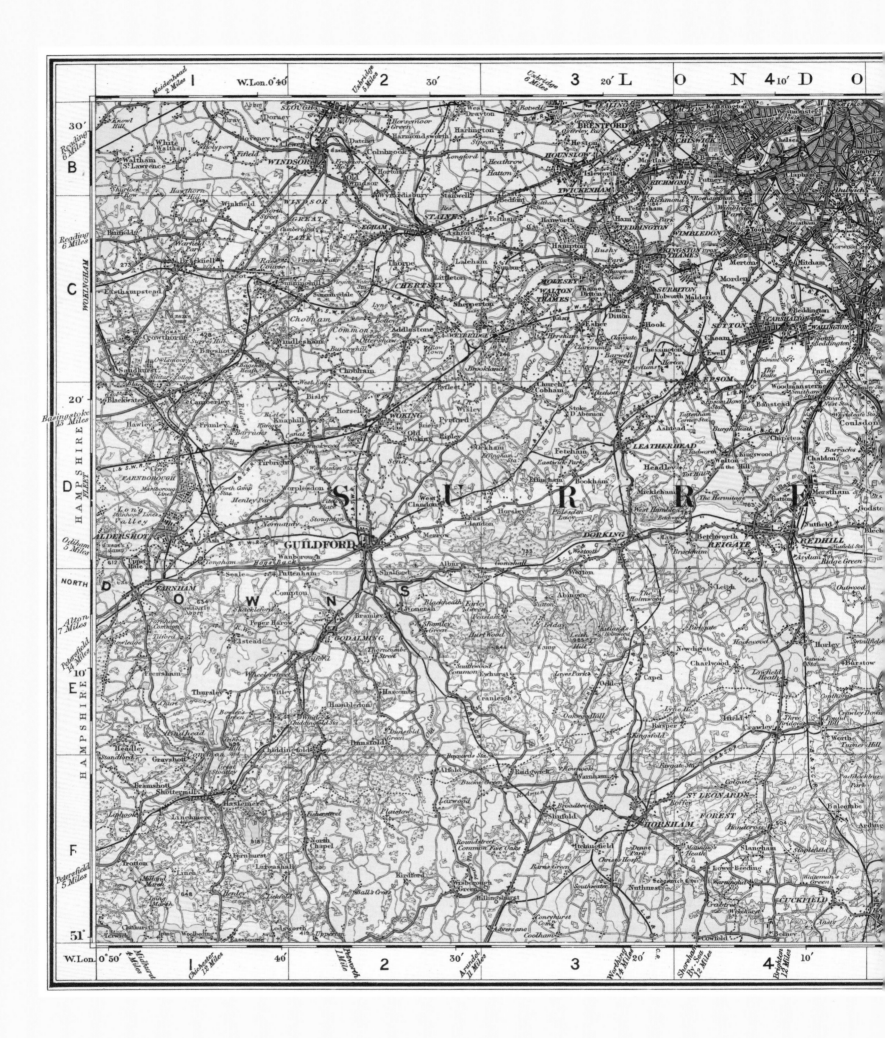

UNTIL 1888, WHEN THE county of London was formed, all London south of the Thames was in Surrey or Kent. As a result, from the Tudor period onwards, all Londoners who wished to have country houses within easy reach of the capital were drawn naturally to Surrey, and so London's southern Home Counties have always been remarkably well endowed with the fruits of successful commercial enterprise in the city. The attractions were ease of access, pleasant countryside with good farmland and good social connections, plus the fashionable appeal of spa towns such as Epsom and Tunbridge Wells. There are plenty of grand medieval and Tudor houses in the region, but it was not until the late 17th century that the first serious country-house boom took place, with the emphasis on outer London villages such as Richmond, Mitcham and Addiscombe. The next boom was in the late 18th century, with the houses of this period being built slightly further out, near towns such as Guildford, Farnham and Dorking, and along the slopes of the North Downs.

However, it was in the 19th century that country-house-building in the region was at its most frenetic, fired by the wealth and enthusiasm of a new generation of successful merchants and industrialists. The first half of the century produced ambitious houses such as Deepdene, Albury Park and Nutfield Priory, but it was in the latter part of the century that the most remarkable developments took place. By now railways had made the whole area quickly accessible from London, and aspiring and actual country-house owners made the most of this. The architects they employed were often the rising stars of their day, and so their legacy is a wealth of houses by designers who are now household names. The pioneering building was Philip Webb's Red House in Beckenham, completed in 1859 for William Morris, which led to other commissions for Webb in the area. Others soon followed, including Norman Shaw, with at least nine important houses, and C F A Voysey with six. However, the architect who really master-minded the last great country-house boom was Sir Edwin Lutyens, and before 1905 ten of his most distinctive houses were standing in Surrey and Hampshire.

①

②

③

⑤

④ ⑥

1 WINDSOR
Castle Hill, The Guards 1914
This view of a ceremonial parade by the Guards down Castle Hill – the broad thoroughfare linking the castle with the town – captures much of the atmosphere of Edwardian times. Within a year many of these soldiers were to die on the battlefields of Flanders.

2 CRYSTAL PALACE *1900*
Sir Joseph Paxton's great iron-and-glass palace, made originally for the Great Exhibition of 1851, was subsequently re-erected in a large public park at Anerley, in south London, where it became an exhibition and concert hall. Served by its own railway station, the Crystal Palace was still popular when this photograph was taken. However, after World War I its fortunes declined, and it was destroyed by fire in 1936.

3 MOLESEY LOCK
Houseboats 1896
Boating on the Thames was a favourite activity during the late Victorian and Edwardian eras, and this view of Molesey lock in Surrey shows a variety of popular craft, including punts and elegant steam launches. In the foreground the passengers on a particularly smart launch admire the scenery, while down below on the stern the maids plan the next meal.

⑦

⑧

⑨
⑩

4 GRAVESEND *The River 1904*
In this view, looking eastwards along the wide Gravesend Reach, are many of the varied craft that regularly used the Thames in the Edwardian period: rowing boats, fishing boats, yachts, sailing barges, tugs and, in the distance, large trading schooners. The town pier, built originally in 1834, was bought in 1895 by the London, Tilbury & Southend Railway for their Thames ferries from Tilbury.

5 COBHAM
The Old Oak Tree Restaurant 1911
The extensive network of railways spreading outwards through London's Home Counties made the exploration of Surrey's leafy lanes quite easy. The bicycle was the favourite means of travel, with frequent stops at roadside tea-shops. By 1911 such establishments were also catering for the needs of motorists, while this particular restaurant also has an interesting side-line in rustic garden furniture.

6 DORKING *1888*
This view of Dorking taken from the Downs shows the town spreading along the Mole valley, its growth encouraged by the increasing habit of commuting from London. Then, as now, the skyline is dominated by the spire of Woodyer's huge church, completed only fourteen years before the photograph was taken. In the distance is Thomas Hope's Deepdene House, since destroyed.

7 OXTED *Town Farm Corner 1908*
This rural scene in a typical Surrey village illustrates the continuing dominance of agriculture in the Home Counties in the years leading up to World War I. Dirt roads empty of cars have been replaced by a busy traffic intersection.

8 REIGATE HEATH *1906*
Set on a circular ragstone base, this fine weather-boarded post mill is typical of the many still at work on the Downs in the Edwardian era. Reigate Heath is now not nearly so remote and rural and this mill has disappeared, although Reigate does still boast a restored tower mill on Wray Common to the east of the town.

9 HORSHAM *Town Hall 1900*
In the 19th century Horsham's town hall, built originally by the Duke of Norfolk in 1812 and re-built in 1888, must have seemed particularly bizarre in what was otherwise a typical Wealden market town. Today, it remains an oasis of quirky individuality.

10 KINGSTON-ON-THAMES
1893
Kingston received its first charter in 1200 and eight centuries later it was still a relatively independent Thames-side town. The busy market place, dominated by the Italianate former town hall of 1840 (originally yellow brick, but now painted) and the Shrubsole memorial statue, erected in 1882, was the setting for the weekly market.

KENT'S REPUTATION AS the Garden of England was already established in the Victorian era, with fruit and hops among the county's staple products. Dependent directly upon the hopfields – with their distinctive oast-houses – were the breweries in towns like Faversham and Maidstone, some of which had been in existence for centuries. However, throughout the 19th century there were other important areas of industrial activity in the region, all of which have either ceased to exist or have since changed. One that does survive today is paper-making, now centred around the Sittingbourne area with its large dock complex in Milton Creek to the north, but formerly far more widespread with mills in Maidstone, Aylesford and other Medway towns.

Just as important in the 19th century but now a part of history was the making of gunpowder and other explosives, an industry established in the marshes north of Faversham in the 16th century and at its peak in the late Victorian period. By the 1930s all the mills had closed. The gunpowder industry existed partly to serve the huge naval dockyards at Chatham which were greatly expanded in the 19th century. From this period date many of the huge slips in which warships could be built or repaired completely under cover. Also guarding the Thames estuary was Kent's other naval base, at Sheerness on the mouth of the Medway. Established in the 17th century, this was also at its peak in the 1800s.

Today, there is no naval presence at either dockyard, but Sheerness has joined the long list of cross-Channel ports, the most important of which is Dover. In the Victorian era Dover hardly featured as a cross-Channel port, its development occurring largely during World War I. Many were developed as a result of competition between the rival railway companies for a share of the lucrative cross-Channel freight and passenger traffic, including Newhaven, Folkestone, Ramsgate, Queenborough (on the Isle of Sheppey), Port Victoria (on the Isle of Grain) and Harwich, giving the Victorian traveller to the Continent a greater choice of routes than his modern counterpart.

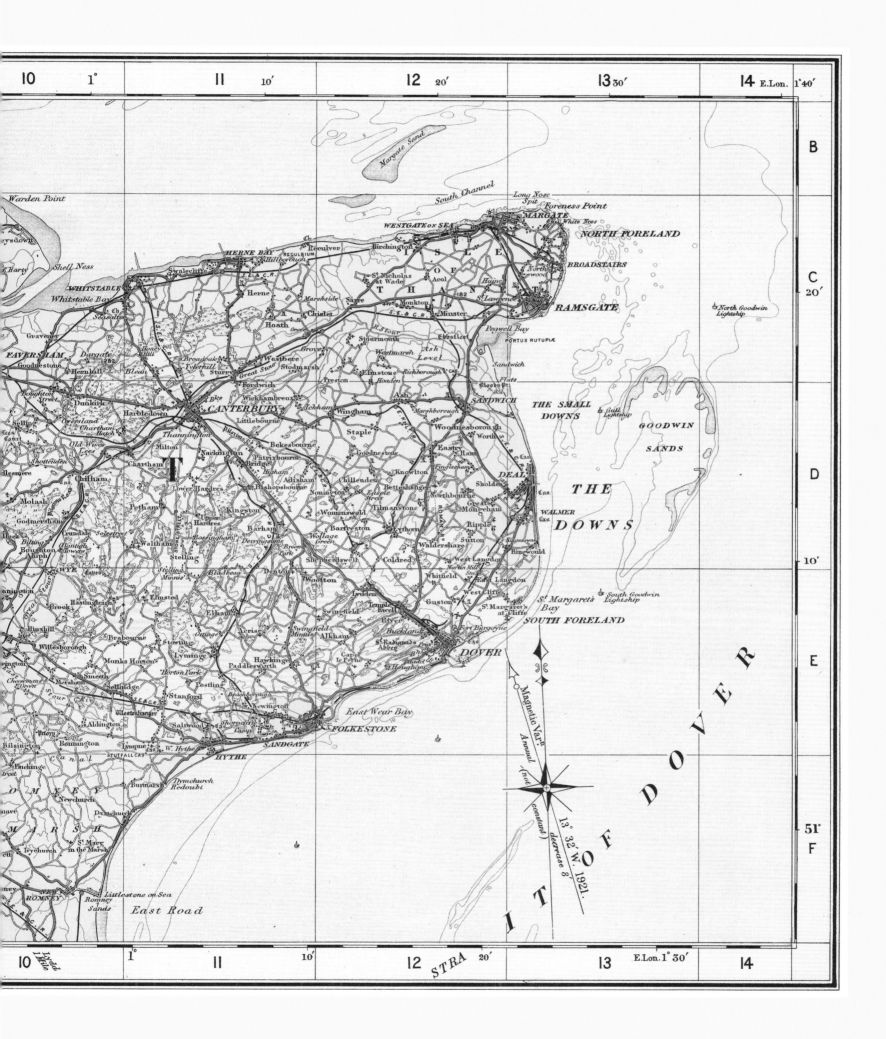

①

②

③

④

1 BROADSTAIRS *1907*
The small town of Broadstairs that grew up around the little harbour during the 1800s was greatly expanded at the end of the century when the fine beach turned it into one of the new generation of fashionable holiday resorts. This crowded scene of tents, bathing-machines and conventionally well-dressed holiday-makers captures the atmosphere of the period.

2 CRANBROOK *High Street 1903*
The leisurely pace of small-town life in the Edwardian era is reflected by this view of Cranbrook's main street with its simple terraced houses, traditional Kentish weather-boarding and lack of traffic. Then, the only intruding element into a scene of architectural harmony was the ponderous late Victorian brick of the pub.

3 ROCHESTER
Castle and Cathedral 1894
One of the great views of Kent has always been the sight of Rochester's castle and cathedral across the Medway. Thankfully this can still be enjoyed today, but probably gone forever is the sight of the two-man crew of a loaded Thames sailing barge dipping the mast with its red sails to pass under the Medway bridges.

4 ASHFORD *Cattle Market 1905*
A market town since the Middle Ages, Ashford continued to be one well into the 20th century, despite the coming of the railway works and its accompanying new town in the 1850s. The scene of sheep being driven to market along an urban street was one that could be regularly enjoyed before World War I.

5 CANTERBURY *West Gate 1890*
Canterbury's West Gate, completed in 1381, was originally built to guard the entry to the city across the River Stour. West of its towers the road to London began, flanked in this photograph, as now, by fine 17th- and 18th-century buildings.

6 GOUDHURST
Hop-pickers 1904
The cultivation of hops has long been a major feature of Kentish agriculture, with the harvest as the high point in the calendar of small villages such as Goudhurst. A labour-intensive activity, hop-picking was traditionally undertaken by families from London who moved down to Kent for the season, combining a bout of healthy outdoor work with some useful cash.

7 DOVER *Esplanade 1892*
Dover's development as a resort in the 19th century was short-lived, eclipsed by the growth of the harbour – initially as a naval base and later as a cross-Channel port. This traditional view of beach, boats, seaside terraces and the towering cliffs, crowned by the great castle, is an interesting reminder of Dover's past.

8 AYLESFORD *1898*
At the end of the 19th century Aylesford was still a busy inland port, with sailing barges carrying their cargoes up and down the tidal River Medway. Today, this view of the medieval bridge, ragstone church with its chunky tower, and terraces of brick cottages remains much the same, but the barges have gone.

⑤

⑥

⑦

⑧

THE CONTRAST BETWEEN
modern and 19th-century south Glamorgan could
hardly be greater, for in the Victorian era this was
one of Britain's most heavily industrialised regions,
devoted to the making of metal. Swansea, a busy
port and known for its potteries, was also the
traditional centre for the copper-smelting industry.
Iron and tin were also staple products, associated
particularly with Merthyr Tydfil, Llanelli, Port
Talbot and Neath. Pontypridd made its fame and
its fortune, not from rugby football, but from its
chain works. Established in 1816, this forged the
great anchor chains for many famous liners and
naval vessels. All these industries were dependent
on coal, and this was available in abundance from
the coalfields to the north, and transported down
the valleys initially by canals and later by a network
of mineral railways. Coal was also exported from
the ports built by Victorian industrialists, along
with the finished products of the metal industries.

The centre of the industry was Merthyr Tydfil,
whose Dowlais Iron Company had been founded in
1759. By the end of the 18th century there were four
great dynasties of ironmasters established in the
town, the Guests, the Homfrays, the Hills and the
Crawshays and Merthyr was the largest town in
Wales, with a population of 7,700. By 1861 the
population had grown to 50,000, but by then the
great days of iron-making were already past their
peak. The late Victorian and Edwardian periods
marked the town's steady decline, even though the
new steel industry had brought a boost to the
region. In 1900 Keir Hardie won the Merthyr seat
for the Labour Party, and it has been a labour
stronghold ever since, its political colour underlined by the impact of the Depression of the early
1930s, when over sixty per cent of the population
were unemployed or working part time.

At their peak, south Glamorgan's heavy industries created prosperity and employment, but the
cost in environmental terms was horrific. Today,
these industries are mostly a part of history, with
only the modern steel works maintaining the metal-
making tradition. The pits have closed, the canals
have gone and the ports are quiet.

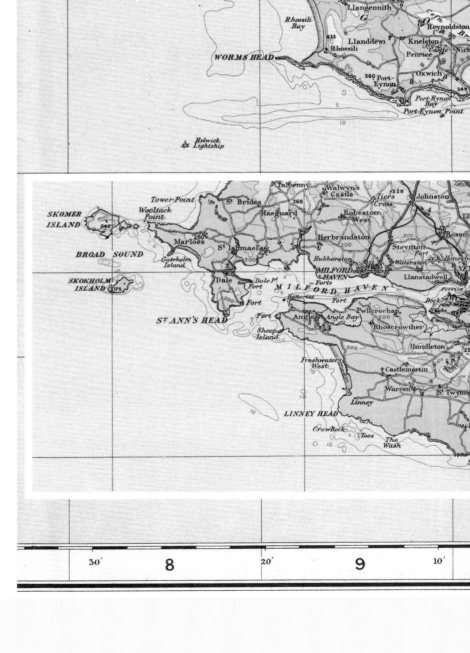

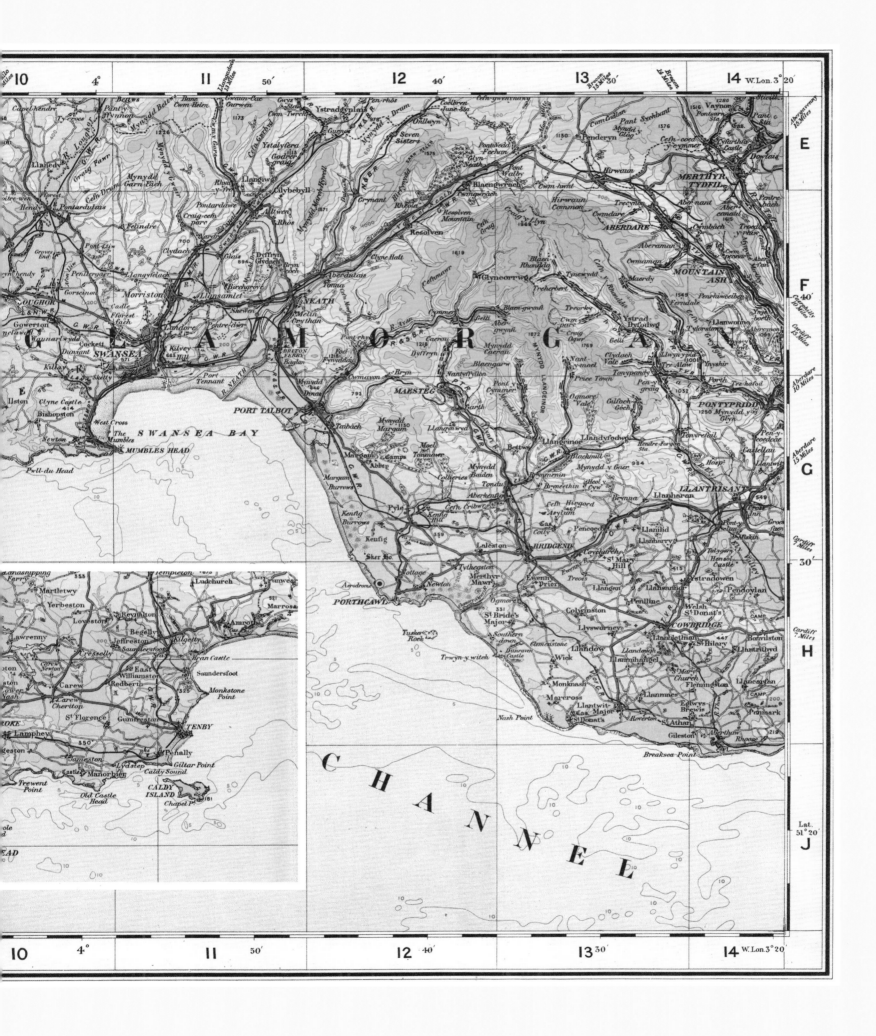

①

②

③   ④

⑤

1 SWANSEA *The Sands 1910*
The wide expanse of Swansea's beach made the town a popular Edwardian resort. This view of a funfair on the beach reveals many of the distinctive features of holidays in south Wales at that time, notably the formal dress and the universal wearing of hats. Even the girls riding the bicycle roundabout in the foreground have kept their hats on.

2 THE MUMBLES
From Quarry 1898
This view south along the sweep of Swansea's bay was taken from the little resort of Oystermouth and looks towards the rugged cliffs of the Mumbles. The track of the famous Mumbles Railway, closed in the early 1960s, can be seen following the curve of the bay and in the distance is the lifeboat pier.

3 PORTHCAWL *John Street 1901*
Porthcawl's rather dour stone terraces and simple shops, seen clearly in this view, reveal the origins of the town as a resort for the local mining communities. The wider appeal of its beaches and harbour was not exploited until later in this century, particularly with the coming of the caravan park and holiday camp.

4 BRIDGEND *1910*
This view of the stone bridge over the Ogmore River shows Bridgend as an old market town, rather than the major industrial centre it was to become after World War I.

5 MERTHYR TYDFIL
High Street c.1906
Limestone, coal and iron prompted Merthyr Tydfil's growth into what was at one time the largest town in Wales. Victorian wealth is reflected by the grandiose buildings in the High Street, but by the time this view was taken the town had passed its peak. Closed and decaying buildings, and the horse-drawn bus in the age of the tram, reveal the decline.

6 TENBY *Fishwives 1890*
Tenby was one of the first of south Wales's little ports to be developed into a resort and the Regency houses that overlook the harbour still have plenty of early 19th-century charm. However, fishing has always been Tenby's major industry and these traditionally dressed fishwives with their hats, shawls and baskets shows how the more picturesque elements of an ancient craft were beginning to be exploited for the benefit of visitors.

7 SWANSEA *1896*
Castle Square and Vivian Statue
This view, with its blend of medieval and 18th- and 19th-century buildings, reflects Swansea's development from market town to industrial centre in the Victorian period. Swansea's city centre was radically changed by World War II bombing and so the atmosphere of this photograph has gone, along with many of the buildings.

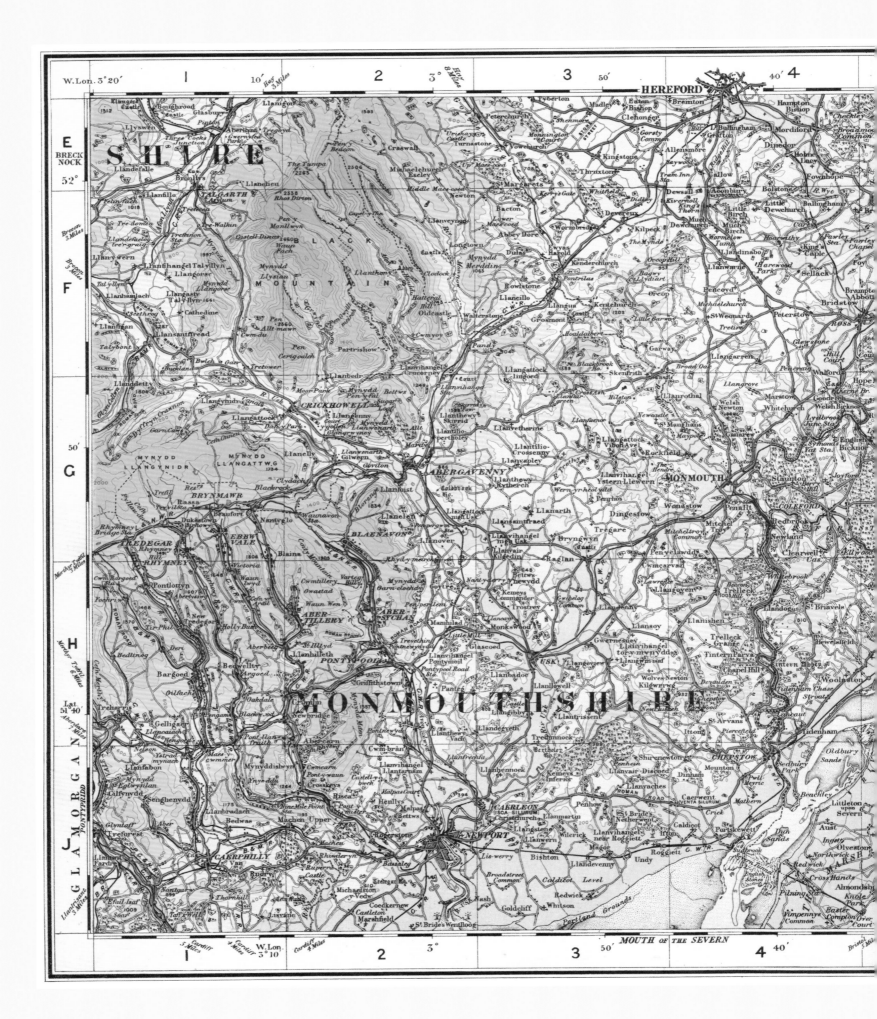

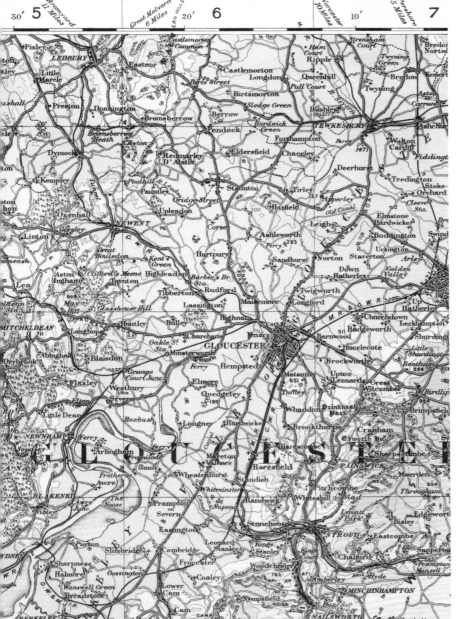

With its picturesque scenery and its tangible remains of many periods of civilisation, the Wye valley has been appreciated for centuries. Settled since the Stone Age, it was probably at the peak of its development in the late 18th and early 19th centuries. The river was then a busy navigation, with locally-built barges and trows carrying cargoes of coal, stone, iron, timber and agricultural produce between Hereford and the Wye's junction with the Severn at Chepstow. Limekilns, ironworks and boatyards flourished along the banks, but these did not diminish the river's scenic appeal, and it was one of the first waterways in Britain to exploit its tourist potential. Visitors were drawn by the picturesque qualities of the Wye's winding course through dramatic landscape, and the historic sites en route such as Goodrich Castle and Tintern Abbey. By 1827 up to eight boats a day were leaving Ross to take parties of visitors on the two-day Wye tour to Chepstow. It was also a river of considerable appeal to artists, both professional and amateur, and many of the Wye's 19th-century visitors would certainly have travelled with their boxes of watercolour paints.

By the late Victorian period the valley had changed considerably. Commercial traffic on the river had virtually ceased, along with much of the riverside industry, but the economic life of the valley had been kept alive by the coming of the railway along the Wye. This, closely following the river's winding course from Chepstow northwards to Monmouth and Ross, now brought increasing numbers of visitors to the region.

Today, the scene has changed again. The railway has in turn disappeared, and much of its route is now part of the fifty-two-mile Wye valley footpath between Hereford and Chepstow. Except for short stretches, the fast-flowing river is now navigable only by canoe, and most visitors come by car or coach. However, the one feature of the Wye that has greatly improved since the Victorian period is the salmon-fishing. In the late 19th century salmon had been virtually driven from the river by excessive netting, poaching and the building of weirs, but protection measures instigated since 1906 have helped to turn the Wye back into one of Britain's finest rivers for game and coarse fishing.

3 MONMOUTH *1890*
In the late Victorian period, Monmouthshire's former county town had a sleepy, even primitive atmosphere. The street here is unsurfaced and lined with plain 18th- and early 19th-century buildings that have seen better days, and a lone gas lamp is the only sign of modernity in an old market town largely untouched by industrial wealth.

4 CRUMLIN *Viaduct 1893*
The Taff Vale Railway, opened in 1840 to carry minerals from the Welsh valleys to the coast was, by the end of the century, one of south Wales's most profitable companies. Its major engineering feature was the steel lattice-work Crumlin viaduct, which carried the line over Ebbw Vale. Today nothing remains of either line or viaduct.

1 TINTERN ABBEY *1893*
The scenic qualities of the Wye valley (the ruins of Tintern Abbey in particular) have been enjoyed by visitors at least since the 18th century. This unchanging view, photographed at the end of the 19th century, can still satisfy the thousands who each year follow in the footsteps of Turner and Wordsworth.

2 GLOUCESTER
Southgate Street 1904
This busy street scene seems remarkable today because of the number of horses and the complete lack of motor traffic. The only sign of the modern age is the electric tram passing the street's oldest building, a fine 16th-century timber-framed structure which still stands.

5 CHEPSTOW *1893*
Chepstow, seen here with its great castle dominating the Wye's winding course, still looks as good today. In the foreground is the iron bridge designed by John Rennie in 1816.

6 CAERLEON
Museum and Church 1890
At various times Caerleon has been a major Roman base, a Bishopric and, traditionally, King Arthur's capital, but by the late 19th century it had become the large village that remains today. The grand, classical museum building celebrates Caerleon's Roman past, while the 15th-century church is more in scale with the town.

⑥

⑤

7 NEWPORT
Bridge and Castle 1903
This view of Newport seen across the Usk has changed considerably since the photograph was taken. The castle, then in a poor state of repair, has been restored but now stands isolated from the town by a new road system that swept away many of the buildings seen here.

8 CRICKHOWELL *1893*
For centuries Crickhowell's main glory has been its fine stone bridge over the Usk, and this late Victorian view still looks much the same today.

⑦

⑧

THE LIMESTONE OF Oxfordshire, the Cotswolds and Northamptonshire has long been prized as a building material. Endlessly varied in colour, durable and capable of being finely carved, the stone has been widely used since the Middle Ages for all kinds of buildings. It was used locally, for churches, houses, cottages and barns, and elsewhere for major structures such as Windsor Castle. By the 17th century the stone's varied colour, from the golden honey tones of the west to the iron-stained reddish browns of the north, had established a distinct pattern of local architecture, determining the character of Cotswold towns and villages. The main quarries, at Taynton, Burford and along the Windrush valley, had been in use at least since the Middle Ages, along with those at Hornton and Edge Hill which yielded the redder Northamptonshire stone, and many were still active in the 19th century. Stone continued to be an important industry throughout this period and many stonemason's yards were to be found scattered round the region. Many were kept in business by restoration projects for medieval and later buildings of historical interest. Weathering had always been a problem with limestone and in the 19th century industrial pollution often speeded the process of natural decay. At the same time the great boom in new church building from the 1840s onwards, for both Anglican and Nonconformist sects, kept the masons hard at work. The tradition of using local materials survived well into the Victorian era, keeping many of the quarries in use, and even the improved transport networks were not able to affect seriously the economic advantages these materials offered. A continuing local demand was for agricultural buildings, and for the miles of stone-walling that are a feature of the region.

Another distinctive Cotswold feature is the steeply-pitched roof with its array of carefully matched stone slates. Until the early 1900s when the quarries and mines were finally abandoned, the village of Stonesfield was the centre of this industry. Dug from deep underground, and left in the fields to be split by the action of frost, the slates were then worked into the required shapes and sizes.

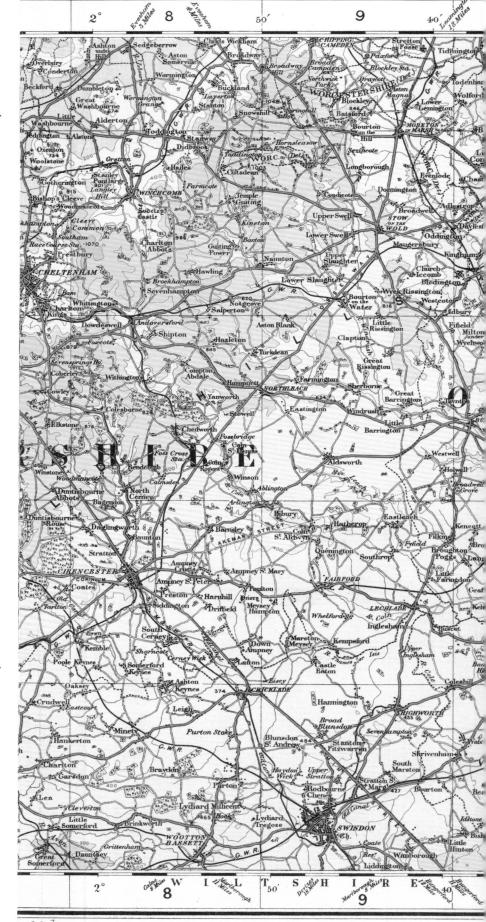

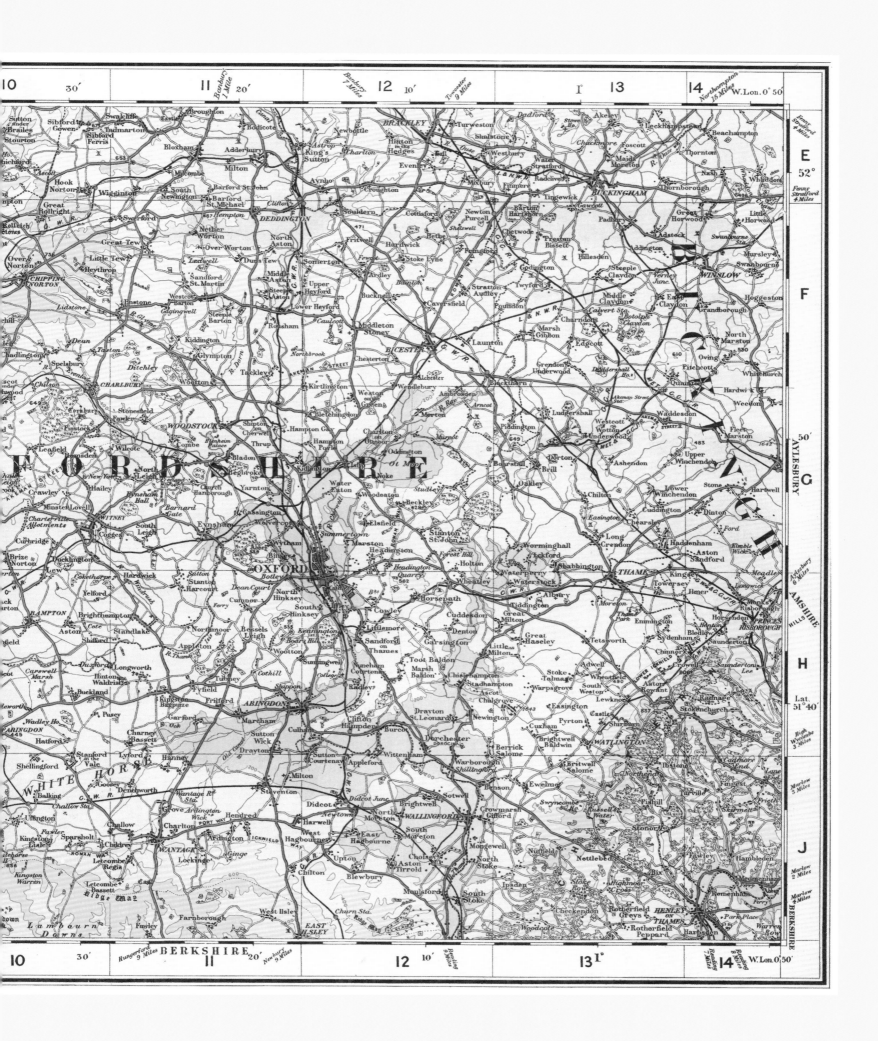

①

②

1 OXFORD *High Street 1900*
This view looks along the High towards Carfax and the tower of St Martin's Church, the body of which had been demolished four years previously. In the foreground is the Baroque portico of All Saints', and next to it the Victorian Gothic buildings of the county bank, completed in 1866.

2 CIRENCESTER
Market Place 1898
The magnificent tower and three-storey porch of the great wool church in Cirencester's market place still dominate the scene as

they do in this view, and the weekly market maintains traditions established in the Middle Ages.

3 HENLEY-ON-THAMES
Regatta 1890
In the late Victorian period the Henley regatta, established in 1839, was already the social and sporting highlight it is today. The Thames is crowded with skiffs and punts, and smartly-dressed spectators line the banks – attending an event that epitomised the late Victorian passion for boating on the river.

④

③

⑥

⑤

⑦

⑧

4 CHELTENHAM
College Playing Fields 1907
Another important event in the Edwardian social calendar was the school cricket match. Here, at Cheltenham College, which was founded in 1841, the game is being played against the background of the Gothic revival buildings that characterised this Victorian school. On the right is the former chapel. Built in the 1850s, it was replaced by the new chapel in 1896.

5 OXFORD
View of the Cherwell 1906
The habit of punting on the Cherwell was essentially late Victorian and had become universally popular by the Edwardian era. Parasols and elegant dresses make it look like a Tissot painting, and it is only the costumes that put this scene apart from its modern-day equivalent.

6 CLIFTON HAMPDEN
Barley Mow 1890
Another favourite late Victorian pastime was exploring the villages and inns of the upper Thames. Typical was the Barley Mow, whose thatched, half-timbered style was in keeping with Clifton Hampden's picturesque cottages. The inn survives today, but somewhat changed, while the village's Victorian buildings by the architect Gilbert Scott are now as famous as the thatched cottages.

7 WALLINGFORD
Market Place and Church 1893
Important since the Saxon period because of its river crossing, Wallingford was, by the end of the 19th century, a quiet market town. This view of a deserted market place on a sunny afternoon shows the 17th-century town hall with its open ground floor and the tower of St Mary's Church, still with its pinnacles of 1660.

8 BROADWAY *1898*
The fine Cotswold-stone houses and the wide main street were already attracting visitors to Broadway in the 1890s, but it was the motor car that really brought the village into the prominence it suffers from today. Here, bicycles are the only means of transport, while the plough is a reminder that Broadway was still primarily a farming village.

69

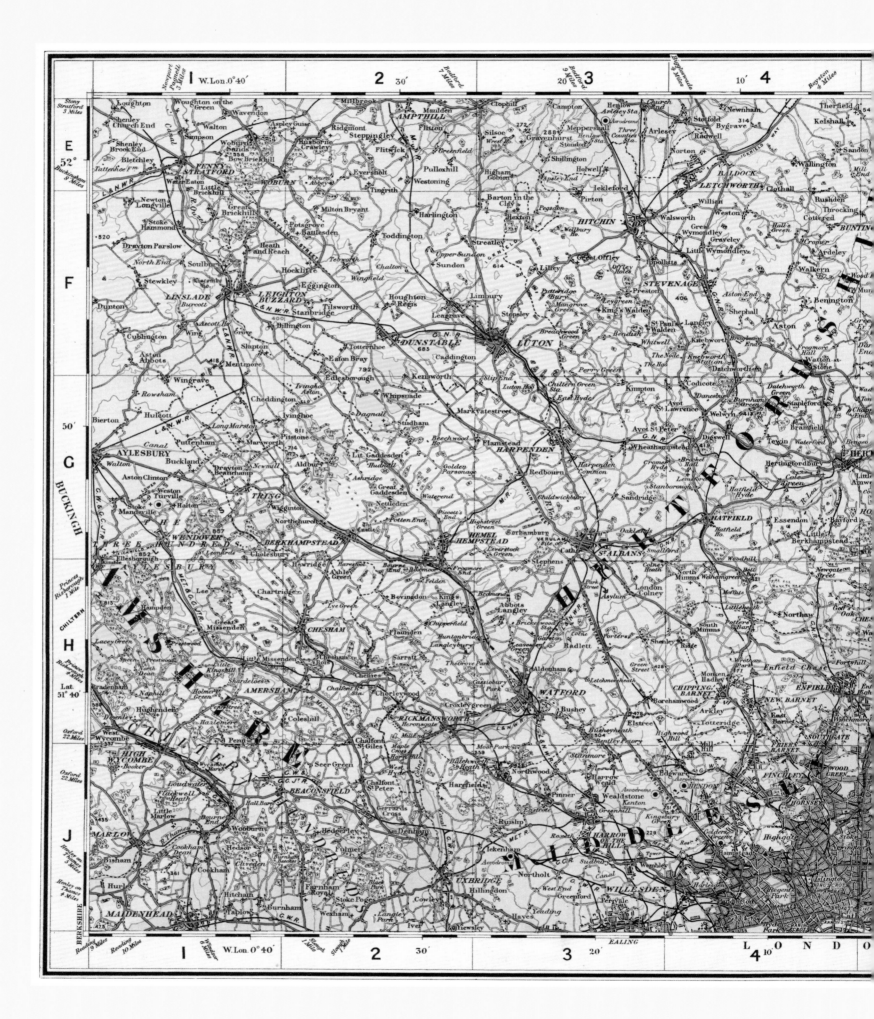

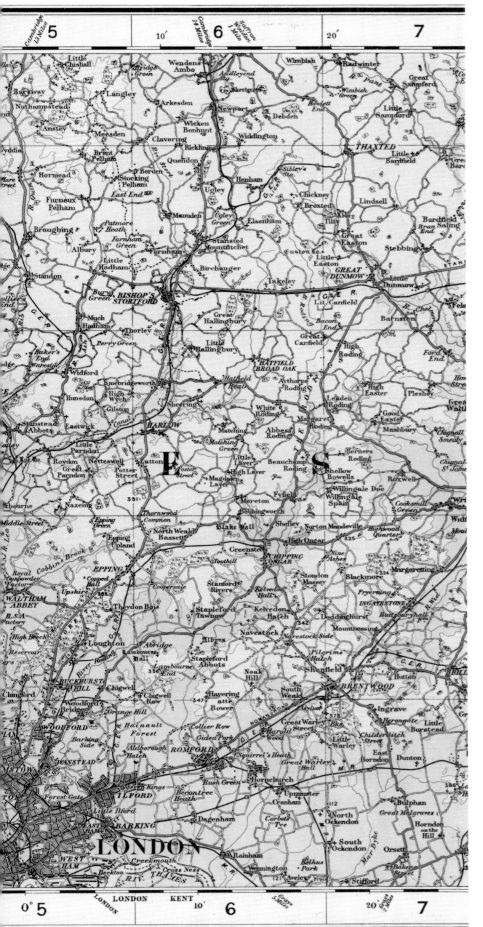

AT THE END OF THE Victorian period the attractions of the countryside became both more alluring, and more accessible, to city dwellers. Writers, artists, philosophers and, increasingly, politicians were creating an image of the rural way of life as something healthy, clean, carefree and pleasantly traditional, and so living in the country came, for the first time, to be seen as a positive virtue for the increasingly dominant middle classes. As the realities of country life remained rather at odds with this ideal, ways were developed to bring the country more into line with the needs of an urbanised population. Most important was the expanding network of railways, underground and tramway systems radiating out of London that brought the country closer to the city. By this time many small and previously independent market towns such as Aylesbury, High Wycombe, Leighton Buzzard, Dunstable, Luton, St Albans, Hertford, Bishop's Stortford and Brentwood, were well under an hour's travel from the centre of London, and so commuting to work was not only possible, but desirable.

This new habit, perhaps the greatest force for social change in late 19th-century Britain, was actively encouraged by the railway companies in their battle for traffic. Some towns were served by more than one company and the smallest villages acquired stations. Where the railways went, housing developments soon followed. The activities of one of the most ambitious of these companies, the Metropolitan Railway, inspired the use of the term Metroland to describe the rapid urbanisation of previously rural regions. The virtues, imaginary and real, of country life, were also promoted by the railways and tramways in their advertisements.

Another approach was epitomised by the garden city movement whose creator, Ebenezer Howard, believed that the ideal was a city built from scratch in a green and pleasant land, combining urban convenience with rural health and tranquillity. His theories were first put into practice at Letchworth, and the garden city built there from 1903 was to be followed by many more, along with the inspiration for modern concepts such as the green belt and town and country planning.

①

②

③

④

⑥

1 LONDON BRIDGE c.*1890*
This view, looking northwards across the 1832 London bridge which was replaced by the present structure in 1973 and exported to the United States, shows a major late Victorian traffic jam, without a motor vehicle in sight.

2 LONDON
Piccadilly Circus 1890s
Far less crowded, by contrast, is Piccadilly Circus – seen here soon after Sir Alfred Gilbert's *Eros* fountain had been erected in its original setting in 1892. This view from Piccadilly towards Leicester Square shows the Palladium on the left and the Criterion on the right. Today, the façades of these buildings look similar, but *Eros* has been resited outside the Criterion, and Piccadilly Circus is now more in the nature of a crossroads than a roundabout.

⑦

⑧

⑤

⑨

⑩

3 THAMES *Ship-building c.1910*
Ship-building was a major industry on the Thames throughout the 19th century, with yards producing both naval and commerical vessels. One of the most famous products of the Thames-side yards was Brunel's *Great Eastern*.

4 ROMFORD MARKET *1908*
Romford still has its generous market place but the town's heyday as one of London's leading provincial markets is long gone. Captured here is the scale and diversity of the market, with stalls selling all kinds of produce, livestock, agricultural and garden implements, baskets, clothing, ladders and much else beside.

5 TRING *High Street 1897*
Queen Victoria's Diamond Jubilee of 1897 was an event of great national celebration and the flags, bunting and lanterns that decorate Tring's High Street are typical of those that brought colour to many of Britain's towns and villages.

6 CHINGFORD *1906*
The expanding tramway network encouraged the spread of London during the Edwardian period and many outlying suburbs and villages gained the mixed blessing of a direct link to central London. Here, at the end of the line in Chingford, a tram waits to set off back to the Lea Bridge Road.

7 WATFORD
Cassiobury Park and Canal c.1914
Canals were an important part of the national transport network until World War II. Here, a pair of butty boats are about to leave a lock on the Grand Union Canal as it passes through Cassiobury Park.

8 BISHOP'S STORTFORD
1899
Prominent in this view of a small Hertfordshire market town are the pyramid-shaped kilns of the malt houses, one of Bishop's Stortford's major industries since the opening of the River Stort navigation in 1769. Dominating the skyline is the tower of St Michael's Church.

9 LUTON
George Street 1897
In the Victorian period Luton was a small Bedfordshire market town famous for hat-making, but it changed radically after 1907 when Vauxhall began to make cars near by. This view looking along George Street towards the old town hall is practically unrecognisable today. A new town hall was built 1938, along with a whole range of public buildings to suit Luton's new status as an industrial centre.

10 LETCHWORTH
Norton Road 1908
From 1903 Letchworth was laid out as a new garden city to the designs of Parker and Unwin and by 1908, when this photograph was taken, the characteristic cottage-style of terraced housing was already well established, along with the pattern of wide roads radiating out from the centre. The telegraph poles dominating the scene are a sign of the changing times.

COLCHESTER CLAIMS TO BE Britain's oldest town, and its Roman ancestry was well appreciated by the Victorians along with the relics of later periods of civilisation to be found there and in the surrounding Essex countryside. Rural Essex had changed little in the intervening centuries and it was not until the late 19th century that the foundations of modern Essex were laid down. Most noticeable were changes along the coast, where a series of emergent resorts were among the first in Britain to experience the impact of popular leisure and tourism. From the 1850s rapid access by train and steamship turned the Thames estuary and the Essex coastline into a kind of London-by-the-Sea, with new resorts competing to appeal to both holiday-makers and day-trippers. These resorts were a Victorian phenomenon and yet they remained, by modern standards, very small until the period of rapid growth after World War I.

First to develop was Southend, whose origins as a resort date back to the 18th century. The Princess of Wales stayed in 1803, and expansion soon followed this royal seal of approval. At first it remained a rather exclusive place, but from the 1850s the railway, the large hotels and finally the pier, turned the town into a popular resort. Next came Walton, developing from the 1830s, and then Clacton and Dovercourt – Harwich's resort. Last to arrive was Frinton, a development of the 1890s that managed to retain its initial aura of exclusivity in a region by then devoted to popular tourism.

Another feature of the Essex coast in this period was the many small ports. Maldon, Brightlingsea, Tollesbury and Manningtree, for example, were kept busy by their railway connections, and by the fleets of characteristic red-sailed Thames barges that carried every kind of cargo along the vast network of tidal rivers and marshland creeks from which the Essex coastline is formed. Today, the few barges that survive are carefully preserved in sailing centres such as Maldon, and only Colchester, Harwich and Felixstowe survive as major commercial ports. Yachts and pleasure boats now fill the others, and the sailing centre of the region is Burnham-on-Crouch which, in the Victorian era, barely existed at all.

Holton
St Mary
Higham
Stratford
St Mary   East Bergholt   Bentley Sta.   Tattingstone
Wedham   Brantham   Holbrook   Stutton   Harkstead   Shotley   Trimley   Walton
Lawford   Mistley   Seafield Bay   Hall   Holbrook
Bay   RIV. STOUR   HARWICH   FELIXSTOWE   Erwarton
MANNINGTREE   Bradfield   Wrabness   Dovercourt   Orwell
Haven   Ferry
Harbour   Aerodrome
Fort
Ramsey   Mill Bay   Cork Lightship
Horsleycross
Street   Wix   Great
Oakley   Horsley Cross   Stone's Green   Beaumont   Hamford   THE NAZE
CHESTER
OLONIA   Little
Bentley   Tendring   Weeley   Thorpe
le-Soken   Kirby-le-Soken   Walton
Hall   Tower   WALTON-ON
THE-NAZE
Frating   Great Bentley   Weeley
Heath   Kirby Cross   FRINTON
Little
Clacton   Great
Holland   Little
Holland
BRIGHTLINGSEA   Gt Clacton
Point
Weley   St Osyth   CLACTON-ON-SEA
Mersea
Flats   St Osyth Marsh   Colne Point
Sunk Lightship

Gunfleet

Dengie
Flats   Buxey

Ray
Sand   Sunk Sand
Foulness
Sands   Bar   Kentish Knock
Lightship
Holliwell
Foulness
Point   Magnetic Var.
Annual
Knot
decrease 8′
14° 7′ W. 1921.
constant)

Edinburgh Lightship

The Shingles   Tongue Lightship

Mouse Lightship

E

F   50′

C

40′

H

J   Lat.
51° 30′

①

②

③

1 SOUTHEND *Pier 1898*
Although Southend's development as a resort started in 1767, it was not until the coming of the railway that it became a popular holiday destination. Hotels soon followed, along with an esplanade, but it was the pier above all that brought Londoners to the town in their thousands. This view of the pier was taken shortly after its completion in 1895. Rebuilding took place in the 1920s.

2 FELIXSTOWE *1907*
The rapid development of east coast resorts was a phenomenon of the Edwardian era and Felixstowe's gentle bays soon brought the small village its share of hotels and seaside apartments. The donkey- and goat-carts seen here reflect the genteel qualities of this little resort long before the days of amusement arcades.

3 CHELMSFORD
High Street 1895
This view along Chelmsford High Street towards the 18th-century shire hall is full of the pleasant small-town atmosphere and interesting variety of architecture often driven into oblivion by the combined assaults of the car and thoughtless redevelopment. Four years after this photograph was taken Marconi set up the world's first radio factory in Hall Street.

④

⑤

⑥

4 WITHAM *Chipping Hill 1900*
The oldest part of Witham surrounds the 14th-century Church of St Nicholas, and the picturesque qualities of these timber-framed cottages and barns were appreciated even in the 19th century. The area still survives today, but the heavy hand of the restorer has replaced rural charm with suburban self-consciousness.

5 WALTON-ON-THE-NAZE
1900
A little Essex resort since the 1830s, Walton never developed sufficiently to match its nearby rival, Clacton. The hotels and seafront terraces were few and far between, although one early example, the Cliff Hotel and White Lodge of the late 1830s, can be seen in the distance in this view. The beach, quiet and uncrowded, has its quota of bathing-machines.

6 FRINTON-ON-SEA *c.1910*
Frinton was developed from the 1890s as a discreet and rather private resort, with smart houses and estates spreading inland towards the railway station. The dunes attracted a more casual growth of beach huts which continued to spread along the foreshore until the 1920s.

7 COLCHESTER
High Street and Town Hall 1902
This view was taken almost immediately after the completion in 1902 of Colchester's extraordinary town hall, designed by Sir John Belcher. By the standards of other buildings in the street the town hall is vast, and its 162-foot-high tower dominates the skyline. In the distance is one of Colchester's other more eccentric buildings, the red-brick water tower dating from 1885.

⑦

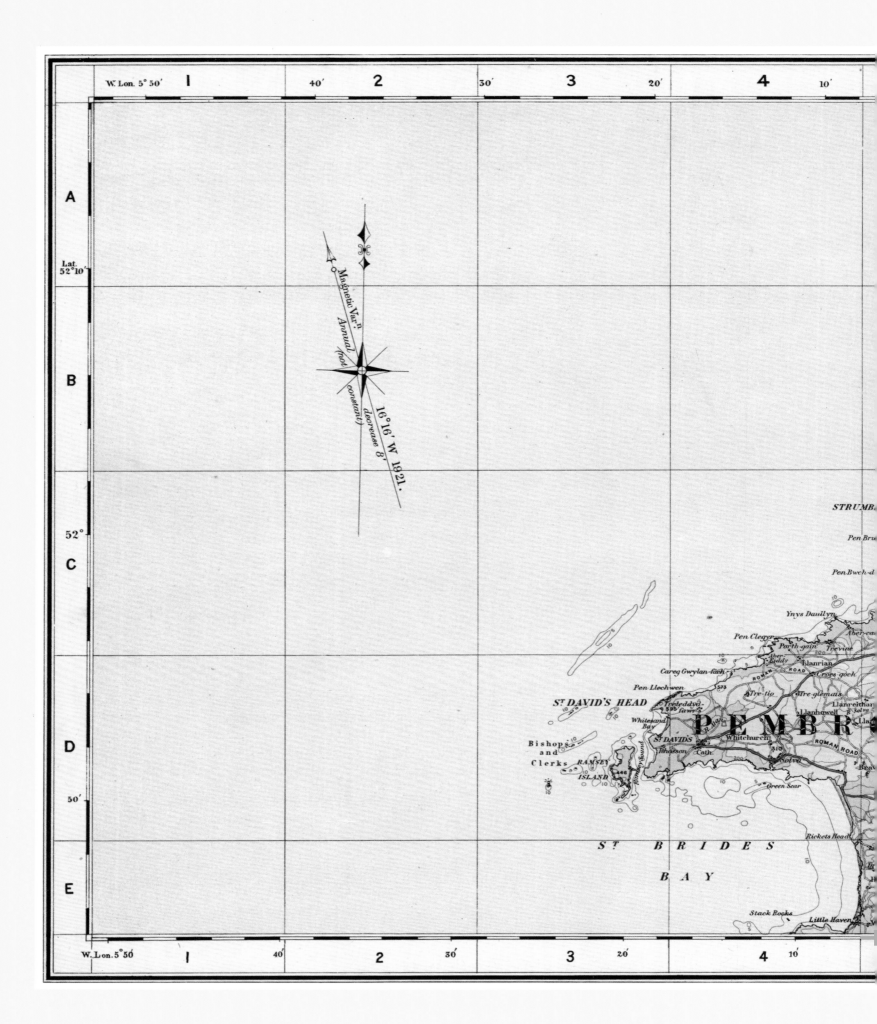

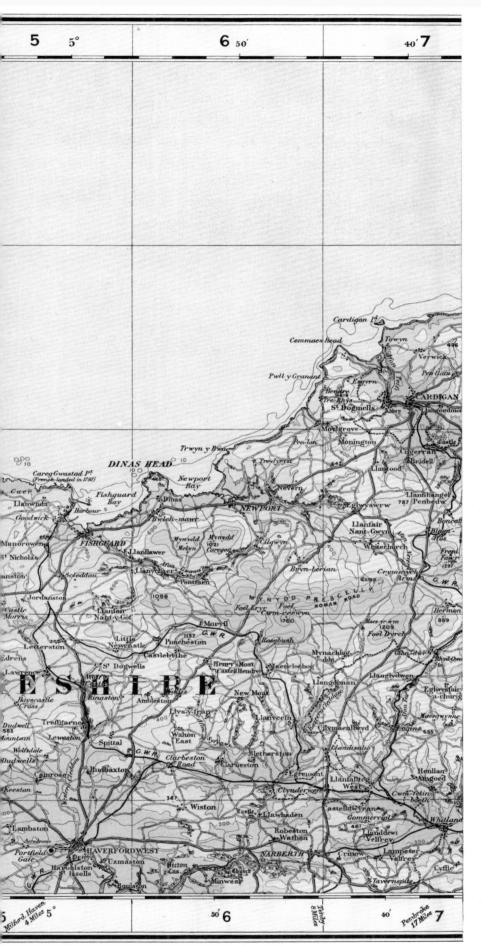

IN THE 19TH CENTURY Pembrokeshire was a remote and rarely visited region, appreciated more for its history than its landscape and dramatic coastline. Its spirit of independence had been formed partly by geography and partly by its distinctive history upon which many periods of civilisation had left their mark. However, it was not until the Victorian period that the serious study of Pembrokeshire's past began to separate real history from the hazy traditions of Celtic and Druidic mythology. This was the age when modern methods of archaeology were first applied to the relics of prehistory, and pioneering work was carried out in south Wales with its wealth of cromlechs, or burial chambers, and stone circles. In 1912 a human skeleton that had been discovered in 1823 in the Paviland caves in the Gower was proved to belong to the Cro-Magnon era, contemporary with the first cave paintings in southern France.

The Roman and Celtic periods were studied with equal intensity, along with the pattern of early Christian settlement that had led to the building of St David's Cathedral, and the shrines to St Non, the mother of Wales's patron saint. This growing appreciation of local history, and the realisation of its importance for Britain as a whole, fired the new spirit of Welsh independence that came to life again in the Victorian period after being dormant for several centuries. The Welsh language was revived along with other aspects of Welsh culture – such as the eisteddfod – but it was the spread of Welsh Methodism that really expressed the new independent fervour. The movement began in the 18th century, contemporary with English Wesleyanism, but it did not take over the country until the 19th century. Chapels were built throughout the land, but south Wales was in the forefront of the movement. A 1910 survey revealed that there were over 4,700 chapels in Wales, most of which were built in the Victorian era by the various Nonconformist sects, such as the Calvinistic Methodists, who alone claimed in 1895 to have 2,794 chapels, the Baptists, the Independents, the Unitarians, the Congregationalists and many others.

①

③

1 HAVERFORDWEST *1906*
This view down one of the steep streets in Haverfordwest that climb up from the river underlines the agricultural nature of Pembroke's county town at the turn of the century. Traditional provincial attitudes prevail, with the horse the only means of transport and the wearing of hats still universal. Locally-made children's chairs can be seen for sale outside the shop in the foreground.

2 ST DAVID'S *Cathedral 1890*
Even to the Victorians St David's must have seemed an extraordinary building in so isolated a spot, but the attractions of this remote cathedral made it popular throughout the 19th century. Clearly seen in this view of the cathedral from the ruined Bishop's Palace is the west front, rebuilt in 1862 to the designs of Gilbert Scott.

②

3 HAVERFORDWEST
Castle from the river 1890
This view of Haverfordwest's cottages and warehouses clustered on the bank of the Cleddau River below the towering bulk of the Norman castle shows the town at its most picturesque. Today, part of the river has been dammed and there are riverside walks along its banks. The town gaol, seen here inside the castle walls, is now the county museum.

4 LOWER FISHGUARD *1899*
This view shows the original harbour as a small fishing and trading port. In 1907 major redevelopment of the harbour was undertaken by the Great Western Railway to try to turn Fishguard into a port of call for transatlantic liners. This scheme never really got off the ground, but the new harbour did subsequently become a major ferry port for Irish traffic.

④

In the late 1860s the Central Wales Railway finally completed its line that ran north-west from Carmarthen through dramatic scenery to Knighton, and the impact on the towns and villages along the route was immediate. Llandeilo and Llandovery, traditional market towns for centuries, now became even more important as distribution points for the agricultural produce of the region, and in particular for the great herds of black cattle that were now transported by train to be sold in England. However, it was the spa towns, Llanwrtyd Wells, Llandrindod Wells and Builth Wells, that really felt the benefit.

The curative and improving effects of the saline streams and sulphurous wells of the region had been well known at least since the 18th century. The first to be developed was Llanwrtyd Wells, where in 1732 the Reverend Theophilus Evans cured his scurvy, but the other two soon followed. Llandrindod Wells had its first spa hotel in 1749, while at Builth Wells development was encouraged by the presence of two wells, one salt and one sulphur. Visitors were also drawn to Builth by its important place in Welsh history, a subject of increasing interest to the Victorians. It was near here that Llewellyn, the last Prince of Wales, was killed in a skirmish with soldiers from the garrison in the Norman castle at Builth, and with him perished the Welsh Royal line.

By the end of the 18th century the habit of taking the waters was well established in the region, along with the other fashionable activities traditionally associated with spa towns. However, the relative inaccessibility of the region limited its potential until the railway came, but from that moment growth was dramatic. All three towns were at the peak of their prosperity in the late Victorian and Edwardian eras, when large hotels were built to cater for the thousands of visitors who came to take the waters, and to enjoy the flourishing life and culture brought into being by the pump rooms. In its heyday Llandrindod Wells was the largest, and smartest, of the three, attracting 80,000 visitors a year. However, the other two did not lag far behind, appealing as they did to a broader social span.

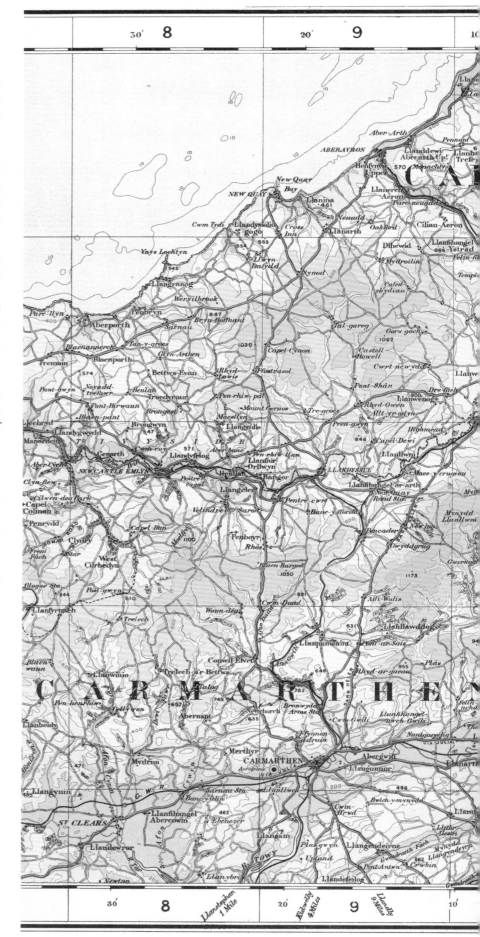

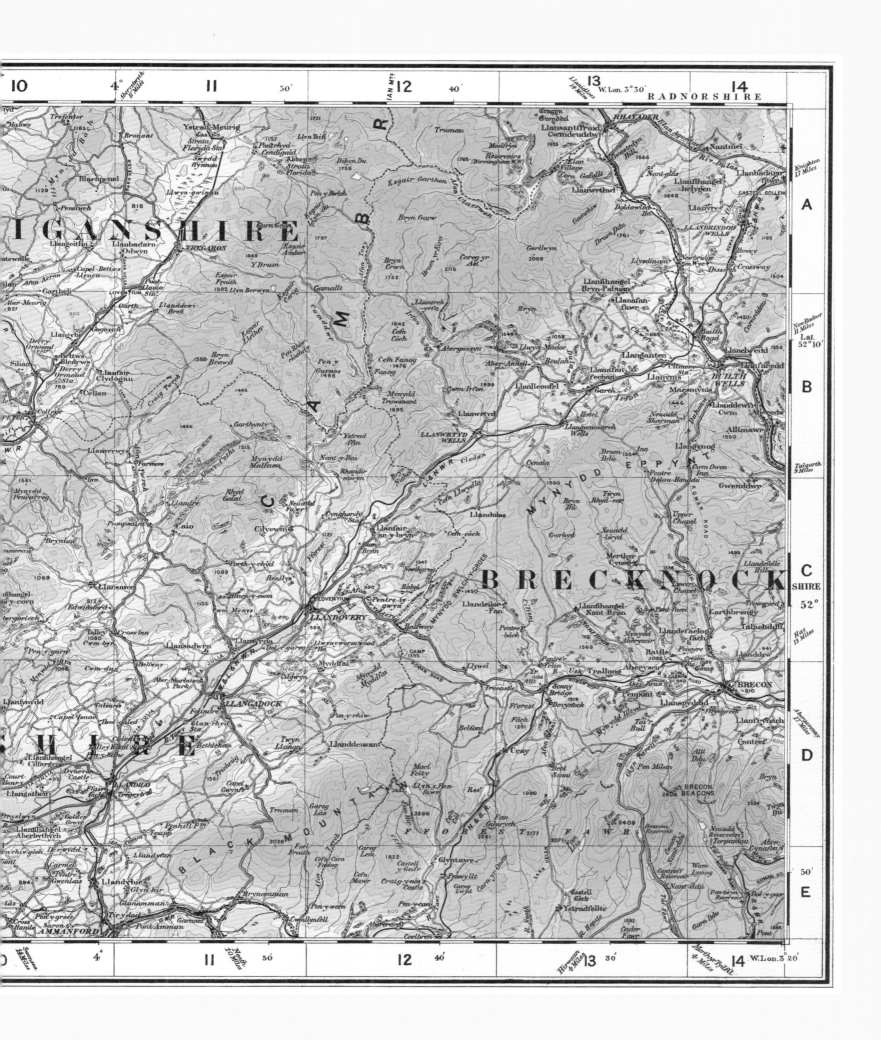

①

③

1 BRECON *High Street 1910*
An important town since the Middle Ages, Brecon still offers its visitors a pleasant blend of Tudor, Georgian and 19th-century architecture. This view of the High Street shows how the tower of St Mary's Church dominates the town, as it still does today. However, it was not this church but the Priory Church of St John, to the north of the town beyond the remains of the Norman castle, that was designated Brecon's cathedral in 1923.

2 CARMARTHEN
Lammas Street 1893
Carmarthen's longest and widest thoroughfare is still Lammas Street, but it is seldom seen so empty today. In the centre of the street is the Royal Welch Fusiliers' Crimean war memorial.

3 CARDIGAN *Priory Street 1860*
This view, looking along Priory Street to the parish church of St Mary, clearly illustrates the rural nature of Welsh towns in the Victorian period. At this point Cardigan's fortunes were at a rather low ebb, the coming of the railway having greatly reduced the town's significance as a port. Quiet domestic architecture surrounds the rather bizarre Gothic-style town hall, whose little bell-tower can be seen on the left.

②

④

4 BRECON *Bridge 1899*
Relatively unchanged today is this view of Brecon's five-arched bridge over the River Usk, still the only river crossing in the town. The castellated buildings beyond the bridge are part of Christ's College school.

5 CARMARTHEN *Coracles 1898*
Salmon-fishing has long been a feature of Welsh rivers such as the Towy and the Teifi, and the coracle fishermen of towns like Cardigan and Carmarthen were well known in the 19th century. These distinctive craft, of wickerwork and tarred canvas, were a local speciality. Surprisingly, there are still a few coracle fishermen working from Carmarthen and examples of coracles are sometimes displayed in the market. There have been changes to the town's waterfront since this view was taken, and there is a new concrete bridge across the Towy.

⑤

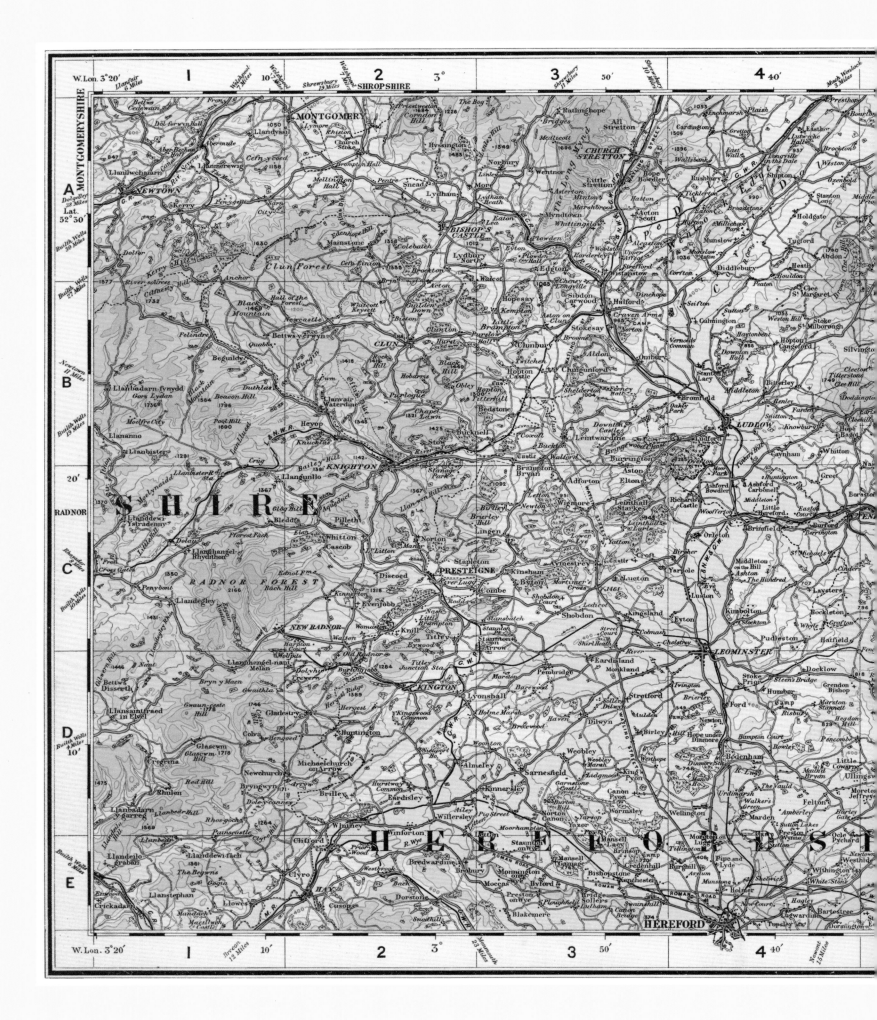

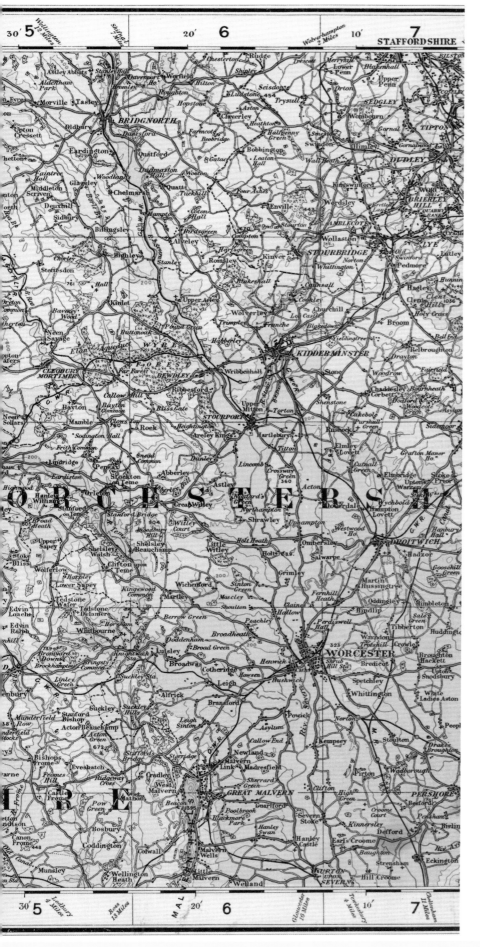

THERE WERE MANY THINGS that brought visitors in the late Victorian period to Herefordshire and Worcestershire, and to the Welsh Marches. With their keen sense for both local and national history, they enjoyed the long line of Border castles, Offa's Dyke and the varied architecture of the region, from the great cathedrals and abbeys to the traditional black-and-white buildings. Also popular were the lush fields of the Severn valley that were famous, then as now, for their fruit, hops and cider.

Many of the pleasures that appealed to the Victorians in the region can be enjoyed today, but less familiar now is something that would have been taken for granted in the late Victorian period. Until the latter part of the 19th century much of the produce, the raw materials and the manufactured goods of the region, was transported by water, and the River Severn was a busy artery at the centre of a network of navigable waterways. Many of these had been developed in the late 18th century, but the building of canals continued well into the Victorian period and even into the railway age.

Early this century, the Severn itself was still navigable as far north as Ironbridge, and large vessels sailed regularly to the docks in Worcester and Stourport where they could load or unload cargoes into the fleets of narrowboats that travelled regularly to and from Birmingham and the Black Country. The best-known parts of this Severn-based waterway network were the Worcester & Birmingham and the Staffordshire & Worcestershire Canals, still used by pleasure boats today.

Little-known today are the other waterways, the canals that linked Droitwich, Hereford and Leominster to the Severn, and thus to the national waterway network. The Droitwich Canals were busy throughout the 19th century, but have been long closed. Less active was the canal completed between Hereford and Gloucester in 1843, which had only a short life before succumbing to inevitable railway competition, while the canal planned to connect Leominster to the Severn was never even completed. The short section that did carry traffic was abandoned in 1859 when part of its route was taken over by a new railway.

②

④

1 WORCESTER
Guildhall and High Street 1899
Worcester's most unusual building is probably its 1723 guildhall, one of the most splendid of Britain's 18th-century town halls. The extravagance of the carved detail seen here can still be enjoyed today, especially as the High Street is now a pedestrian precinct. The rather extraordinary lamps that top the gate have disappeared, but otherwise the scene is much as it was in 1899.

2 GREAT MALVERN *1893*
Set on the steep slopes of the Malvern Hills, Great Malvern is a largely 19th-century town, its growth and popularity based on the Victorian fashion for taking the waters. This view shows the early 19th-century terraces of the High Street and some of the later

hotels that marked the town's importance as a spa. Malvern's other claim to fame, the 15th-century priory, lies to the south.

3 UPTON-ON-SEVERN c.*1910*
Upton's charm comes from its position beside the river, its range of Georgian buildings, and the tower of the old church whose height, with its copper cupola on top, gives a focus to the whole town. Little has changed since this view was taken except that the bridge was replaced in 1940 and the rest of the old church was pulled down in 1937, leaving the tower isolated on a little green.

4 HEREFORD *High Town 1891*
Hereford's High Town, an open space at the city centre, was created after the Middle Ages and some of its most important black-and-white timber-framed buildings were destroyed or altered. A surviving example surrounded by more conventional 18th- and 19th-century buildings, can be seen in this photograph. Beyond is All Saints' Church with its tall steeple. In the centre hansom cabs wait for customers, while behind the cab rank is one of those timber-built refreshment cabins for cabbies that were once common in all British cities.

③

⑥

⑤

5 BRIDGNORTH *The Lift 1898*
The cable-hauled cliff railway was a popular feature of late Victorian Bridgnorth, offering a quick connection between the High Town around the castle and the Low Town by the Severn. The railway still operates today, but these Victorian cars with their open driving position have been replaced by enclosed models with rather quaint Art Deco streamlining.

6 LEOMINSTER *High Street 1904*
The varied architecture of Leominster's attractive High Street can be seen here, including an early timber-framed building that still survives. Particularly interesting are the displays of agricultural and domestic equipment hanging outside the shops, underlining Leominster's importance as a market town whose wealth was based on wool.

7 BRIDGNORTH
From Castle Walk 1898
Hill towns are rare in Britain so Bridgnorth had a particular appeal for the Victorians who enjoyed the splendid panoramas from the ruined castle. This view of the winding course of the Severn and the six-arched bridge of 1823 has hardly changed, but there has been considerable development

across the river away from the town. The tall warehouse by the bridge is a reminder that the Severn was still navigable towards Shrewsbury in the early 19th century.

8 LUDLOW
Lower Broad Street 1892
Remarkably, Ludlow is still one of Britain's most attractive small towns and the qualities that made it popular among Victorian and Edwardian visitors still stand. Then, as now, the best approach to Ludlow was from the old bridge over the Teme and up Lower Broad Street, to enter the town through 13th-century Broad Gate. The tower of St Laurence's Church crowns the skyline.

⑦

⑧

THE SHAKESPEARE INDUSTRY has turned Stratford into one of Britain's most visited towns, a shrine for tourists from all over the world, but few of today's visitors are aware of their debt to the Victorians who were the first to develop the cult into an international business. Indeed, the poet was so little considered in the 18th century that the house in Stratford where he spent the last five years of his life was demolished without a murmur in 1759. Today, hundreds of thousands come each year to stare at the recently exposed foundations of New Place. Shakespeare was not commemorated on a national scale until 1769, when the actor David Garrick staged the first Shakespeare festival to be held in Stratford, and it was not until the 19th century that the playwright became a figure of national importance.

In 1824 the Shakespeare Club was formed in the town and twenty three years later the forerunner of the modern Shakespeare Birthplace Trust bought the house in Henley Street where Shakespeare had been born in 1564. The price paid for this decayed and virtually derelict building, described by the agent as the 'most honoured monument of the greatest genius that ever lived' was a staggering £3,000. This, more than anything else, marked the birth of the Shakespeare business and the house, completely rebuilt, was soon opened to the public. From this beginning, the industry grew rapidly, receiving an additional impetus from the national celebrations held to commemorate the tercentennary of Shakespeare's birth in 1864.

In 1879 the first permanent Memorial Theatre was opened, with its adjacent museum and art gallery, and in 1888 the famous Gower statue which shows the seated playwright flanked by representations of Hamlet, Lady Macbeth, Falstaff and Henry V was unveiled. This theatre was destroyed by fire in 1926, and the present building was completed six years later. With visitors now coming in their thousands to Stratford, the town soon found other Shakespearean relics to keep them busy. Anne Hathaway's cottage was acquired in 1892 from descendants of the Hathaway family, and by the end of the Victorian period the Shakespeare cult was firmly established.

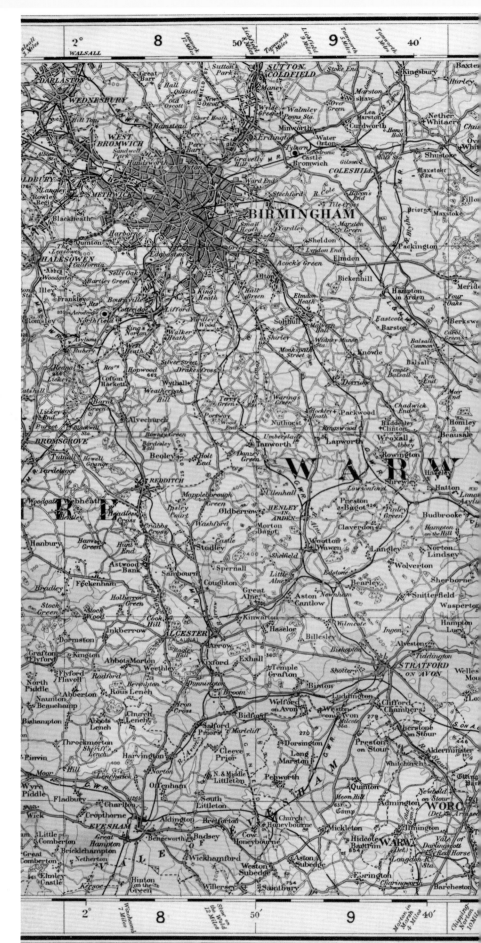

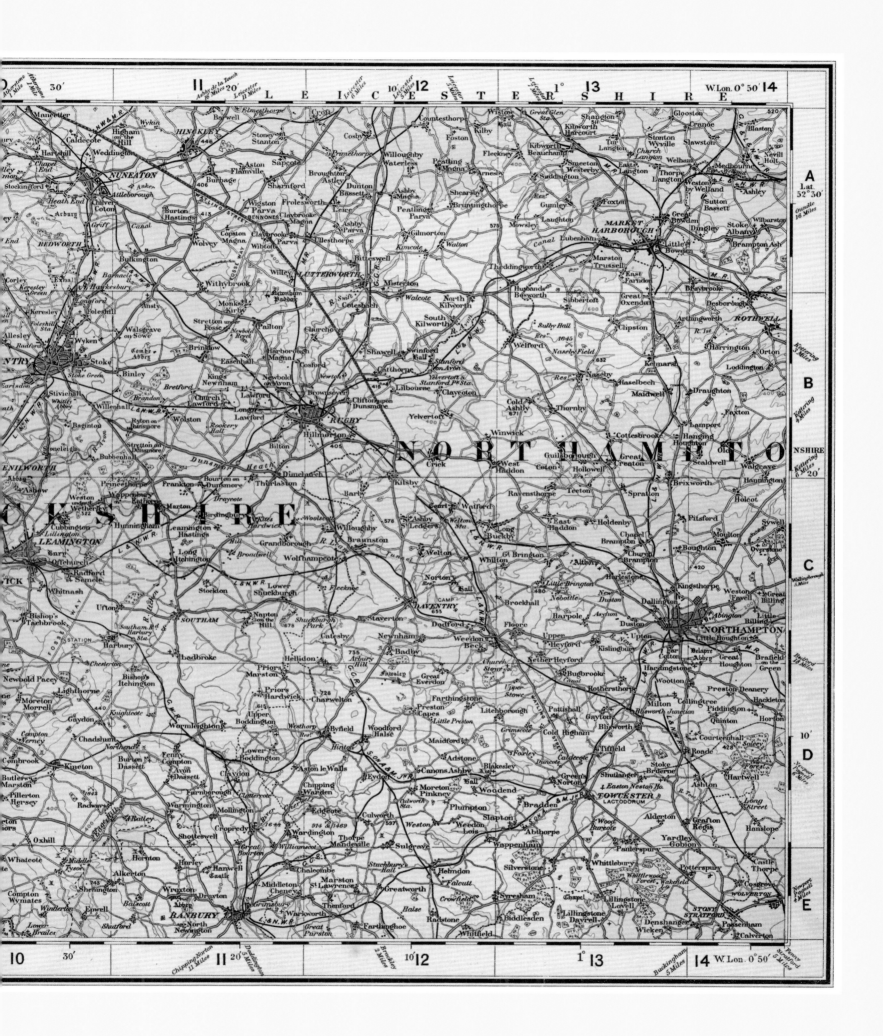

①

②

④

③

1 KENILWORTH
Village 1892
Sandwiched as it is between the spreading suburbs of Coventry and Warwick, Kenilworth could hardly be called a village today. Yet in the late 19th century it was just that, although the railway and the increasing popularity of the castle had begun the inevitable pattern of development. This view shows a rural village, set in woodland, with few roads and, half hidden, the simple 1841 church.

2 WARWICK
Castle from Bridge c.1914
By contrast, this famous view of Warwick's medieval castle towering above the River Avon is still one that can be enjoyed today. Then, pleasure-boating on the Avon was a popular pastime but boats are rarely seen on this stretch of river nowadays.

3 STRATFORD ON AVON
Memorial Theatre 1892
Stratford's first Shakespeare Theatre, a simple structure, was opened in 1827. In 1879 this was replaced by the far more ambitious theatre seen in this photograph, an extraordinary blend of Flemish Gothic with local timber-framing, topped by a belfry-like tower. This was burnt down in 1926 to be replaced in turn by the present rather bland Art Deco brick box.

⑥

⑦

4 WOLVERTON
Stratford Road 1910
The little village of Wolverton was changed beyond recognition after the London & Birmingham Railway built its carriage works here in 1838. The result was a new railway town with streets of brick houses built on a grid pattern, some of which can be seen in this view of the works. Notable is the steam tram, with its two double-decker trailer cars.

5 BIRMINGHAM
Corporation Street 1890
Corporation Street was created from scratch between 1878 and the early 1900s as part of a scheme to construct a grand urban boulevard in the city centre. By the time this photograph was taken the wide handsome street was lined with tall Gothic and Italianate buildings of stone and terracotta, with modern shops on street level. The new law courts, completed in 1891, were also part of this new expression of Birmingham's civic pride. Corporation Street survives today, but considerably changed.

6 LEAMINGTON
Parish Church 1892
Leamington's massive parish church was built steadily through the 19th century. Work started in 1843 and a number of architects subsequently added to the building in a variety of generalised European Gothic styles. This photograph shows the church before the addition of the tower, completed in 1902. The horse-drawn tram adds an interesting period touch.

7 STRATFORD ON AVON
Market Place 1892
This view of the market place, still quite recognisable today, underlines the importance of Stratford as a major market town in the 19th century – quite apart from any associations with Shakespeare. In modern terms the Shakespearian industry was then in its infancy, although it had been given a boost by the celebrations surrounding the tercentenary of the playwright's birth in 1864.

8 COVENTRY
Butchers' Row 1892
This view captures well the flavour of pre-industrial Coventry, when narrow cobbled streets were lined with medieval and later buildings. Few such buildings survive today for most of the city's heart was wiped out by the bombing raid of 14 November 1940. When this photograph was taken the bicycle and the motor car were already changing the face of Coventry but their impact had still to be felt in streets like Butchers' Row.

⑤

⑧

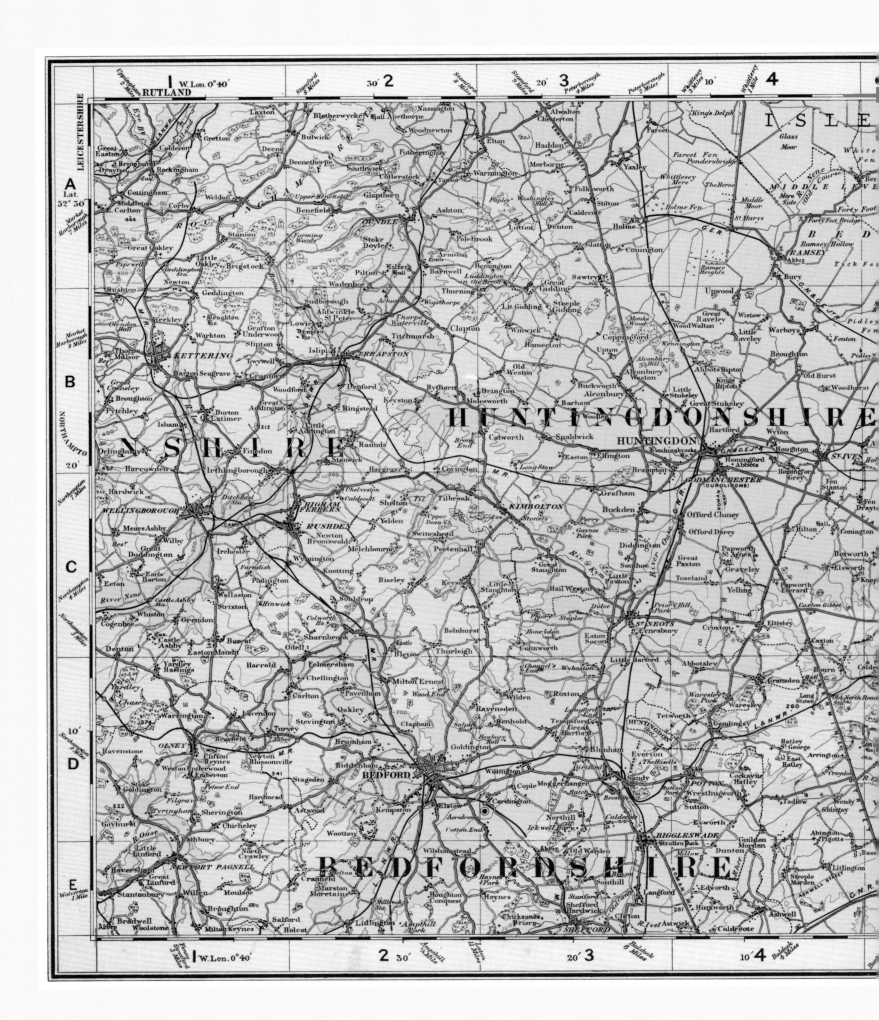

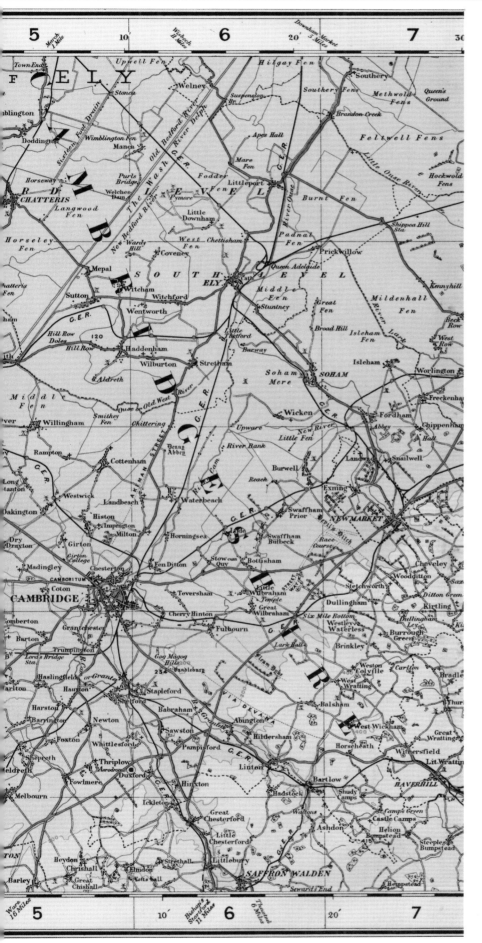

PRIOR TO THE VICTORIAN period village life in Britain had changed little since the Middle Ages, but in the 19th century the village began to lose some of the self-sufficiency that had made it so successful as a tightly-knit community. First, social divisions which had seemed unimportant in previous periods were now more obvious, thanks in part to the declining power of the church whose dominant position was being increasingly challenged by the rise of Nonconformist religions. The chapel was a major addition to many Victorian villages.

Fragmentation was also caused by changing patterns of employment. Agriculture was still the economic backbone of most villages, but mechanisation and changes in farming methods were reducing the number of workers required by local farms. The result was often poverty and hardship, and so many people left the village to seek employment in the large towns and local industries. Leaving the village on a temporary or a permanent basis was in any case made easier by new means of transport. Villages that had a railway station immediately lost their traditional isolation, and the train became an escape route for workers seeking employment elsewhere. It also made it easy for villagers to visit the nearest market town, forcing the local shops to make the most of improved distribution systems and carry more stock. Similarly, local craftsmen were no longer dependent upon the village for their raw materials – or their customers. Universal styles of brick and tile replaced more traditional building materials, again provoking a loss of individuality.

At the same time, there were new forces that helped to maintain the village as a community. Universal education was an important Victorian principle and so the school became a vital cohesive element in the village. All the local children were educated together, and so they tended to grow up together. Until the end of the 19th century well over fifty per cent of village marriages were between couples from the same parish, but this pattern was soon to change, thanks to increased leisure, greater mobility in employment and the bicycle, which greatly facilitated long-distance courting.

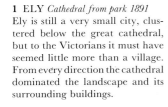

1 ELY *Cathedral from park 1891*
Ely is still a very small city, clustered below the great cathedral, but to the Victorians it must have seemed little more than a village. From every direction the cathedral dominated the landscape and its surrounding buildings.

2 SAFFRON WALDEN
Bridge Street 1907
This enjoyable view of a quiet East Anglian market town in the pre-car age shows the wide range of architecture that gave towns such as Saffron Walden their appeal. Timber-framing and pargetting show the traditional side of such towns, old buildings in pleasant harmony with the later structures that surround the nearby market place. Cars apart, such views can still give pleasure today.

3 ST NEOTS *High Street 1897*
In the late 19th century St Neots was a pleasant, small market town, with the scant remains of a Benedictine priory and a fine late medieval church. In the Middle Ages its Easter Fair was one of the four busiest in England.

④

⑥

⑦

⑤

4 CAMBRIDGE
View on the Granta 1914
The leisurely exploration of the River Cam and its tributaries by punt or canoe was a favourite activity, then as now. This delightful scene, taken during the summer of 1914, is particularly evocative, for within a few weeks the world was at war and the Edwardian era was swept away for ever.

5 CAMBRIDGE *Petty Cury 1909*
Petty Cury, with its shops and bicycles, is still one of Cambridge's busiest streets, but traps and delivery carts give it far more appeal than their modern equivalents.

6 BEDFORD
Bunyan and St Peter's Church 1898
Despite its apparent simplicity, St Peter's is one of Bedford's earliest buildings, with clear Anglo-Saxon origins. This was not really appreciated in the 19th century and so the focus of attention in this photograph is the statue of John Bunyan by Sir J E Boehm, set up here near the river twenty four years earlier.

7 GODMANCHESTER *1898*
The best view of Godmanchester is from the islands in the middle of the River Ouse, approached by the so-called Chinese bridge of 1827 which can be seen in this photograph, with the tower of St Mary's Church in the background. Victorian Godmanchester was a small place, despite its Roman origins, and it is not that much bigger today.

8 ST IVES *Houghton Mill 1899*
Houghton lies to the west of St Ives on the Great Ouse and this rather Constable-like view of its mill is typical of the many such buildings to be found at work on rivers all over Britain. Water power remained important for local industry at least until World War 1, particularly on river navigations where barges could be used to transport the grain and the milled flour.

⑧

TODAY, SUFFOLK'S LANDSCAPE is enjoyed for many reasons, not least of which is the great variety of habitat it offers to wildlife. The observation and enjoyment of wildlife in its natural setting is something taken for granted now, yet in the 19th century this popular pastime was practically unknown. From the 18th century onwards creatures were appreciated as part of the British landscape but little attempt was made at any form of individual study. Artists depicted birds and animals as accurately as possible, but only as components in a much larger picture, and they generally worked from dead specimens.

A general interest in nature became more widespread in the early 19th century, but it was still seen as a gentlemanly activity unconnected with science. Gilbert White was one of the first naturalists in the modern sense of the word, but his methods were still based entirely on observation and there was no attempt at more scientific means of study and classification until the publication of works by Darwin. Even then, study was based on dead creatures rather than on species in the wild. Throughout the 19th century the only way to study birds and animals was to shoot them first. As a result, there was little interest in the way wildlife actually existed until the end of the century, when advances in photography made it practical to study living examples.

The Victorian naturalist was primarily a collector and his trophies might be preserved as skins or skeletons, or they might be stuffed by taxidermists. Indeed, the collecting of stuffed birds and animals was a major branch of Victorian naturalism, as was the collecting of birds' eggs. The basis of scientific study was the formation of as complete a collection as possible of eggs, butterflies, beetles, dried flowers or whatever, and there was simply no understanding of the link between these types of collections and the possible threat to the species as a whole.

Naturalism as a science and the development of modern attitudes towards conservation are entirely of the 20th century, and so the bird sanctuaries along the Suffolk coastline could not have existed a hundred years ago.

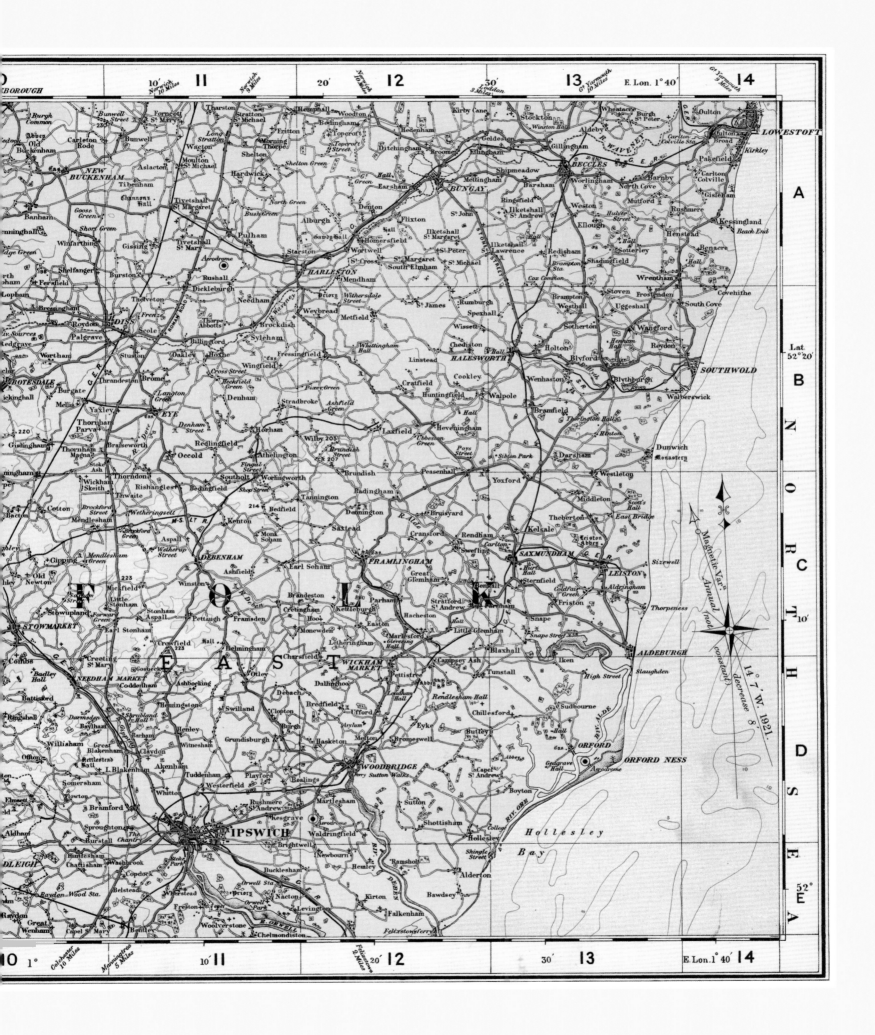

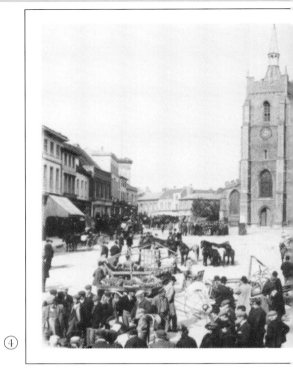

1 ALDEBURGH
Lifeboat Winchester 1903
The Royal National Lifeboat Institution was founded in 1824 and by the end of the century lifeboat stations had been established all round Britain's coast. In 1903 oars and sails were still the dominant source of power, and Aldeburgh's boat is typical of the craft in service at that time.

2 LOWESTOFT *Yacht Basin 1896*
Sailing for pleasure became a major interest at the end of the 19th century and Lowestoft, with its direct connections both to the sea and to Norfolk's network of Broads and rivers, was one of the first towns with a basin for private yachts. It is interesting to see how many of the yachts in the photograph have been developed from sailing trawlers and smacks, and other working boats.

3 IPSWICH *Butter Market 1893*
Butter Market is one of the principal streets of Ipswich and its most striking feature, then as now, is the so-called Ancient House – a 16th- and 17th-century building whose façade is decorated with a mass of ornate plasterwork.

4 SUDBURY *Market 1904*
Sudbury is still a prosperous and attractive market town and in the Edwardian period it was the centre of a large agricultural community. This view of the weekly market shows busy trading in produce, livestock and farm machinery and equipment. Elegant 18th- and 19th-century buildings surround Market Hill, the open space that drops gently from St Peter's Church – Sudbury's focal point. Today a statue of the painter Gainsborough stands in front of the church.

5 WOODBRIDGE
Church Street 1906
Church Street links the River Deben and the railway station to the centre of Woodbridge, and seen here is a typical East Anglian street flanked by 17th-, 18th- and 19th-century buildings. Gas lights and, in the distance, the milk cart, underline the leisurely Edwardian atmosphere.

6 BURY ST EDMUNDS
Market Place 1898
The two gatehouses are all that remain of Bury St Edmunds' magnificent abbey, destroyed by Henry VIII in 1539, but these were sufficient to draw many visitors to this Suffolk market town in the Victorian era. The Saxon king St Edmund, King Canute and King John, all associated with Bury, added to the town's appeal. This view, however, shows Bury's

more domestic face, which can still be enjoyed in the town's markets and old shopping streets.

7 IPSWICH *The Docks 1893*
Ipswich has flourished as a port since the 13th century, benefiting from its good position at the head of the tidal River Orwell, and even today the town's docks are still busy. This view, taken during the period of transition from sail to steam, shows the great variety of vessels that traded around the coasts of Britain in the late 19th century, including sailing barges, trading schooners and coasters.

8 SOUTHWOLD *High Street 1896*
Southwold is one of Suffolk's most picturesque seaside towns and the appeal of its little streets with their surprisingly fine and varied architecture, and its beach, was considerable in Victorian times.

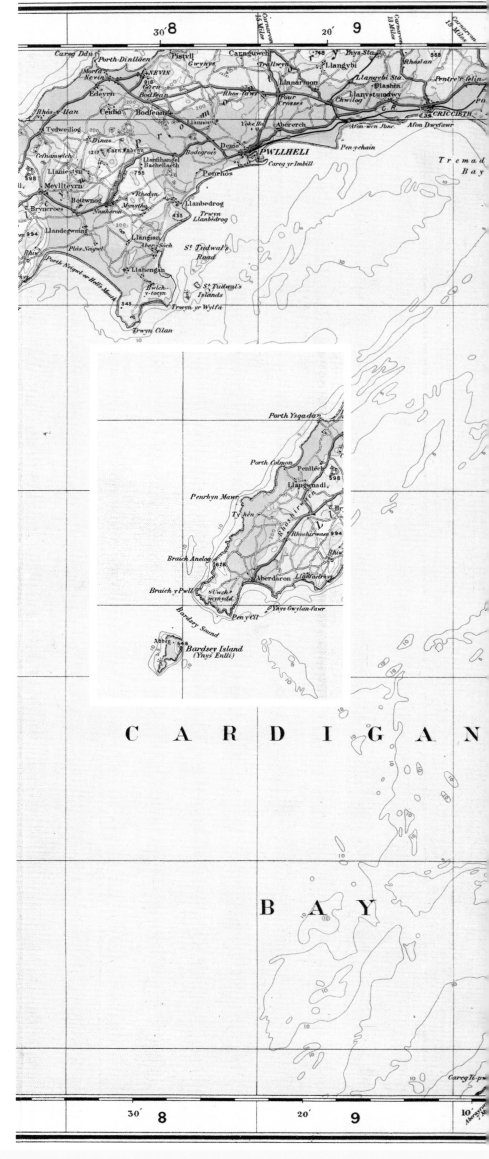

So many visitors come to mid and north Wales today to enjoy the wild and mountainous scenery that it is easy to forget that the appreciation of this type of landscape is a relatively recent phenomenon. Until the middle of the 18th century this region was regarded generally as inhospitable and unappealing, and the few visitors who came approached by boat via the little ports along the Cambrian coast. However, from that date artists began for the first time to explore the scenery of Britain and painters such as Richard Wilson, trained in the Italianate style of classical landscape, were among the first to try to capture the qualities of Cader Idris and other local views. Mountains, steep river valleys, waterfalls and ruined castles all feature in the paintings of this period and, as appreciation of the Welsh landscape spread, so more and more artists made their way into the mountains, encouraged by the popularity of the picturesque movement which delighted in wild and angular scenery, old ruins and all the decorative features of a primitive way of life. Initially the painted views were part imaginary and part based on the actual landscape, with the picturesque elements deliberately heightened. At the end of the 18th century watercolour began to take over as the dominant medium for landscape painters, and this new technique brought a greater degree of reality. Portable and quickly achieved, watercolour proved to be ideal for artists working in the open air in relatively inaccessible areas, and by the beginning of the 19th century views of Welsh mountains, valleys, estuaries and castles were to be seen in every watercolour exhibition.

Where the professional artists prepared the ground, the amateurs were quick to follow, and by the middle of the century virtually every visitor came equipped with a paintbox. Companies such as Rowney's and Winsor & Newton became well-known at this time for their extensive ranges of fully equipped and beautifully made painting sets, all neatly fitted into handsome wooden travelling cases designed to accompany the artist on his travels into even the most inhospitable of landscapes. At the same time, the artist could draw on an increasingly wide range of technical manuals, and so it is often quite hard to draw any clear line of quality between professional and amateur production. Sketching in Wales became a popular form of holiday, deemed to be particularly suitable for ladies of all ages for whom competence with watercolour and an appreciation of landscape and ancient buildings were considered to be vital parts of a well-rounded education.

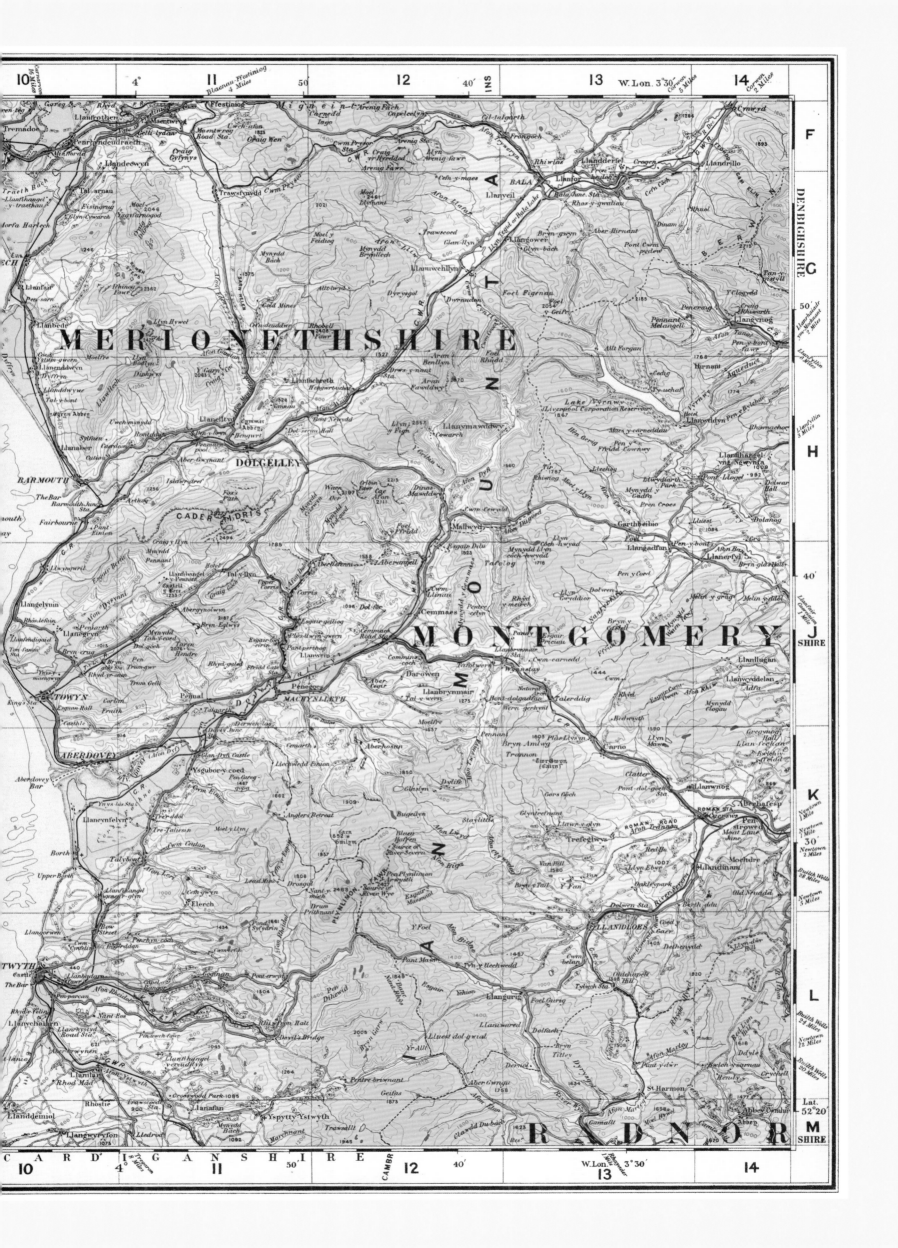

①

②

③

④

⑤

1 PORTHMADOG *Harbour 1908*
Porthmadog's harbour was created during the 19th century by the MP William Madocks in the hope of capturing the Irish trade. This plan failed, but the port thrived as the outlet for the massive slate quarries at Blaenau Ffestiniog. When this view was taken the harbour, now a marina, was still busy with the slate and timber trades.

2 MAENTWROG *1889*
The dramatic scenery of north Wales has been enjoyed since the 18th century and the Vale of Ffestiniog was particularly popular.

This view of the winding course of the Dwyryd, with the picturesque village of Maentwrog in the distance, was probably taken from the Ffestiniog Railway, a slate line to Blaenau that carried passengers from 1865.

3 BARMOUTH BRIDGE *1896*
Built in 1867 by the Cambrian Coast Railway, this long viaduct across the estuary of the Mawddach linking Barmouth with Morfa Mawddach is now the only major timber structure of its type still in use on the British railway network. Soon after this photograph was taken the section of the bridge in front of the train was replaced by a steel-girder opening bridge, to allow the passage of ships. In the distance is Cader Idris.

4 ABERDOVEY *From Pier 1901*
Aberdovey's harbour, now used only by pleasure craft, was still a busy port in the early years of this century – as can be seen from the coastal trading vessels in this photograph. Later, sandy beaches turned the town into a popular holiday centre. Much of the simple Georgian architecture around the port survives.

5 PWLLHELI
West End Promenade 1898
When this photograph was taken Pwllheli was at the point of transition from small market town serving the Lleyn Peninsula to major resort. The Victorians' love of the seaside and the five miles of sandy beaches facing southwards across Cardigan Bay gave the town its popularity. Later, the great holiday camps arrived, destroying for ever the exclusive atmosphere.

6 MACHYNLLETH
Corris Railway 1899
Built originally as a slate line, the narrow-gauge Corris Railway enjoyed a second period of prosperity in the late Victorian and Edwardian eras, carrying tourists into the hills below Cader Idris. Long closed, little survives today except the railway's route along the Dulas River, and a museum in Corris.

7 BORTH *From Upper Borth 1895*
Borth, originally a remote village with one straggling street, was turned into a resort by the coming of the railway. The good beach soon brought visitors to the area and rapid development took place in the early years of this century.

8 HARLECH *Castle 1913*
Harlech Castle has been regarded as one of the wonders of north Wales for centuries, due to its magnificent site and the views that could be enjoyed from its ruined towers. This view of Harlech, seen from what is now the busy A49, has not greatly changed.

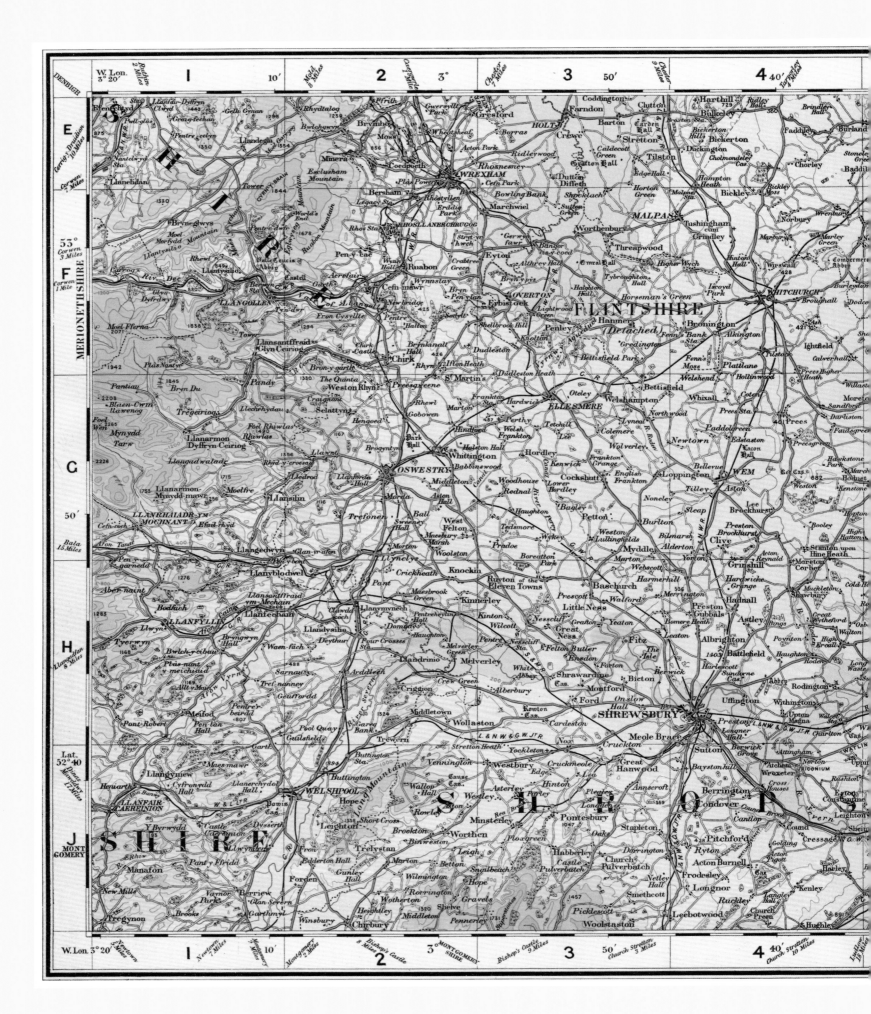

VICTORIAN STOKE-ON-TRENT
was no more than one of the closely grouped, but
fiercely independent, six towns in north Staffordshire famous for the making of pottery since the
17th century, as the city that brought them all
together was not formed until 1910. The nature of
the ceramic industry in the 19th century was very
different from that to be seen in the city today, and
its atmosphere was well described in Arnold
Bennett's novels. It was a dirty place, with
hundreds of the bottle-shaped ovens pouring smoke
and fumes into the sky day and night. Close by were
the coal mines, adding their share of smoke and
dust. Every street had its factory, some just tiny
family concerns, others huge enterprises employing
thousands of men and women whose specialist skills
had made the British ceramic industry the best in
the world in the Victorian period.

Pottery-making is one of the few industries in
which women have always played an important
role and in the 19th century girls went into the
factories when they were little more than children,
usually to take on the more menial and repetitive
tasks. It was also a dangerous industry in the days
before the passing of the modern factory acts, and
lead-based glazes were still in common use. Public
health was of little concern in an industry in which
fortunes could be made, and lost, very quickly.

The most successful Victorian companies,
Minton, Doulton, Davenport, Copeland and
Wedgwood, were able to sell their wares all over the
world. Thanks to local deposits of clay and coal,
and to efficient canal and railway networks that
brought in other raw materials such as flint, bone
ash and Cornish clay, then took away the finished
products, the Staffordshire industry was at its peak
in the Victorian period. Hundreds of factories in the
region made every type of ceramic from basic bricks
to the most costly and elaborate porcelains.

Naturally there were at that time other centres of
production, such as the Severn valley, Derby and
Nottingham, Yorkshire and the North East, London, Bristol and north Wales, where Ruabon was
famous for its bricks and tiles, but none could
compete with Staffordshire at its best.

①

1 MARKET DRAYTON
Tyrley Locks 1911
The Tyrley flight of locks near Market Drayton, midpoint on the Shropshire Union Canal connecting the Black Country to Chester, Ellesmere Port and north Wales, was always busy. Here, a loaded narrowboat climbing the flight waits to enter a lock.

2 SHREWSBURY
Nag's Head 1891
One of the chief glories of late Victorian Shrewsbury was its wealth of black-and-white timber-framed buildings, reflecting its importance as a wool town in the 16th and 17th centuries. Many have subsequently been demolished, altered or over-restored

and so this kind of view, where the only things later than the 18th century are the people and the gas lamp, has gone forever.

③

⑤

3 WOLVERHAMPTON
Victoria Street 1910
Victoria Street is still one of Wolverhampton's busiest shopping streets, although the huge new Mander shopping centre, completed in 1970, has helped to change the appearance of this part of the town. Edwardian Wolverhampton was a thriving metropolis, drawing its wealth from the Black Country and enjoying the recently-built theatre, museum and art gallery, library and town hall.

4 IRONBRIDGE *1892*
When this photograph was taken Ironbridge was still a working industrial town – a far cry from the massive museum complex it has now become. In the distance are the smoking chimneys of the tile works and in the foreground is one of the Severn barges that in those days could still navigate the river to Ironbridge. However, this view of the 1779 iron bridge, now a powerful symbol of the Industrial Revolution, has hardly changed.

5 IRONBRIDGE *Waterfall 1892*
The application of water power was a vital ingredient in the industrialisation of the Severn valley. This great overshot iron waterwheel, probably built to power a forge, is typical of the relics of 18th- and early 19th-century industry that still littered the Ironbridge region when this photograph was taken. The waterwheel has long disappeared, but many similar memorials to an industrial past have been preserved by the Ironbridge Gorge Museum Trust.

6 WREXHAM *Church 1903*
In the late 19th century the prosperity of the capital of north Wales was built on leather, coal, bricks, iron and brewing, but a legacy of Wrexham's earlier wealth as a market town is the grand 15th-century Church of St Giles whose 136-foot-high tower is regarded as one of the wonders of Wales. Equally admired today are the wrought-iron gates, made in the 18th century by the local Davies brothers.

⑥

④

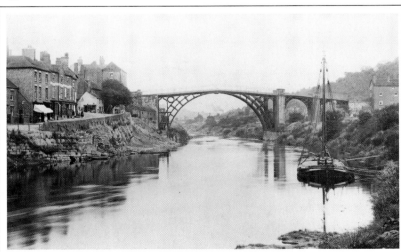

VICTORIAN MELTON MOWBRAY
was famous for its cheese, its pies and its hunting.
The town had long been the traditional centre for
Stilton cheese and pie-making started in 1831, but
the real reason for its fame was its important
position at the centre of Britain's best-known
hunting country. The Quorn, the Belvoir and the
Cottesmore meet on the boundaries of Melton
Mowbray, and all around are the country houses
that caused the area to be known as the Dukeries.

The east Midlands in the 19th century was
predominantly a landscape of rolling farmland and
woods, countryside that easily contained the
pockets of industry that were then quite small. The
traditional textile trades of Derby, Leicester and
Nottingham – silk and wool, hosiery and footware,
lace and knitting – had been expanded by the use of
new machinery but they did not change the face of
what were still old market towns until the latter
part of the Victorian period. Equally traditional
was the making of beer in Burton-on-Trent, an
industry dating back at least to the Middle Ages,
while cheese had long been associated with Derby
and Leicester. Thriving markets and the survival of
traditional events such as Nottingham's Goose Fair
helped to keep new developments at bay, and it was
not until the 1920s that industry began to alter
significantly the character of these towns.

At the same time, other industries that had
developed in the late 18th century, coal-mining,
pottery-making and engineering, were increasingly
making their mark on the region. By the 1860s
Derby's railway works was probably better known
than its porcelain factory, and in the 1870s and
1880s two new industries in Nottingham, cigarette-
and bicycle-making, were setting a pattern for the
future.

Through the centre of the region flows the Trent,
linking many of the major towns and cities.
Lichfield, Burton, Derby, Nottingham and Newark
are all either on the river or connected to it by
tributaries and canals, and in the 19th century the
course of this great waterway underlined the blend
of countryside and industry that was, at that time,
both harmonious and characteristic of the region.

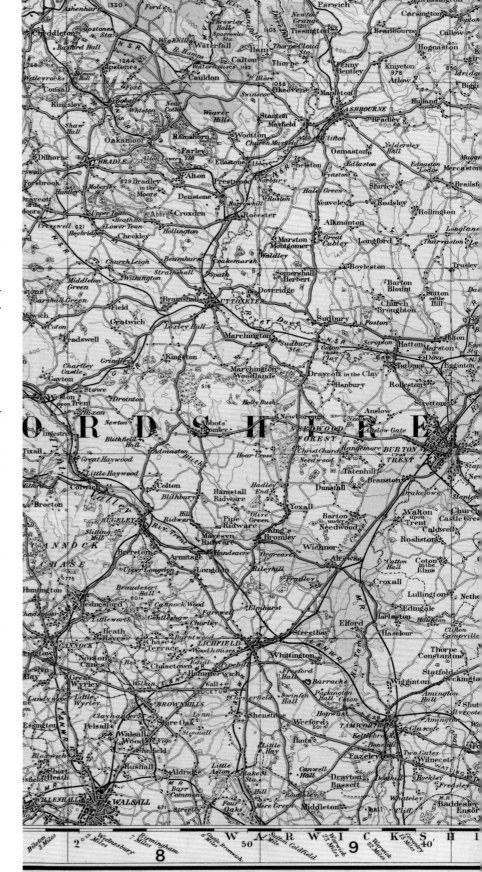

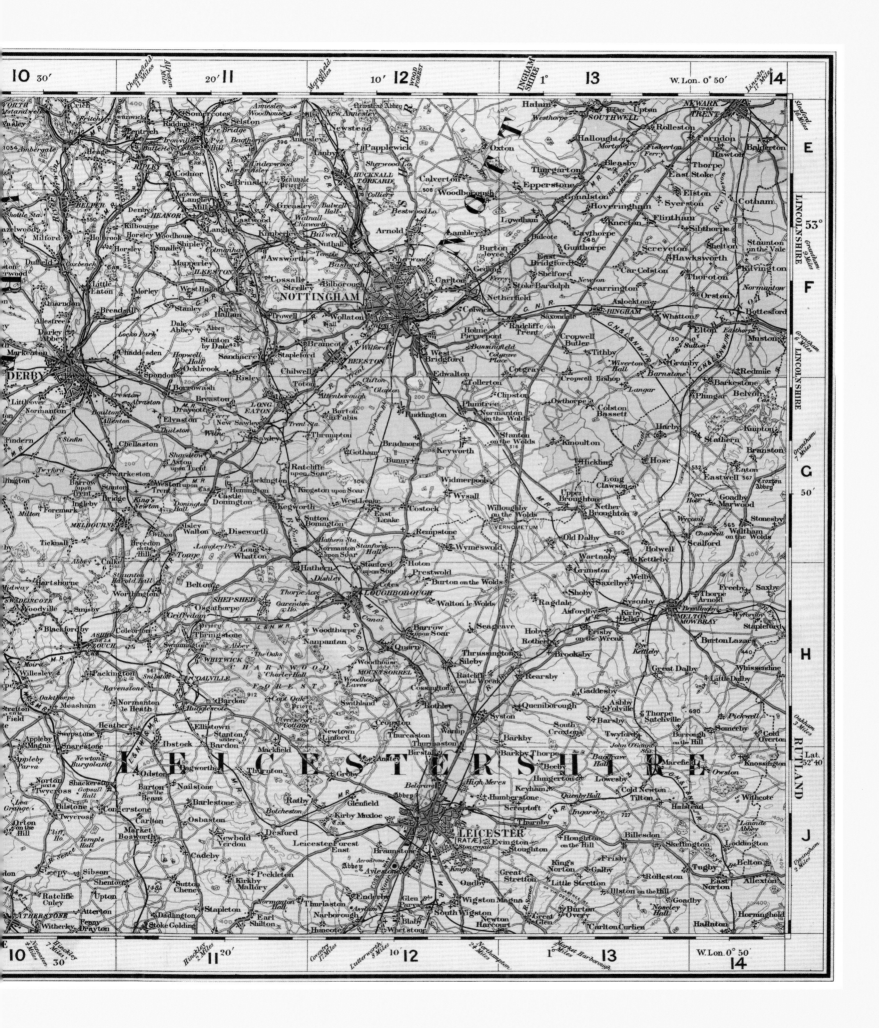

①

②

1 BELVOIR CASTLE *1890*
Set high on its hill above surrounding woodland, Belvoir Castle has long been regarded as one of Leicestershire's finest buildings. Yet, when this view was taken, the castle was actually well under a hundred years old. The medieval castle had disappeared under subsequent rebuilding programmes and most of what can be seen here dates from the early 19th century, including the principal tower and the spiky Gothic of the chapel. The Victorians loved all castles and particularly those they could call their own.

2 ASHBOURNE
Green Man and Black's Head 1886
Ashbourne is now a handsome town on the fringes of the Peak District National Park, well known for its stone buildings and old-fashioned atmosphere. When this photograph was taken the few visitors who came to this small Derbyshire market town would probably have stayed at the Green Man and Black's Head. Surprisingly, this inn stands virtually unchanged.

③

3 LICHFIELD *Cathedral 1897*
Lichfield's 13th-century cathedral, with its three distinctive spires, has always been famous for the display of sculpture on its west front. Ironically, it was easier to appreciate the hundred-plus statues when this photograph was taken, for during the past century the soft stone has been badly affected by weathering and atmospheric pollution.

4 NOTTINGHAM *Cheapside 1890*
Late Victorian Nottingham, a thriving textile town, still retained its medieval core whose atmosphere can be judged from this view. Much of this was to change in the 20th century as new industries took over and the shop in the foreground draws attention to one of these, the tobacco trade. John Player opened his first factory in 1877, ten years later John Bowden started making Raleigh bicycles and the Boots family opened their first chemist's shop.

5 DERBY *Cornmarket 1896*
Derby's Cornmarket, a handsome street flanked by elegant 18th- and 19th-century brick-and-stone buildings, is here seen pleasantly uncluttered. In the distance is the tower of All Saints' Church, made Derby's cathedral in 1927. In this view the tram track and the electric street lamps are a hint of things to come.

④

⑤

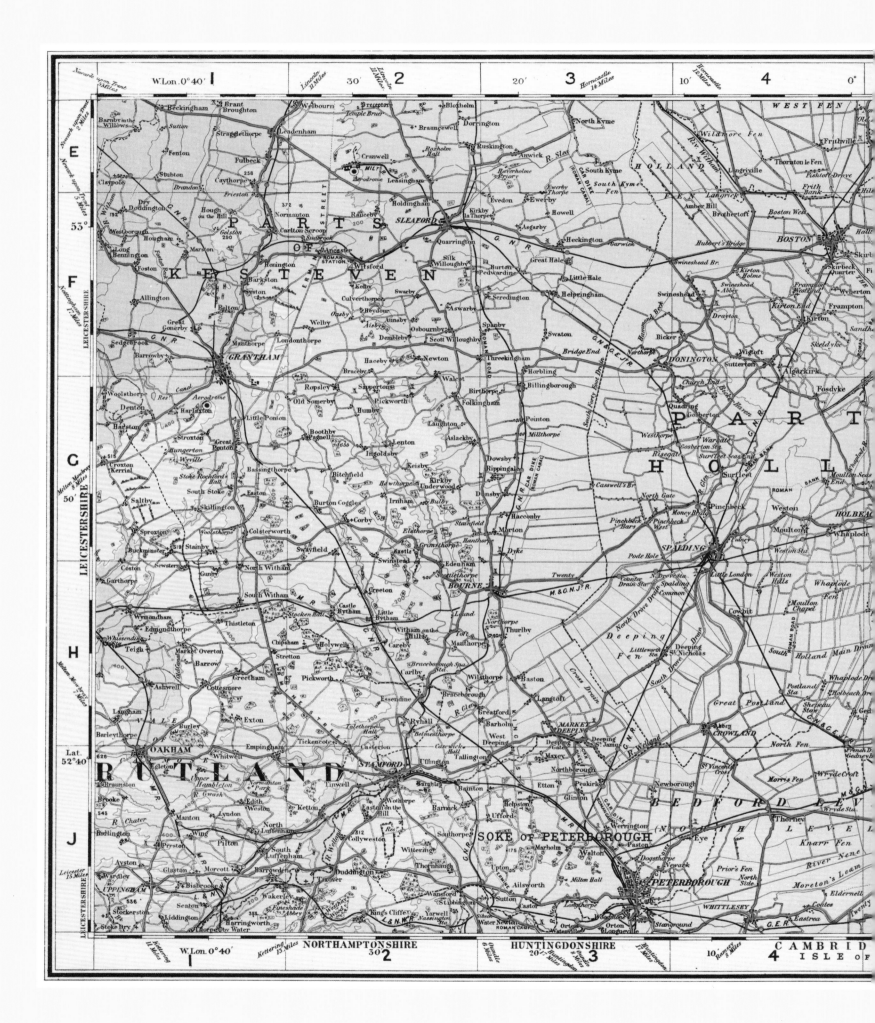

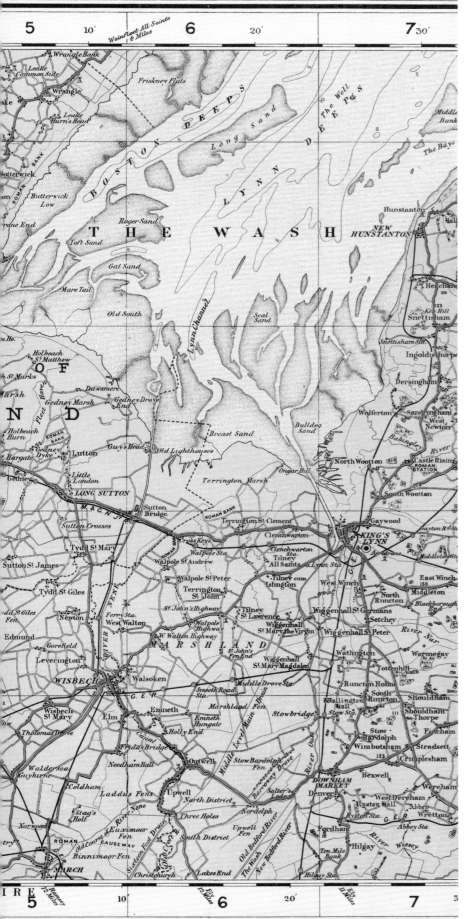

By the 19th century the fenland landscape that is familiar today had largely been formed. Drainage and land reclamation on a grand scale had started in the 17th century, and great advances were made throughout the 18th century with the help of the hundreds of wind-driven pumps which kept the water levels under control in an area that was steadily sinking as the peat dried out. This old technology had reached the limits of its powers towards the end of the century, but the reclamation process was revitalised by the application of the steam engine. The first steam pump was installed in 1821 and many others quickly followed. At the same time, greater efficiency was achieved by the new centrifugal pumps that replaced the old system of scoops mounted on great wheels. By the 1860s the tall engine house with its towering chimney had become the most dominant feature in the flat landscape. Steam power was also applied to the dredgers that kept open the huge network of drainage channels and waterways.

The cutting of new channels and the straightening of rivers continued apace into the Victorian period. For example, the Ouse's straight route between Ely and Littleport was completed in 1827. Major works such as this not only improved the flow of water, but also maintained and expanded the miles of navigable waterways upon which trade and communication within the region depended until the coming of the railways.

Throughout the 19th century the fertile reclaimed land was used for the production of vegetables and flowers, and the remaining acres of natural heathland continued to disappear under the plough. Crops such as cereals, potatoes, cabbages and daffodils would have been familiar to the Victorians, as they are now, while others then equally commonplace have disappeared. Until the latter part of the century when railway transport enabled slate to take over from thatch as the dominant roofing material, the cultivation and cutting of reeds was a major industry. Longer lasting was peat-digging, an exploitation of the region's primary natural resource that continued on a considerable scale until well into this century.

①

1 PETERBOROUGH

Market Place and Cathedral 1904
There have been considerable
changes to Peterborough's market
place since this photograph was
taken, but still to be enjoyed is the
partly Norman outer gate, or great
gate, that leads to the cathedral
precinct, along with the massive
west front of the cathedral itself. In
the foreground is the tower of the
memorial fountain, then brand
new, having been erected in 1898.

2 WISBECH

Clarkson Memorial 1904
Seen here in its original setting
at the head of Bridge Street,
Wisbech's famous 1881 memorial
to Thomas Clarkson, a local anti-
slavery campaigner, is still a
feature of the town. Behind it are
the elegant terraces that line the
quays of this still-busy inland port
with, at the centre, the fine classical façade of the 1811 town hall.

③

②

④

⑤

⑥

3 KING'S LYNN
Custom House 1898
One of the glories of the handsome Norfolk port of King's Lynn is the Custom House. Completed in 1683, this distinctive building with its tall lantern is still to be enjoyed in its isolated position overlooking the quays on the Great Ouse. It is now in rather better condition, but otherwise this view is much the same today.

4 GRANTHAM *Town Hall 1893*
Isaac Newton is Grantham's most famous citizen and his statue is seen here in front of the town's most unexpected building, the French-château-style town hall of 1869. When this photograph was taken both were still relatively new, and an understandable expression of civic pride in a town best known for its medieval architecture.

5 BOSTON *Market Place 1899*
Boston's greatest feature, and a reminder of the town's wealth as a major port in the Middle Ages, is the grand parish church – one of Britain's largest – with its 272-foot tower. Known as the Stump and visible for miles across the flat landscape, it is still used as a navigating mark by ships far out at sea. When this view was taken Boston's great days as a port were long over, but their legacy was a pleasant old-fashioned atmosphere.

6 HUNSTANTON *Green 1907*
The development of this north Norfolk resort occurred rapidly after the arrival of the railway in 1862. Large hotels and the pier soon followed, but the green was kept as an open space at the town's centre. The universal popularity of cricket in the Edwardian era is reflected by the almost all-female game in progress in this photograph.

NORFOLK'S COASTAL PORTS
and villages have been famous for their fish since
Roman times, but it was in the 19th century that
the fishing industry reached its peak. Great
Yarmouth, then still distinct from Gorleston and
Caister, was home to one of Britain's largest herring
fleets whose catches were greatly expanded at the
end of the century as the traditional sailing luggers
were replaced by a new generation of steam drifters.
Cromer and Sheringham were famous for crabs,
Wells-next-the-Sea for whelks, and Stiffkey for
cockles, while cod and flatfish were sold in both
local and London markets.

Norfolk's fish was then better known than its
hotels and beaches, for most resorts were not
developed until the early years of this century. The
earliest was Great Yarmouth, fashionable for its
sea-bathing from the late 18th century until the
1850s. The first pier was built in 1853, and from
then on the town began to appeal to a wider
market. Cromer and Sheringham were fishing
villages rather than resorts until the 1890s, even
though Jane Austen had commented favourably on
the quality of Cromer's sea-bathing.

Tourism as a whole did not significantly affect
Norfolk until the Edwardian era, and the Broads
remained remote and undeveloped until well into
this century. This network of inland lakes and rivers
represented the balanced harmony between agriculture and wildlife that was to be destroyed in the
20th century by overcrowding and pollution.
There were few yachts and pleasure craft to be seen
among the fleets of black-sailed wherries – distinctive craft which were vital in maintaining the
transport and communications infrastructure of the
region until the coming of the motor lorry.

The Victorian vision of Norfolk's landscape of
rivers and Broads, farmland and mills, was pre-
cisely that depicted by the artists of the Norwich
School. Crome, Cotman, Stannard and their
followers were inspired by their common liking for
East Anglia's landscape to work as a cohesive
group, and throughout the 19th century the style
they created remained one of the few in the history
of British art to have so strong a regional affinity.

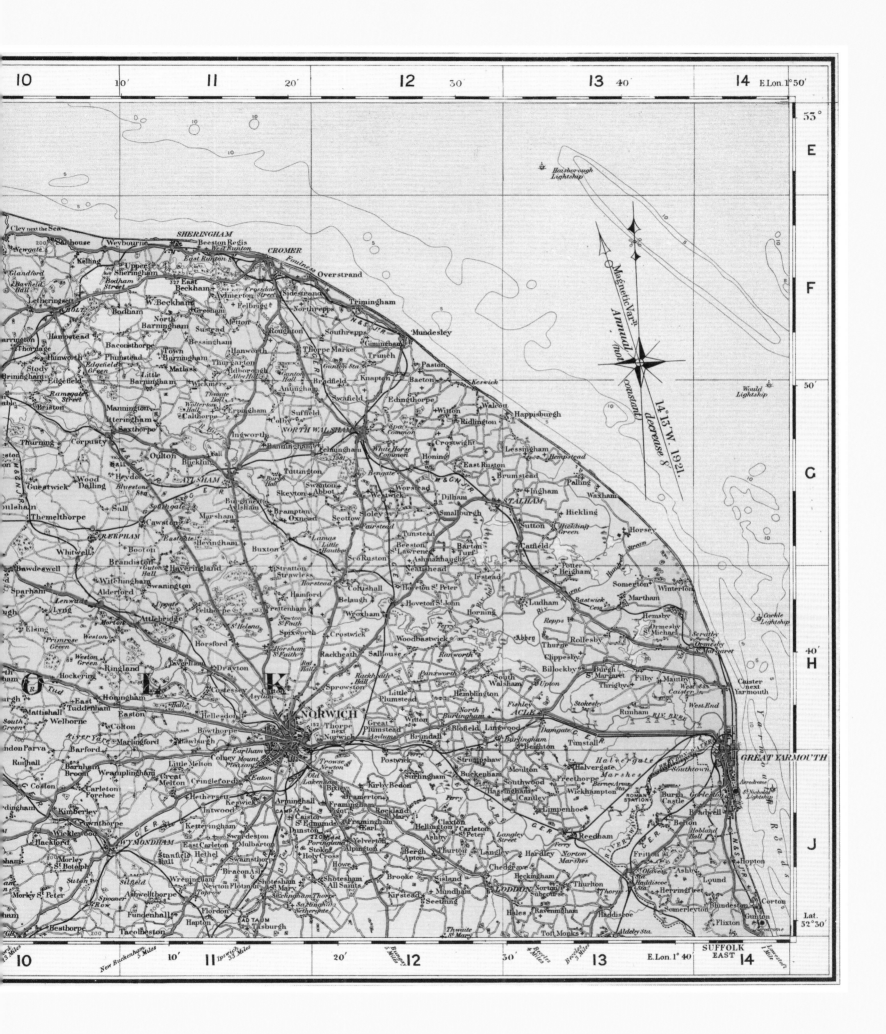

2 GREAT YARMOUTH
The Market 1908
In the Edwardian era Great Yarmouth was still a fashionable resort, although its traditional smartness was already being altered by the demands of popular tourism. The busy market place was then, as now, the town's centre where elegantly-dressed visitors came face to face with a new breed of holiday-maker.

3 CROMER *From the Sands 1899*
Another fashionable Norfolk resort was Cromer, seen here at the height of its popularity when grand hotels expanded the town well beyond its traditional core clustered around the Church of St Peter and St Paul. Bathing-machines and smart clothes capture the atmosphere of a resort before the days of mass tourism.

4 NORWICH *Cattle Market 1896*
It is some time since Norwich's livestock market filled the open spaces below the castle, but this busy scene was a regular occurrence before World War I. Today it is cars rather than sheep that fill the old market place. The old Norman keep of the castle was refaced in the 1830s.

5 CLEY NEXT THE SEA
Windmill c.1910
When this photograph was taken Cley's great tower mill was among the many in Norfolk still in use. Old terraces and a creek filled with a few boats show how quiet a place Cley was before it became a popular holiday and sailing centre.

6 NORWICH *Pulle's Ferry 1891*
When it was built in the 15th century, this gateway guarded a small canal leading to the cathedral which towers above the roofs of Norwich in the background. Named after an 18th-century ferryman on the Wensum, the gateway has been completely restored since this photograph was taken and the old boat sheds in the foreground have gone.

7 SHERINGHAM *Beach 1901*
In the Edwardian period crab-fishing continued as an important activity in a seaside village still in its infancy as a resort. The round stones of the beach were also a valuable building material.

1 GORLESTON
Harbour 1894
Situated to the south of the estuary of the River Bure, Gorleston has now become a part of Great Yarmouth. When this photograph was taken it was still independent, its quay claiming a share of the huge herring catches brought in by the local trawlers.

IN THE 1820s WORK BEGAN
on the construction, near Bangor, of what was to become one of the most grandiose of north Wales's many castles. With its Norman-style towers and battlements, Penrhyn Castle must have been a wonder even to the Victorians, who were used to such excesses. Designed by Thomas Hopper, Penrhyn was built with the wealth generated by one family from the local slate quarries. Inside are intricately carved floors, doorways, fireplaces and furniture – a lasting reminder that slate was, in the 19th century, the most important natural resource in north Wales, whose quarrying and preparation gave employment to thousands. Penrhyn's wealth came from the quarry near Bethesda that is still the world's largest open-cast slate mine. Near by, at Llanberis at the foot of Snowdon, were the huge Dinorwic quarries, while to the south Blaenau Ffestiniog was the centre for slate-mining, where the material was carved out in blocks deep underground and then transported to the surface for splitting and shaping.

All these quarries had their own railway links to the ports from which Welsh slate was shipped world-wide. The oldest, the Penrhyn tramway, was opened in 1801, but this was followed by the line from Llanberis to Port Dinorwic. Most famous of all is the long Ffestiniog Railway, opened in 1836 to connect Blaenau Ffestiniog with the port of Porthmadog and, from 1863, the first narrow-gauge railway to be steam-hauled. The industry was at its peak in the late 19th century when up to half a million tons of finished slates were produced each year, but by the Edwardian period it was already in decline and today the scale of this Victorian enterprise can only be measured by the great mountains of waste that still surround the former mines and quarries.

Another legacy is the narrow-gauge railways, some of which still survive today. In the late Victorian period those with foresight began to carry passengers as well as slate, for by this time tourism was beginning to emerge as a major industry in north Wales. Increased leisure time combined with a new interest in walking and climbing enabled north Wales to enjoy a different kind of popularity in the years leading up to World War I, and a clear indication of future trends was the opening, in 1896, of the Snowdon Mountain Railway – the first in the area to be built solely for the purpose of tourism.

Notable among those railways enjoying a new lease of life as tourist lines is the Ffestiniog, whose steam trains are once again climbing up the dramatically tortuous route to Blaenau following years of patient restoration largely by volunteers. Near the line's new terminus are the old slate mines, some of which are now open to tourists as museums.

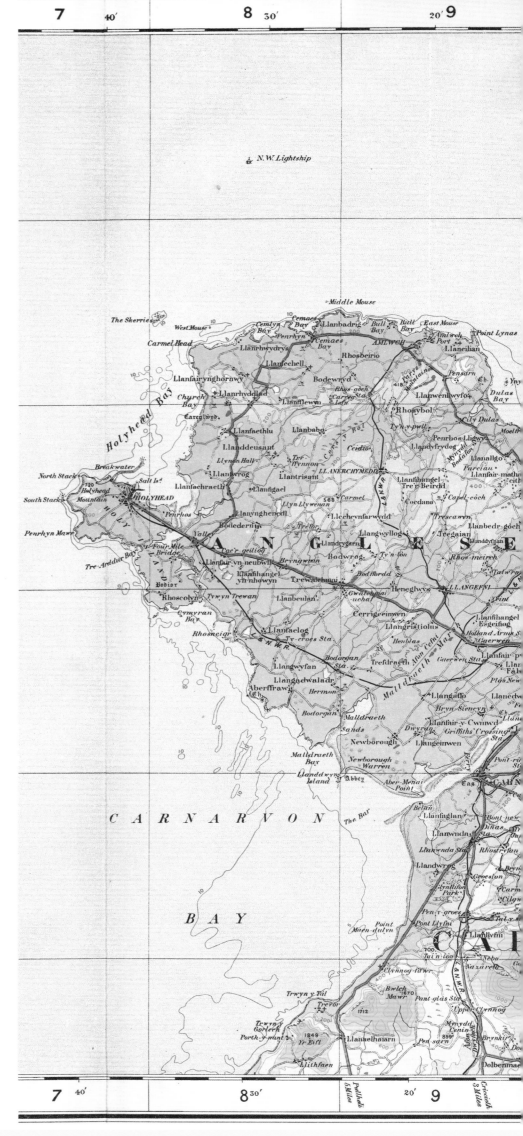

①

②

③

1 HOLYHEAD
South Stack Lighthouse 1892
Set below its sheer cliffs and guarding the entrance to Holyhead harbour is the South Stack lighthouse. Built in 1808, this powerful structure with its accompanying coastguard cottages was already attracting visitors in the Victorian era.

2 BANGOR *High Street 1908*
Bicycles, horses and carts, and an unsurfaced road set the tone for the busiest street of this small cathedral city. A newsagent's placard highlights continuing unrest in South Africa, while further down the street is the prominent sign of the pawnbroker.

3 CAERNARVON *1906*
The formidable walls of Caernarvon's castle stood as proudly a century ago as they do now, although it was not until 1963 that the town became a royal borough. The swing-bridge across the estuary has been replaced, and yachts and pleasure craft have taken the place of the coastal trading vessels seen moored against the castle walls in this view.

①

⑥

⑦

④

⑤

4 LLANBERIS AND SNOWDON *1896*

The magnificent scenery of Snowdonia, appreciated since the 18th century, only began to fulfil its true tourist potential at the end of the 19th century. Railways built originally for the slate traffic were now turning their attention towards passengers and the development of Llanberis as a resort dates from this time. Seen in this view is the old station, with Dolbardarn Castle and the lakes in the distance, taken the year the Snowdon Mountain Railway was opened to the summit.

5 BLAENAU FFESTINIOG *Duffus Station 1901*

At the end of the 19th century Blaenau Ffestiniog was still primarily a slate town even though the industry was in decline by that time. Then, as now, great mountains of slate spoil surrounded the town which was served by three railways, the Great Western, the London & North Western and the narrow-gauge Ffestiniog.

6 LLANDUDNO *Parade 1908*

The fishing village of Llandudno was developed as a resort through the efforts of Lord Mostyn and his plans were completed soon after this view was taken. Grand hotels, the pier, the pavilion with its concerts and the fine beaches quickly made Llandudno fashionable, with smartly-dressed visitors arriving by train and by motor car.

7 RHYL *1914*

The many pleasures offered by Rhyl's beach, pier and pavilion were enjoyed by thousands during the last summer of the Edwardian era. Here, a donkey winds its way among the distinctive basketwork shelters – essential protection against the prevailing winds that have prompted the town to build its more recent entertainment centres under cover.

8 DENBIGH *Castle Ruins 1891*

Edward I built one of his largest castles at Denbigh on a site marked by its magnificent views northwards towards the coast. By the Victorian period the castle was a crumbling ruin, appreciated more for its picturesque qualities than its history by visitors to this small town whose weekly market continues to thrive. Visible in this photograph is the castle's best-preserved feature, its gateway.

⑧

125

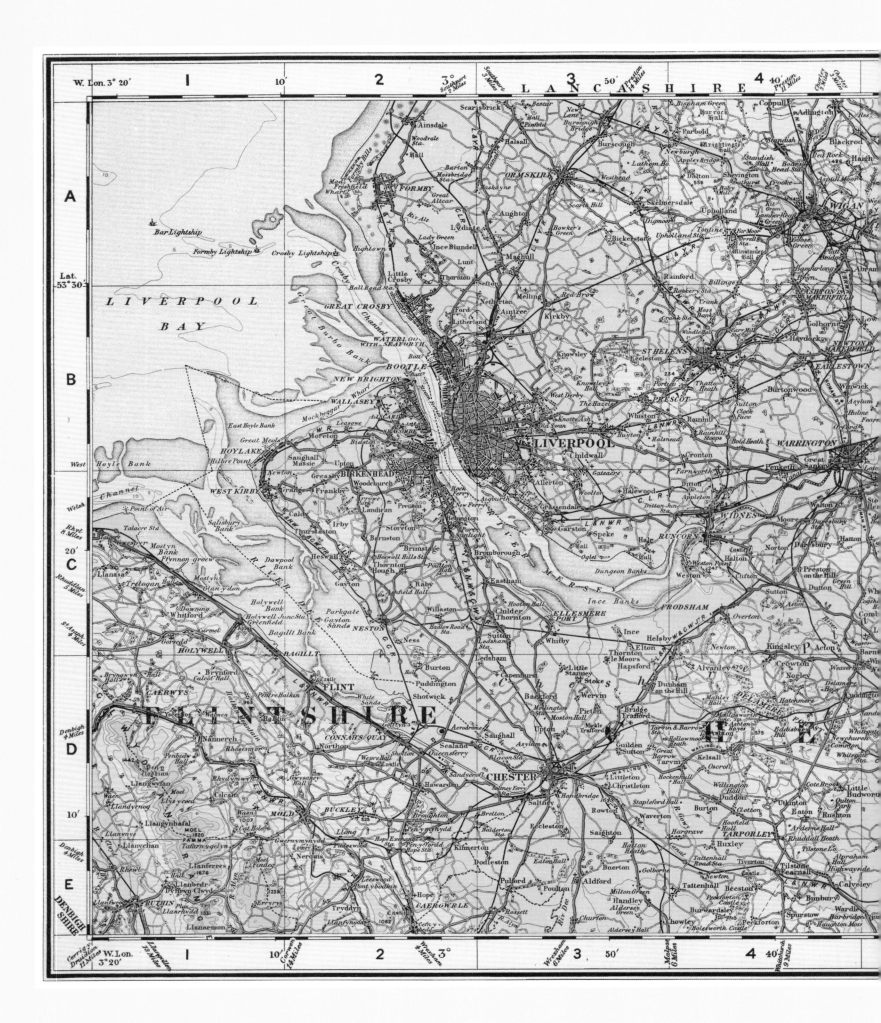

CIVIC PRIDE WAS A powerful force in Victorian Britain, finding expression in a number of ways. A notable form, and one that can still be appreciated today, was the commissioning of grand public buildings. Liverpool, Manchester and the industrial towns of Lancashire were keen to show that there was more to commercial success than tenements, terrace housing, mills and warehouses.

The Victorian period was the great age for public building, with industrial towns that had been little more than villages in the late 18th century now competing with each other in the building of town halls, museums and art galleries, schools, colleges and hospitals, theatres, concert halls, and railway stations. The standard was set by Liverpool which created at its heart a great open space surrounded by classical buildings with, at its centre, the massive Grecian-style St George's Hall. Designed in 1841, this is probably still the grandest public building in Britain. Ranged around the square are the classical façades of the William Brown Library, the Picton Reading Room and the Walker Art Gallery, all dating from the 1860 to 1880 period. With Liverpool a centre for the classical style, Manchester turned to the Gothic, and its masterpiece is its 1868 town hall, but even this extravaganza could barely compete with that erected at Rochdale a few years earlier, one of the most ambitious town halls in England..

Also important were the railway stations – major reflectors of the new industrial wealth. Liverpool and Manchester each had three great termini, the most adventurous being Manchester's Piccadilly of 1862 and Liverpool's Lime Street of 1868. Many of these buildings were designed through public competitions, the winners of which were a new generation of adventurous young architects. H L Elmes was only twenty five when he won the competition for St George's Hall, but the best-known local architect was Alfred Waterhouse, the designer of Manchester's town hall, Liverpool's Lime Street station and a host of other major Victorian buildings, including London's Natural History Museum.

1 LIVERPOOL *Lime Street c.1910*
In the 19th century Liverpool created for itself the most impressive city centre in Britain, a reflection of the city's civic pride at the height of its prosperity. This view of spacious Lime Street, with its hansom cabs and horse-drawn trams, is flanked by the station and St George's Hall. In the distance are the Wellington memorial column and the newly completed Walker Art Gallery and William Brown Library.

2 MANCHESTER
Market Street 1889
Victorian industry and endeavour were also the driving forces behind Manchester's development, and the bluff façades of Market Street are typical creations of this period. Horse-drawn trams, crowded pavements and one or two familar names capture the atmosphere of a long-forgotten era of commercial success.

3 MANCHESTER SHIP CANAL
Barton Bridge and 'Manx Fairy' 1894
When this photograph was taken the Manchester Ship Canal, a vital waterway link to the Mersey that turned the city into one of Britain's busiest ports, had just been built. One of its wonders, completed in 1893, was the Barton aqueduct. Carrying the Bridgewater Canal, this could be swung to allow the

passage of ships. The Barton Bridge is still in use but few ships now make their way to Manchester's docks, and long gone are the ferry services to the Isle of Man.

4 BURY
Market Place and Church 1902
By the end of the 19th century Bury's medieval past had been largely obliterated by the rapid Victorian growth of this cotton town, birthplace of Sir Robert Peel whose 1852 statue can be seen here in the market place. The 1870s church, with its earlier tower, still dominates Bury's market place but modern traffic has taken the place of the solitary steam tram.

⑦

⑧

⑨

5 CHESTER *Eccleston Ferry 1895*
The chain ferry across the Dee at Eccleston, the major estate village attached to the Duke of Westminster's Eaton Hall, was a popular spot in the late 19th century. Seen here is Ferry Farm, newly built in the late Victorian vernacular style used for many of the estate buildings. Today the ferry has gone – along with Waterhouse's Eaton

Hall – but many of the buildings survive, including this farm.

6 BOLTON *Market Hall 1895*
Grand, covered market halls were a Victorian phenomenon thanks to the advances in cast-iron building technology. Bolton's, built in 1855, was like a great cathedral with its nave, aisles, transepts and mass of delicately-pierced cast iron.

7 MACCLESFIELD
Market Place 1898
Macclesfield's large parish church is a testament to the town's importance in the Middle Ages, whereas its 1820s town hall is a reminder of a later period of prosperity, when Macclesfield was the centre of the silk industry.

8 NORTHWICH *1903*
Northwich has been a centre of the salt industry since the Roman period when the vast salt beds beneath the town were first exploited, and many centuries of salt extraction have caused subsidence to affect the buildings.

9 WILMSLOW *Styal Mill 1897*
Styal's Quarry Bank Mill, built in 1784 for the manufacture of silk and steadily enlarged in the early 19th century, still stands beside the River Bollin. However, today it has been restored as a working museum of the textile trade and is owned by the National Trust.

10 ALTRINCHAM
George Street 1900
Now wholly absorbed by Manchester's suburbs, Altrincham was, at the turn of the century, an independent small town that had grown up around the railway after its arrival in 1849. Gas lights and shops selling a fascinating variety of goods have been replaced by a new shopping precinct.

⑩

TODAY, THE PEAK DISTRICT is one of Britain's most popular regions for leisure activities, thanks largely to the National Park. At the same time, the great country houses of the area, Chatsworth and Haddon Hall for example, are enjoyed by thousands of visitors each year.

In the Victorian period things were very different. National parks were not even an idea, let alone a fact, for the first ten – which included the Peak District – only came into existence after the passing of the National Parks Act of 1949. Prior to World War I public access to the whole region was actually very limited. Much of the land was privately owned and laws of trespass were strictly enforced by the major local landowners such as the Duke of Devonshire. As a result there was little public awareness of the qualities of a landscape so widely enjoyed today, and the distinctive towns and villages, which in any case were relatively inaccessible in the pre-car age, were rarely visited. Better known were the traditional spa towns of Buxton and Matlock, both of which were made more popular in the 19th century by the coming of the railway. The warm mineral springs of these towns had been enjoyed at least since Roman times, both for bathing and for medicinal reasons. Buxton became the height of fashion in the late 18th century, thanks to the architectural developments sponsored by the Duke of Devonshire who hoped to turn the town into a second Bath. Expansion continued in the Victorian period, epitomised by the great dome of the Devonshire Royal Hospital, completed in 1879.

The industrial towns lying to the east of the Peak District, far older than the new industrial centres in Lancashire to the west, had developed around the traditional industries of iron, coal and stone. Great expansion took place in the Victorian period, thanks to new technologies such as the making of steel, but growth was still limited by the hilly nature of the landscape. Sheffield, itself contained by hills, was surrounded by a series of small towns in which agriculture and industry were still existing side by side. It is noticeable on the map how small towns like Mansfield, Worksop, Rotherham, Doncaster and Barnsley are surrounded by areas of countryside.

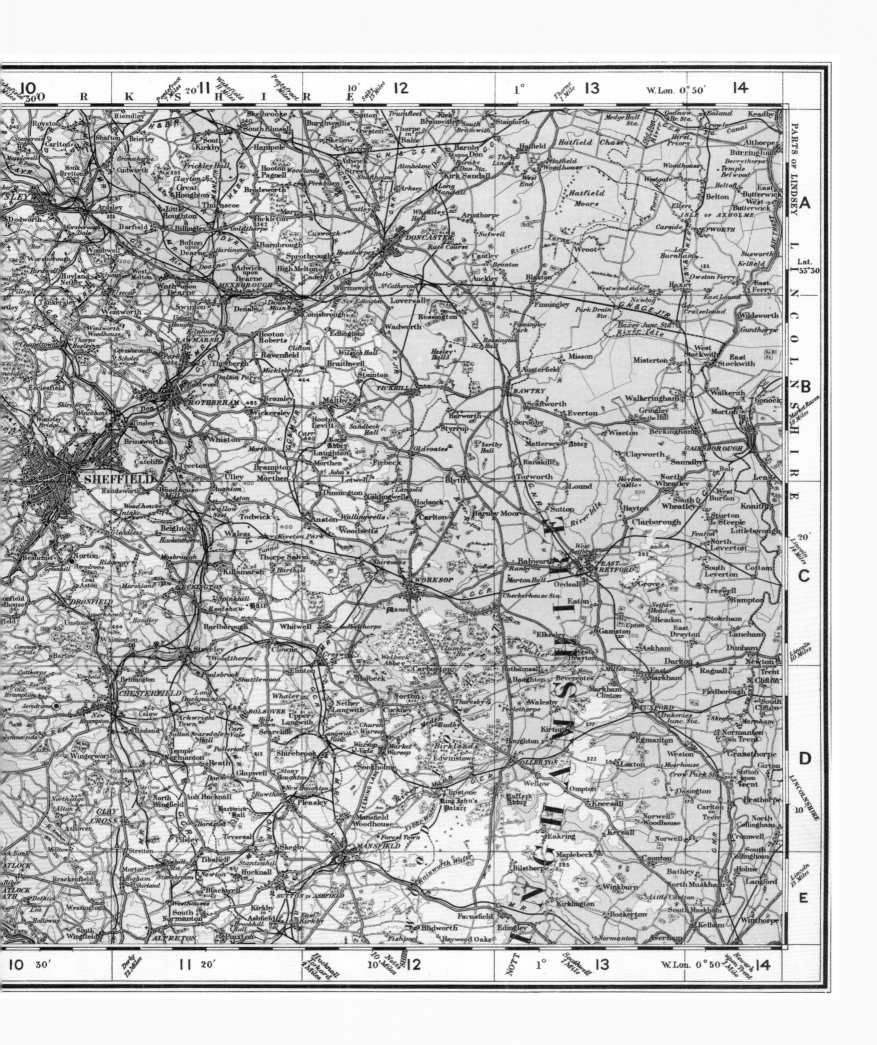

①

②

④

③

⑤

⑥

⑦

⑧

1 DERBYSHIRE PEAK DISTRICT *Cat and Fiddle c.1912*
Still one of England's most isolated inns, the Cat and Fiddle is now a popular stopping place on the A537 across the Derbyshire Peaks. In the Edwardian era the motor car opened up such remote areas. Here, smart chauffeur-driven vehicles look almost out of place outside the rather basic inn.

2 MATLOCK BATH
Footbridge 1886
The small Derbyshire town of Matlock became popular in the Victorian period because of its thermal baths, and one of its huge hydropathic hotels can be seen in the distance. Appreciation of the scenery soon followed, particularly High Tor and the Heights of Abraham that command the twisting course of the Derwent. The notice on the latticework bridge shows that the romantic appeal of the 'Swiss' scenery was already well established.

3 DONCASTER
Parish Church 1893
When this photograph was taken

Doncaster's grand parish church with its tall, pinnacled tower was still quite new, having been completed thirty five years earlier. Today it still dominates the town's skyline, but the River Don, in the foreground, is no longer busy with coal barges serving the south Yorkshire coalfields.

4 CASTLETON *1909*
The little village of Castleton, stuck at the end of a track leading nowhere and overlooked by rocky hills and the walls of Peveril Castle, was almost inaccessible in Edwardian times. Yet the group of huge limestone caverns beneath the village was already attracting visitors, with photographs for sale at the entrance to Speedwell Cavern whose wonders were then, as now, best seen by boat.

5 CHESTERFIELD
High Street 1896
This view along Chesterfield's main shopping street towards the Church of St Mary with its crooked spire reflects the unhurried nature of late Victorian life in this Derbyshire town.

6 CHESTERFIELD
Queen's Park 1902
Queen's Park, a pleasant oasis of public parkland with a lake and playing fields, was evidence that philanthropy and industry were sometimes hand-in-hand in Victorian towns. The values of fresh air were increasingly appreciated in the Edwardian era.

7 SHEFFIELD *Canal Basin 1870*
Sheffield's canal basin was a scene of frenetic activity in the 19th century, filled with the characteristic wooden barges that brought in the coal to fuel the city's iron and steel works. Today the basin is visited only by pleasure craft, but work is underway to improve it.

8 SHEFFIELD
Crimean Monument 1893
The Crimean was the first of the major Victorian wars to promote a series of grand memorials, and Sheffield's was a typically forceful structure of decidedly mixed architectural origins. It followed the tradition of the period in having actual cannons flanking the monument.

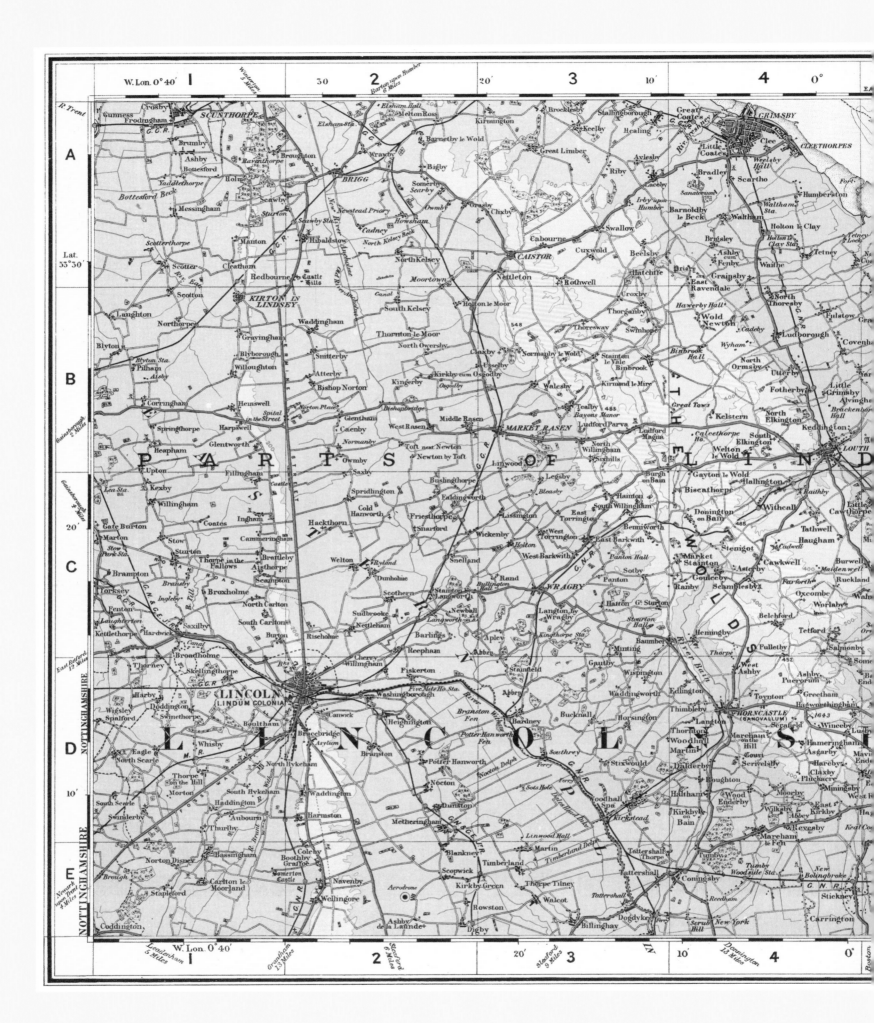

EVEN TODAY, LINCOLNSHIRE is a remote and little-known county, and it was far more so in the 19th century when its flat landscape was broken only by windmills and the towers and spires of churches. There were few towns of any size, and those that did exist were old-fashioned and independent, steeped in their history that often went back to the Roman period. For all that, it is a county upon which Victorian architects and builders made a firm impression.

To a region already richly endowed with churches, the 19th century added much more. There were local architects such as W A Nicholson who designed a number of brick churches in the 1830s and 1840s that were inspired by Louth's magnificent medieval parish church. At the same time, many of the great names of Victorian architecture – Scott, Butterfield, Street, Pearson, Teulon and Ferrey – all made their mark on the county's ecclesiastical buildings. Gilbert Scott worked first at Lincoln in 1838, and then went on to greater things at Saxby and Nocton. Another famous local architectect was Pearson Bellamy, and his forte was the extravagant Italianate town hall, with notable examples in Louth and Grimsby. With its town hall, its campanile-like clock tower and its grand waterfront, Grimsby must have had a definite Renaissance air in the 19th century.

The county also had some fine early railway stations, in Italianate, classical and Jacobean styles, and other Victorian buildings of note included chapels and warehouses. The domestic architecture of the Victorians was not so notable, but the century did contribute one of Britain's most unusual country houses. In the 1830s, at Harlaxton, George de Ligne Gregory set out to build himself the biggest house in the county. Helped by the architects Salvin and Burn, the vast Jacobean pile he created is still a remarkable sight today. However, perhaps the most notable 19th-century addition to this traditional county was the new town and resort of Skegness. Laid out on a grid plan during the 1870s, Skegness soon acquired its church, its chapel, its seaside hotels, its railway station and its pier – essential components for the town's future development into a major 20th-century leisure centre.

①

②

③

1 LINCOLN *The Glory Hole 1906*
The Witham Navigation takes a dramatic route through Lincoln, burrowing through the Glory Hole beneath medieval buildings – a view virtually unchanged today.

2 LINCOLN *Cathedral 1890*
This view of the cathedral high above the city shows the old High Street, with the Tudor gateway of the Stonebrow and guildhall in the distance.

3 GRIMSBY *Fish Pontoon 1906*
Fish has been Grimsby's *raison d'être* for a thousand years and the town still revolves round its fishing fleet, harbours and fish market. Herring was, for centuries, the fleet's mainstay but many other types of fish, as seen here, have maintained Grimsby's staple industry.

4 GRIMSBY *Docks 1893*
Grimsby's harbour was rebuilt in the middle of the 19th century following the arrival of the railway and these two events determined the town's prosperity. This view of the docks shows a range of trading vessels and, in the background, the Italianate dock tower of 1852.

5 SKEGNESS *Pier 1910*
Skegness's 1,843-foot-long pier was completed in 1881, a vital element in the resort's development. The large seafront hotels visible in the distance indicate the town's rapid popularity.

6 SKEGNESS *Lumley Road 1899*
Skegness was developed as a planned resort by the ninth Earl of Scarborough and building started in 1877. Twenty years on much of the town had been built, including the seafront, its hotels and its Jubilee clock-tower, seen in the distance in Lumley Road, the main street from the station to the sea.

④

⑤

⑥

In 1880 the members of the Preston North End Cricket Club decided to amuse themselves during the winter months by playing football, and so formed a football club with the same name. When the Football League was formed eight years later, Preston North End became one of its original twelve members, along with other now famous names such as West Bromwich Albion, Aston Villa, Everton (then known as St Domingo) and Wolverhampton Wanderers. League champion in its first two seasons, Preston also won the FA Cup in 1888–9.

The emergence of football as a major national sport was a feature of the late Victorian period, and the formation, first of the Football Association in 1863, and then of the League and its expansion into two divisions in 1892, was a reflection of the popular support the game enjoyed. At this point, football was linked closely with the industrial towns of the Midlands and the North, and many of the clubs that are now household names were founded during the last decades of the Victorian period. One of the earliest, dating back to 1866, was Sheffield Wednesday – another club formed by cricketers idle in the winter. Manchester United was formed in 1878 as Newton Heath, while Manchester City started as Ardwick in 1887. Liverpool came a bit later, in 1892 – one of a group of Lancashire clubs that included Blackburn Rovers, Burnley, Accrington Stanley and Blackpool.

The North East was also well-represented in the early days, with Newcastle United being formed from the amalgamation of two local teams in 1882, and Sunderland three years earlier. Prior to World War I the northern teams tended to dominate the League, and the various competitions, and the local support they generated was considerable, establishing in many cases the type of loyal following many of these clubs still enjoy today.

Famous names from the south, such as Arsenal, founded in 1886, Tottenham Hotspur, formed in 1882, West Ham United which started in 1895 as Thames Ironworks, and Portsmouth which dates from 1899, had to wait for the 1920s and 1930s before their great days arrived.

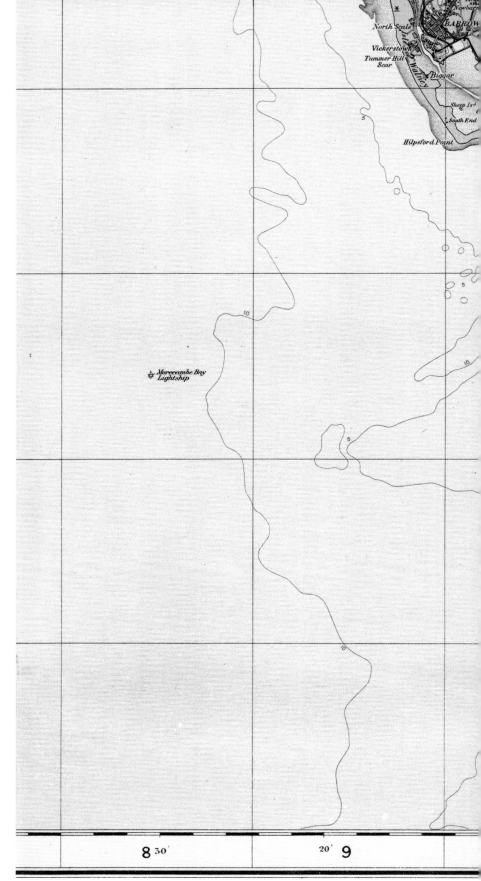

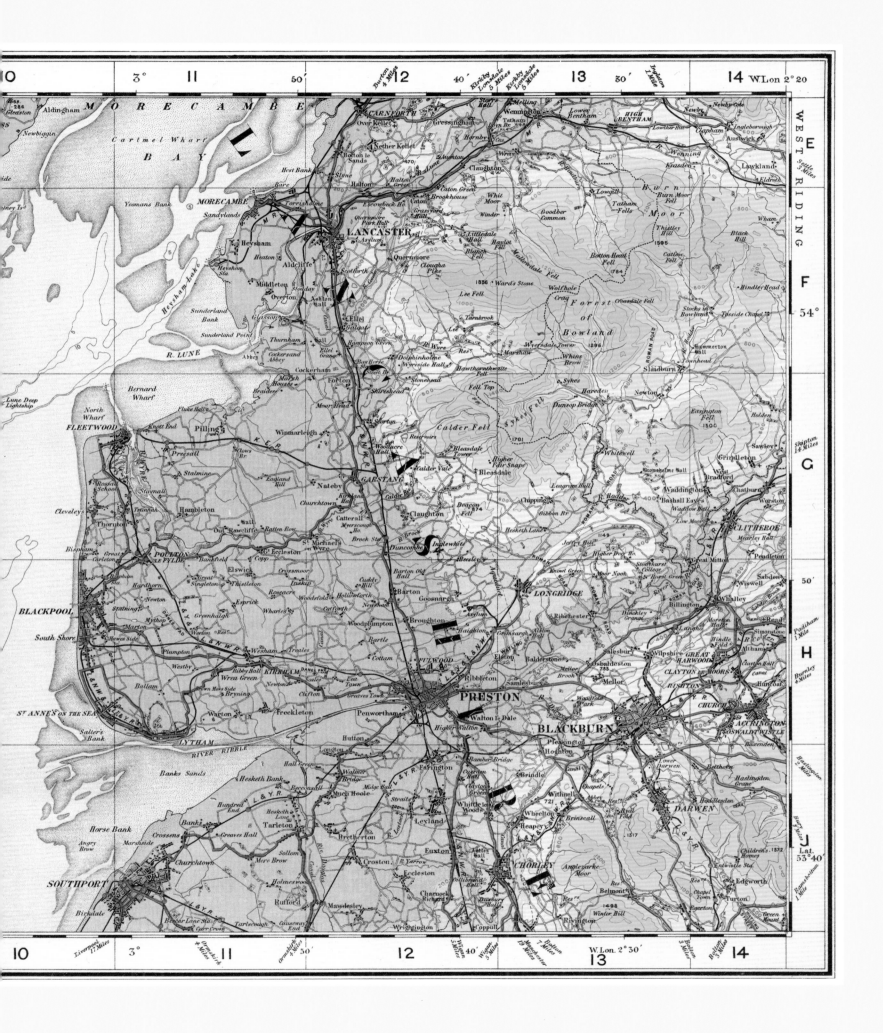

①

②

1 BLACKPOOL
From Central Pier 1899
In 1887 a newspaper commented that Blackpool offered more fun for less money than anywhere else, and this principle seems to have been the essence of this popular resort since its rapid development after the 1870s. This view shows Blackpool's distinctive and unchanging holiday atmosphere.

2 PRESTON *Fishergate 1903*
This view, looking along Preston's principal street towards the distinctive 1850s spire of St John's Church, shows the decorative nature of a typical Edwardian street scene, with its variety of shops signs, displays and delivery vehicles. Interesting also is the widespread use of awnings to shelter both customers and the goods on display from direct sunlight.

③

④

⑤

3 SOUTHPORT *Pier 1902*
Considered a more salubrious resort than its brasher neighbour, Blackpool, Southport grew rapidly in the 19th century and by 1861 had a population of 10,000. The pier, three-quarters-of-a-mile long, is unusual in that it starts well inland, crossing a large lake before reaching the sea. Theatres were a feature of all piers at the turn of the century and particularly popular were the pierrot shows advertised here.

4 LANCASTER
From Skerton Bridge 1891
This view of Lancaster, taken from one of the Lune bridges, shows the town's distinctive skyline formed by castle and church rising high above the surrounding buildings. Although of Norman origin, the castle was extensively rebuilt in the 18th and early 19th centuries.

5 BLACKBURN
Market and Town Hall 1894
A town with an ancient history, Blackburn is best known for its weaving mills; when this photograph was taken about one hundred were in operation. Few survive, but the 1850s Italianate town hall is still at the heart of the city. The market was completely rebuilt in the 1960s.

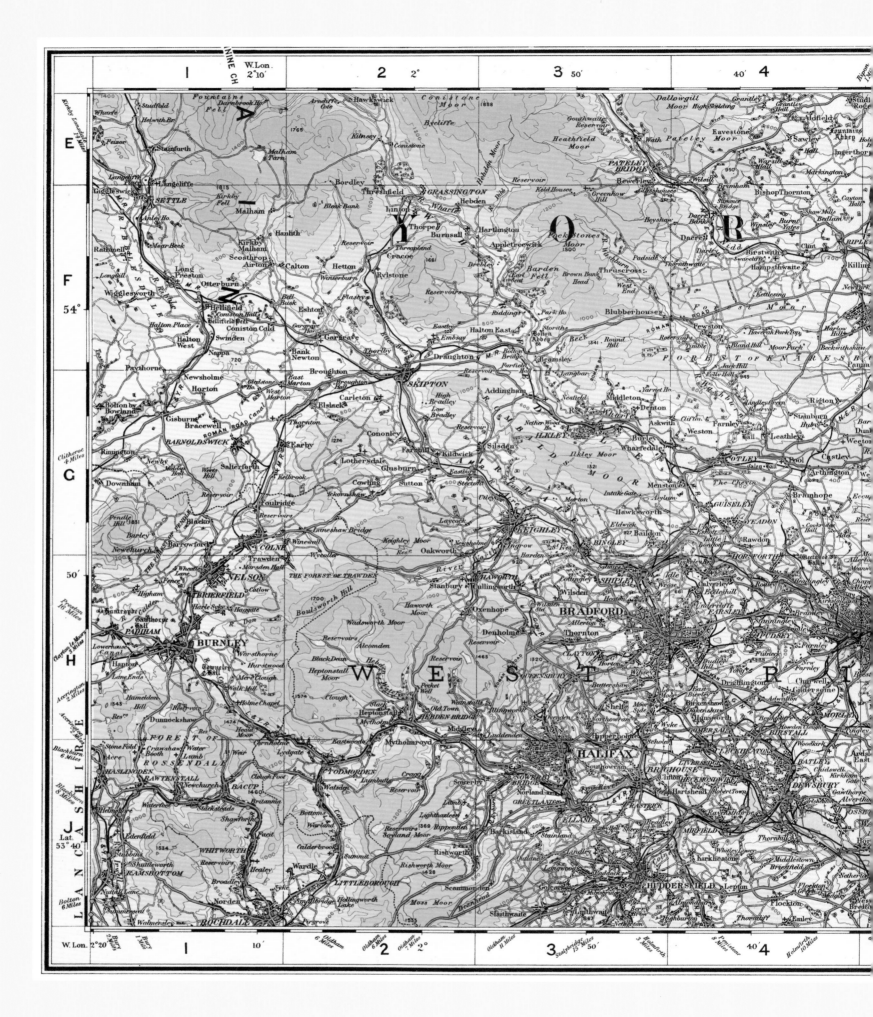

THERE IS PERHAPS NO better reflection of the industrial enterprise of the Victorians than the Yorkshire textile towns. Spinning and weaving had, of course, brought wealth to the region since the Middle Ages, but it was in the late 18th and early 19th centuries that the traditional cottage-based industry was replaced by the large mills that were to give the region its distinctive character. Even today, tall chimneys and the bare mill façades dominate many of the streets of towns like Bradford, Halifax, Bingley and Huddersfield, but what survives gives only a hint of the scale of the Victorian textile industry, and its impact upon its environment.

In the late 18th century development followed the river valleys, for the early mills, such as that built at Golcar near Huddersfield, were dependent upon water power. Within a few decades steam was dominant, and the Victorian mill was born. With its plain brick or stone frontage rising up five or six storeys, and running sometimes the whole length of a street, the mill completely dominated its surroundings, thrusting rampant industrialisation upon what had been small towns and villages. Typical examples are Armley, near Leeds, or Illingworth's in Bradford, both early Victorian, but even more powerful is the massive bulk of Samuel Lister's Manningham Mills, built in Bradford from 1873. Not all were plain, for some mill owners were prepared to spend money on decorating their buildings to show that they were, at heart, cultured.

Other owners were marked by a genuine philanthropy. Halifax's Copley Mills, built between 1847 and 1865, had a school, a library and a pleasant estate of workers' cottages. The self-contained factory estate or village was a not uncommon Victorian phenomenon. Other examples include Haley and Akroydon, built by Colonel Akroyd, and Crossley's West Hill Park, but by far the best known is Sir Titus Salt's new town of Saltaire, created from 1850 in a field near Shipley. The mill was opened in 1853 and all around were the houses (820 of which had been built by 1872), the school, the institute, the congregational church and the shops. There was even a park, but no pubs were allowed in this ideal estate village.

(1)

(3)
(4)

(2)

(5)

1 ILKLEY
Winding path across the Moors 1914
This photograph of the moors south of Ilkley was taken at a time when moorland walking was still in its infancy as a popular activity, partly owing to the limited access tolerated by private landowners.

2 KEIGHLEY *Fair c.1900*
The Fair, held in the streets of this Yorkshire market town, was an important event for the local farming community. The sight of cattle wandering the streets outside Keighley's handsome stone houses is now a part of history.

3 BINGLEY *From Ferncliff 1894*
Bingley, still an important wool town in the late Victorian era, is seen here from the east. The skyline of chimneys and steeples stands against the hills that flank the Aire valley.

4 HALIFAX
Town Hall from Cornmarket c.1900
A thriving cloth town since the 15th century, Halifax was still at the peak of its success when this view was taken. The Italianate

town hall, completed in 1862, was a measure of the town's civic pride and wealth.

5 YORK *Coney Street 1909*
Coney Street, a busy thoroughfare running parallel to the River

Ouse, shows the diversity of architecture in Edwardian York, and its importance as a shopping centre. Also interesting is the range of transport at a time when the motor car was beginning to have an impact on the city.

(6)

⑦

⑧

⑨

⑩

6 LEEDS *Town Hall 1894*
One of Britain's grandest and most imposing Victorian buildings is Cuthbert Brodrick's brown stone town hall. It was completed in 1858 and opened by Queen Victoria.

7 HEADINGLEY
Cricket Ground and Pavilion 1897
The smart new pavilion and stand show that Headingley was already famous as the home of Yorkshire cricket when this photograph was taken.

8 ALDBOROUGH *1907*
This view shows the centre of Aldborough, a picturesque village grouped round its 15th-century cross, but its main claim to fame was already its Roman past. The museum was opened in 1864 with important finds on display even though the major excavations were still to take place.

9 KNARESBOROUGH *1888*
Knaresborough's castellated railway bridge across the narrow valley of the Nidd was completed in 1848 and from that point on its dramatic arches featured in most views of the town. This view, taken from the west, also shows the 12th-century tower of St John's Church.

10 HARROGATE
Royal Pump Room 1907
Harrogate's development as one of Britain's leading spa towns took place in the late 18th and 19th centuries. The Royal Pump Room, now a museum, covered the town's most famous sulphur spring, but it was the Royal Baths that really gave Harrogate its Edwardian popularity.

KINGSTON-UPON-HULL WAS
laid out as a new town in 1293 on the orders of
Edward I, who wished to expand the already
thriving wool trade that had been developed in the
12th century by the monks of Meaux Abbey. From
this date onwards the town enjoyed considerable
success as a port, with the export of wool and
woollen goods its mainstay over several centuries.
However, its growth into one of Britain's largest
seaports and busiest deep-sea fishing bases did not
take place until the Victorian period, when a series
of enclosed docks was added to the old quays that
had flanked the confluence of the Hull and Humber
rivers since the Middle Ages. The first dock,
Queen's, was actually built in 1778, but the main
period of expansion occurred in the early 19th
century with the addition of three larger docks,
Humber, Prince's and Railway – the last-named
indicating clearly the reason for this sudden
expansion.

The railway was the key to Hull's success in the
19th century, and played a major part in the
development of the town's huge fishing fleet.
Thanks to the train, fish landed at Hull could be on
sale in the London markets the following morning.
In 1885 the huge Alexandra dock was opened, with
its fifty three acres of enclosed water, and this was
followed in 1914 by the even larger King George
dock. At their peak, the town's docks eventually
covered 200 acres, with thirteen miles of quays.

Throughout the Victorian period the textile
trade was dominant, but by the end of the century it
was already going into reverse, with Hull importing
increasing quantities of wool from Australia and
New Zealand to feed the Yorkshire mills. While the
railway was crucial in Hull's 19th-century growth,
waterways also played their part. Via the Humber's
connections with the Ouse and the Trent, Hull was
linked directly to the major manufacturing centres
of the North and the Midlands. The inland port of
Goole was the gateway for this trade, and this town
was entirely a 19th-century creation. The first
docks were opened in 1826, following the completion of the Aire and Calder Navigation from
Knottingley, and Goole then expanded rapidly
from its initial population of 450.

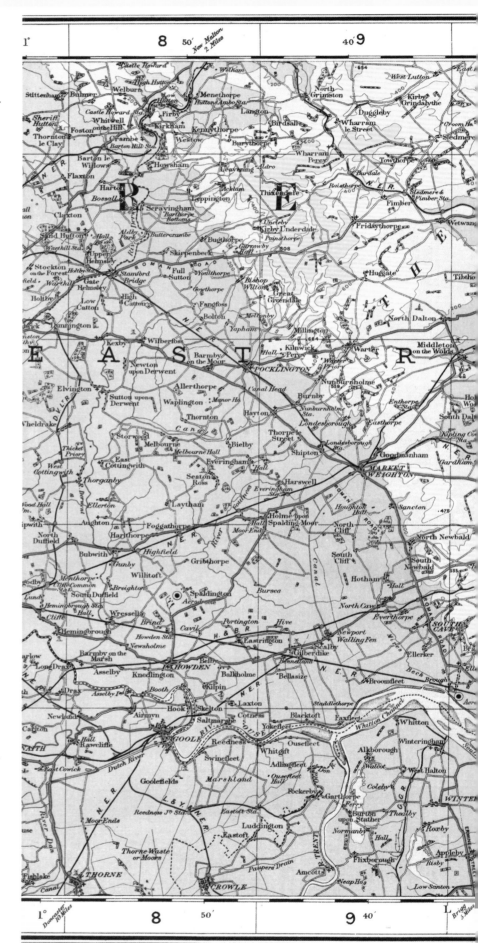

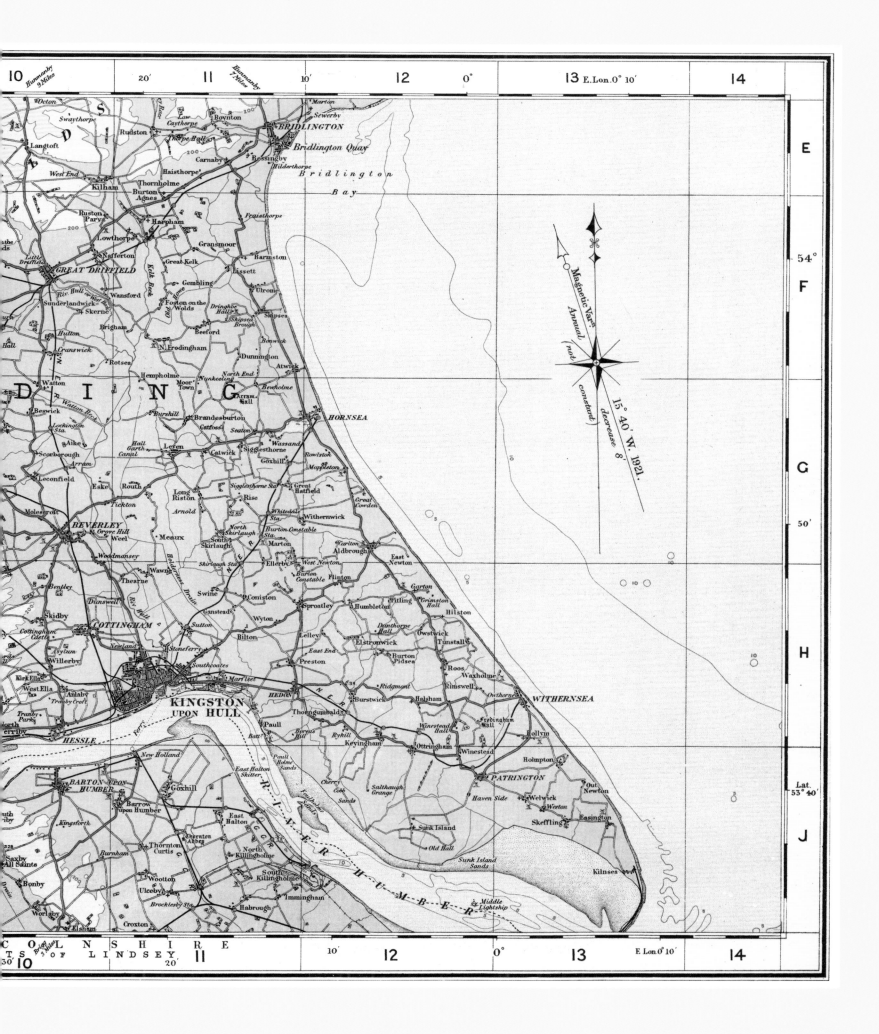

1 BRIDLINGTON *Quay 1893*
The old fishing port of Bridlington was developed as a resort in the late 19th century when the railway made its miles of sandy beaches accessible to thousands of holiday-makers. Seen here are the harbour's crowded quays and boats filled with pleasure-trippers.

2 BEVERLEY *Market Place 1886*
This view, looking northwards along Saturday Market, shows the early 18th-century market cross and, in the distance, the tower of the Parish Church of St Mary. The feeling of late Victorian spaciousness was inevitably affected by the coming of the motor car.

3 BRIDLINGTON
The Terraces 1906
Bridlington's terraced esplanade, backed by large hotels, was the height of fashion when this photograph was taken. Well-dressed Edwardian holiday-makers can be seen strolling with their parasols and picture hats and watching a beach concert.

⑤

④

4 HULL *The Humber 1903*
Hull's docks, built on the junction of the Hull and Humber rivers, have been busy since the Middle Ages and owe their original prosperity to the wool trade. At the peak of their activity in the Edwardian era the docks were used by a great variety of vessels. Seen here are large steamers, tugs, a Humber keel with its distinctive single sail and the ferries that provided the vital link southwards across the Humber to New Holland.

5 HULL *Dock Offices 1903*
When this photograph was taken the grandiose Victorian dock offices were the centre of Hull's commercial life, and the town's prosperity was reflected by the Queen Victoria jubilee statue. On the right is the 100-foot-high column of the Wilberforce memorial, seen here in its original location. Today the dock offices have become the town's museum, while Wilberforce has been moved to Queen's Gardens and now stands near the new technical college.

6 BEVERLEY MINSTER
East End 1886
This unfamiliar view of the Minster is taken from the railway crossing to the east and shows well the delicate tracery of 13th-century Gothic, one of the many periods represented in this famous building.

THE LAKE DISTRICT IS
probably the only part of Britain that owes its
popular development to literature, for the first to
appreciate and to promote the particular qualities
of the region through their writings were the
Lakeland poets. The key figure is, inevitably,
William Wordsworth, who spent his life in the
Lakes. Born in the small town of Cockermouth and
educated in Hawkshead, Wordsworth moved with
his sister Dorothy and his future wife Mary
Hutchinson into Dove Cottage, Grasmere, in 1802.
After brief periods at Allan Bank and Grasmere
Rectory, the family moved to Rydal Mount in
1813, and this remained the poet's home until his
death in 1850.

Wordsworth and his circle – Keats, Southey,
Coleridge and de Quincey – found the Lakeland
scenery a permanent source of inspiration, and
their writings, both prose and poetry, did much to
increase public awareness of the area as a whole.
The result was the start of the conflict between
preservation and accessibility, a battle that has
continued to rage ever since, and with increasing
intensity in the 20th century. Wordsworth himself
was torn: on the one hand he could write that the
Lakes were 'a sort of national property, in which
every man has a right and an interest who has an
eye to perceive and a heart to enjoy' and on the
other he could lead the fight to keep the railways
out. Railways or not, the pressures of tourism were
well established in the Victorian period as more and
more people were drawn to the Lakes both as
occasional visitors and long-term residents.

The literary promotion of the region did not stop
with Wordsworth, for the list of Victorian writers
who wrote about Lakeland or came to live there is
considerable. Walter Scott, Dickens, Matthew
Arnold, Lord Tennyson and John Ruskin all
played a part. Tennyson became a particular
enthusiast, using Bassenthwaite Lake as the inspiration for his epic poem, *The Morte d'Arthur*,
while the Grand Old Man of the Lakes was Ruskin,
who spent his last years in a house near the shores of
Lake Coniston. These Victorian writers were often
great walkers and hill-climbers, setting in train a
pastime that has come to dominate Lakeland-
visiting in the 20th century.

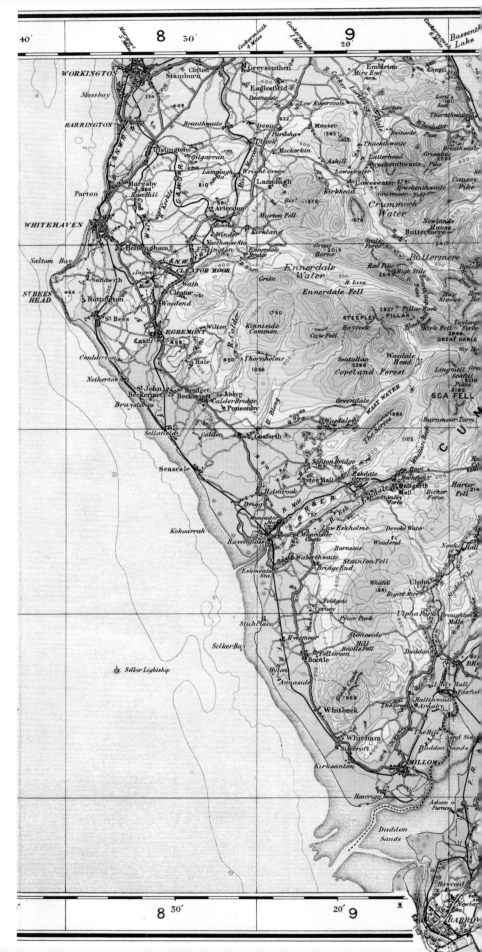

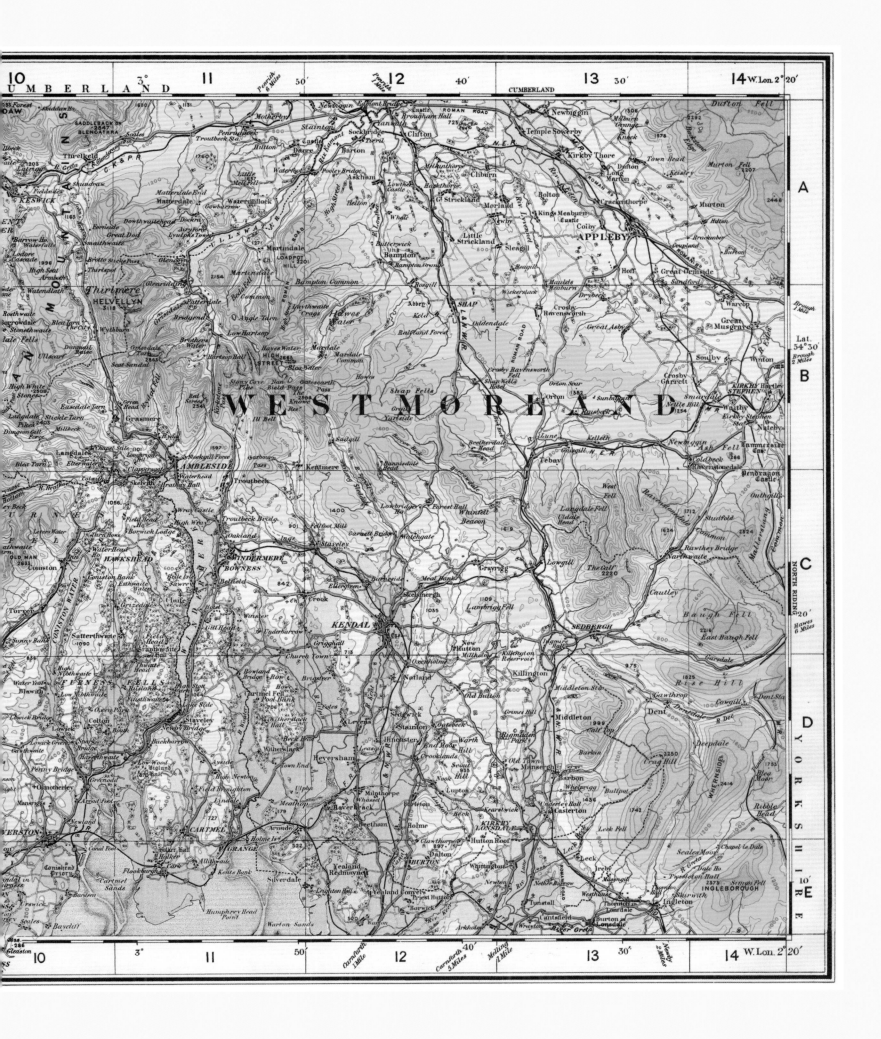

(1)

(2)

(4)

(3)

1 BARROW IN FURNESS
Walney Bridge 1912
The making of iron started at Barrow in the Middle Ages and by the end of the 19th century the town had the biggest steel-works in the world, along with massive dock and ship-building facilities. This view of Barrow across the Walney Channel was taken soon after the formation of Vickers, the name that was to be synonymous with Barrow throughout the 20th century.

2 GRANGE-OVER-SANDS
1912
Formerly a small fishing village, Grange was consciously turned into a resort by the Furness Railway from 1857 and it rapidly acquired the salubrious Edwardian atmosphere that it retains today. Dominant in this view from the sands is the 1854 Church of St Paul.

3 BOWNESS *Ferry Boat 1896*
This view across Lake Windermere, looking from Bowness towards the wooded Claife Heights, shows a rather primitive steam-powered ancestor of the modern vehicle ferry that carries traffic on the B5285 across the lake. The yachts in the distance illustrate the already established popularity of sailing on Windermere.

⑥

⑦

⑤

4 DERWENTWATER
Friars Crag 1889
In the 19th century Derwentwater was still relatively inaccessible, and the particular qualities of its wooded shores were best appreciated on foot or by boat.

5 BUTTERMERE
From Head 1889
This view of the tiny village of Buttermere and Crummock Water beyond underlines the remoteness of much of the Lake District in the Victorian era. Buttermere was then, as now, the starting point for walks to Scale Force, the highest waterfall in the Lakes.

6 CONISTON *Waterhead 1912*
Seen here from Waterhead at the lake's northern end, Coniston was particularly popular in the Victorian era. This was thanks, in part, to John Ruskin who lived beside the lake at Branston from 1871 until his death in 1900. When this photograph was taken there was still a railway to Coniston which connected with the steam yachts that operated on the lake. *Gondola*, built in 1859, is back in service today after restoration by the National Trust.

7 KIRKBY LONSDALE
Market Street 1908
The grey stone buildings of this attractive market town can be clearly seen in this view of Market Street whose quiet pleasures can still be enjoyed.

8 AMBLESIDE *Market Place 1912*
Its strategic position near the head of Windermere at a major road intersection has long made Ambleside a centre for Lake District exploration. In this busy Edwardian view of the town centre wagons full of visitors are setting off on tours, while in the distance an early motor vehicle hints at changes that were soon to alter forever the remoteness, and thus much of the appeal, of the Lake District.

⑧

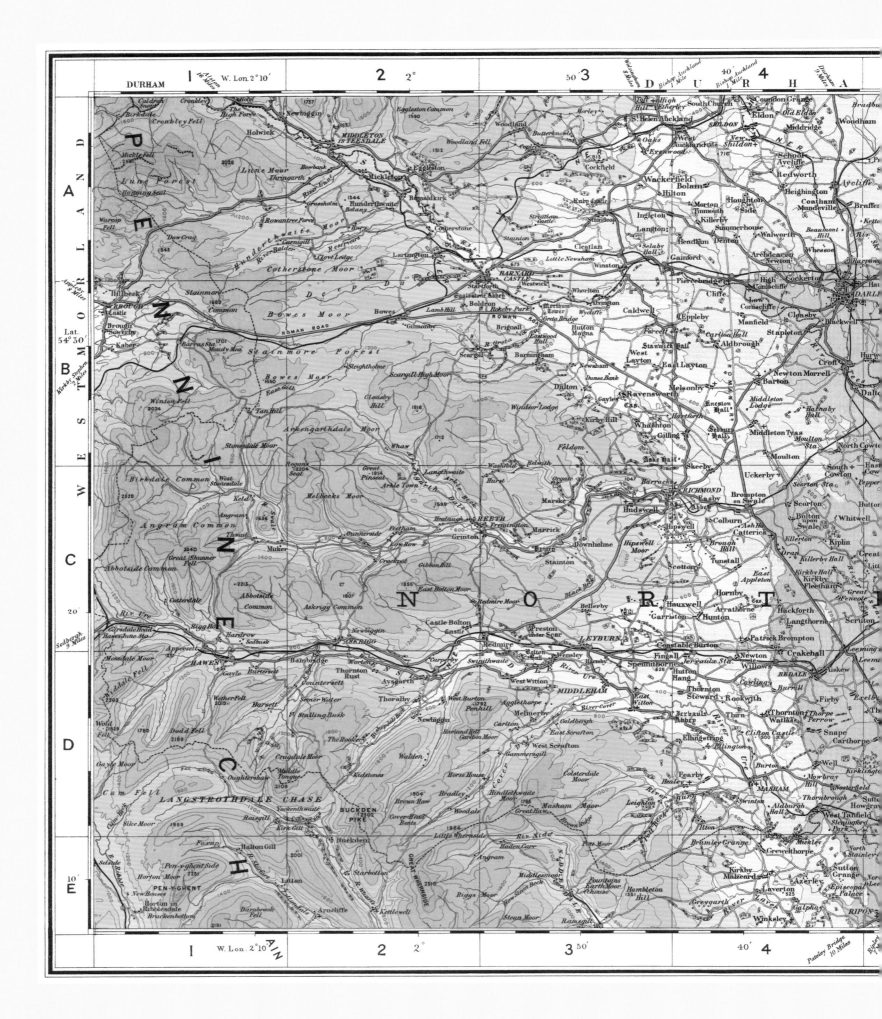

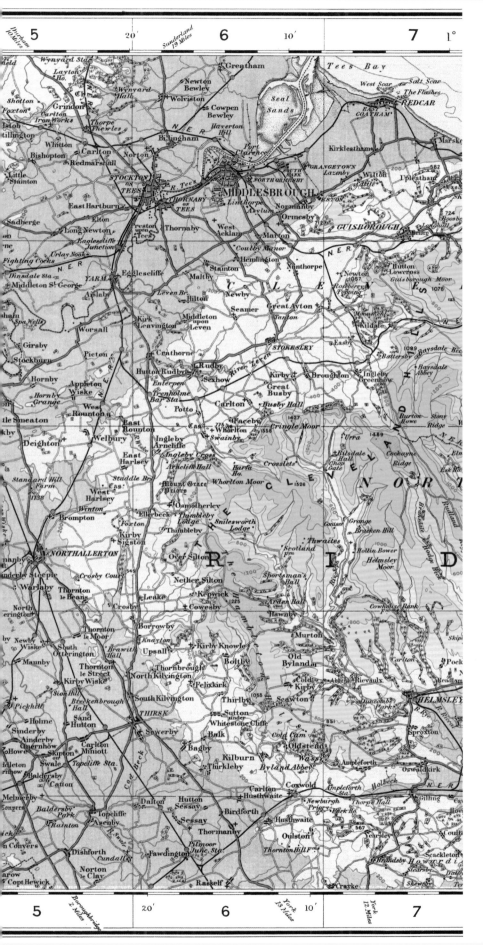

MANY OF TODAY'S VISITORS to the moors and dales of north Yorkshire are drawn by the wild and natural landscape of the region, without realising perhaps just how much of what they are enjoying is actually man-made. Until the late 18th century the landscape was genuinely wild, but the impact of the enclosures greatly changed its appearance. A characteristic feature of the region, and seemingly an integral part of the landscape, are the miles of drystone walls, yet these were mostly built in the late 18th or early 19th centuries as part of a plan to manage the land more efficiently and to improve the control and breeding of stock. Many of the roads that wind their way across the hills and along the valleys were constructed at the same time to improve access and communication.

This pattern of change continued through the Victorian period, and its impact could be measured in many ways. Local markets were seeing for the first time a greater variety of stock as the local sheep, such as the Swaledale and Wensleydale, were being cross-bred with imported breeds. This kind of animal management, so commonplace today, was still quite a novelty in the Victorian period, yet by the end of the century some of the traditional local breeds were already becoming rare. Other changes included the bringing under the plough of centuries-old pastureland.

All this radically altered the appearance of the landscape, but even the hills themselves were not inviolate. The building qualities of the local sandstones and limestones had been exploited locally at least since the Middle Ages, but the ever greater demand for the stone, both for building projects outside the region and for the new roads and railways, brought about a great increase in quarrying. Newly-discovered deposits of ironstone were also rapidly developed by the Victorians, and it was these that led directly to Middlesbrough's emergence as a major centre of the iron industry. From a population of forty in 1801, the town grew quickly to reach 20,000 by 1860. The first foundry was opened in 1841, and most of the famous names rose to positions of pre-eminence during the latter part of the century.

1 HIGH FORCE *1892*
Appreciation of the dramatic Pennine scenery of Teesdale was a relatively new phenomenon during the late Victorian period. The railways opened up these remote regions and hotels then sprang up to cater for visitors drawn by natural wonders such as the High Force waterfall.

2 REDCAR *Sands 1886*
Another resort whose growth was dependent upon the coming of the railway, Redcar is seen here at quite an early stage of its development. Bathing-machines and donkeys decorate the beach and in the distance is the pier, but still to arrive are the thousands of visitors who turned the town into a major holiday and leisure centre after World War I.

3 LEYBURN *1914*
The small market town of Leyburn, notable for its large market square, became popular in the late 19th century as a base for visitors exploring the Pennines, the Dales and the historic buildings of the region. This view, looking away from the market place towards the tower of St Matthew's Church, shows in the foreground a shop with a fine display of photographic souvenir views, including Frith's.

4 STOCKTON-ON-TEES
High Street 1899
The market town of Stockton was turned into a centre of industry from 1825 with the opening of the Stockton and Darlington Railway. This view along the High Street, reputedly the widest in Britain, confirms the town's success.

5 HAWES *1908*
When this photograph was taken Hawes was still primarily a compact, grey-stone market town set below the Pennines – a social and commercial centre for the local farming community. The fine collection of traps and carts shows that the horse was still dominant.

8 MIDDLESBROUGH
Market Place 1913
This view of Middlesbrough's market place on a wet day shows, on the left, the tower of the old town hall and in the centre the Parish Church of St Hilda, with its distinctive steeple. Modern developments have changed this view considerably.

9 SALTBURN-BY-THE-SEA
Inclined Tramway 1901
In a setting notable for its dramatic cliffs, Saltburn's development as a resort was largely due to the efforts of the Quaker iron magnate Henry Pease. The first hotels and the characteristic white-and-red brick terraces date from the 1860s, and the simple pier, seen here with its inclined tramway link to the town, was built in 1868. Thanks to its fine beaches, Saltburn's appeal increased after World War I.

10 RICHMOND
Market Place 1908
Still one of England's most appealing small towns, Richmond's development has always been limited by its hilltop position. In the centre is the generous and still-cobbled market place, whose dominant features are Holy Trinity Church, the market cross obelisk and the view of the castle keep.

6 BARNARD CASTLE *1890*
This classic view of Barnard Castle, with the old bridge, the houses climbing sheer from the bank of the Tees and, high above, the castle ruins, is still one to be enjoyed today.

7 RIPON *Spa Baths 1914*
Ripon has long been known for its cathedral and its streets of pleasant Georgian houses. This photograph is a reminder of a less familiar chapter in the town's history, when the success of nearby Harrogate encouraged Ripon's development as a spa.

⑨

⑩

THE DEVELOPMENT OF NORTH Yorkshire's coastline occurred largely during the 19th century, and was inspired directly by the railways. In any case, with the opening of the Stockton and Darlington line in 1825, railways had come early to the region. Ten years later a line was opened between Whitby and Grosmont, and extended a year later to Pickering. Initially isolated and dependent upon horsepower, this was converted to steam in 1847 and by the 1860s was connected to the national network. The 1880s saw the opening of lines along the coast, and it was these routes that turned fishing villages into resorts.

An important element was also the increase in leisure. During this period the working day was steadily reduced. In the 1860s working hours in factories were six to six, and in offices and shops eight to eight, but by the end of the century a nine-hour day was becoming widespread. The six-day week was progressively reduced by Acts of Parliament making Saturday a half day, and in 1871 another Act instituted bank holidays. At the same time, the industrial habit of closing for a week in summer was increasingly being taken up in other areas. This was inspired both by the need to overhaul machinery and by the survival into the industrial age of traditional festivals such as Wake's Weeks.

At the heart of the region, and quite apart from the other coastal towns, is Whitby, a seaport whose fame spreads far beyond the 19th century. The abbey marks the site of the signing in AD664 of the Synod of Whitby, when the method of determining the date of Easter was established, but the town's more recent associations have all been with the sea. Whitby's links with Captain Cook are well known, as is its fame as a whaling port and centre for ship-building. Although it never really became a resort as such, the Victorians visited Whitby in great numbers, drawn then, as now, by the traditional atmosphere, the kippers and, above all, the jet industry. In its heyday in the 1870s over 1,000 people were employed in the finding, carving and selling of this highly distinctive, glossy, fossilised wood that became the epitome of a particular kind of decorative Victorian jewellery.

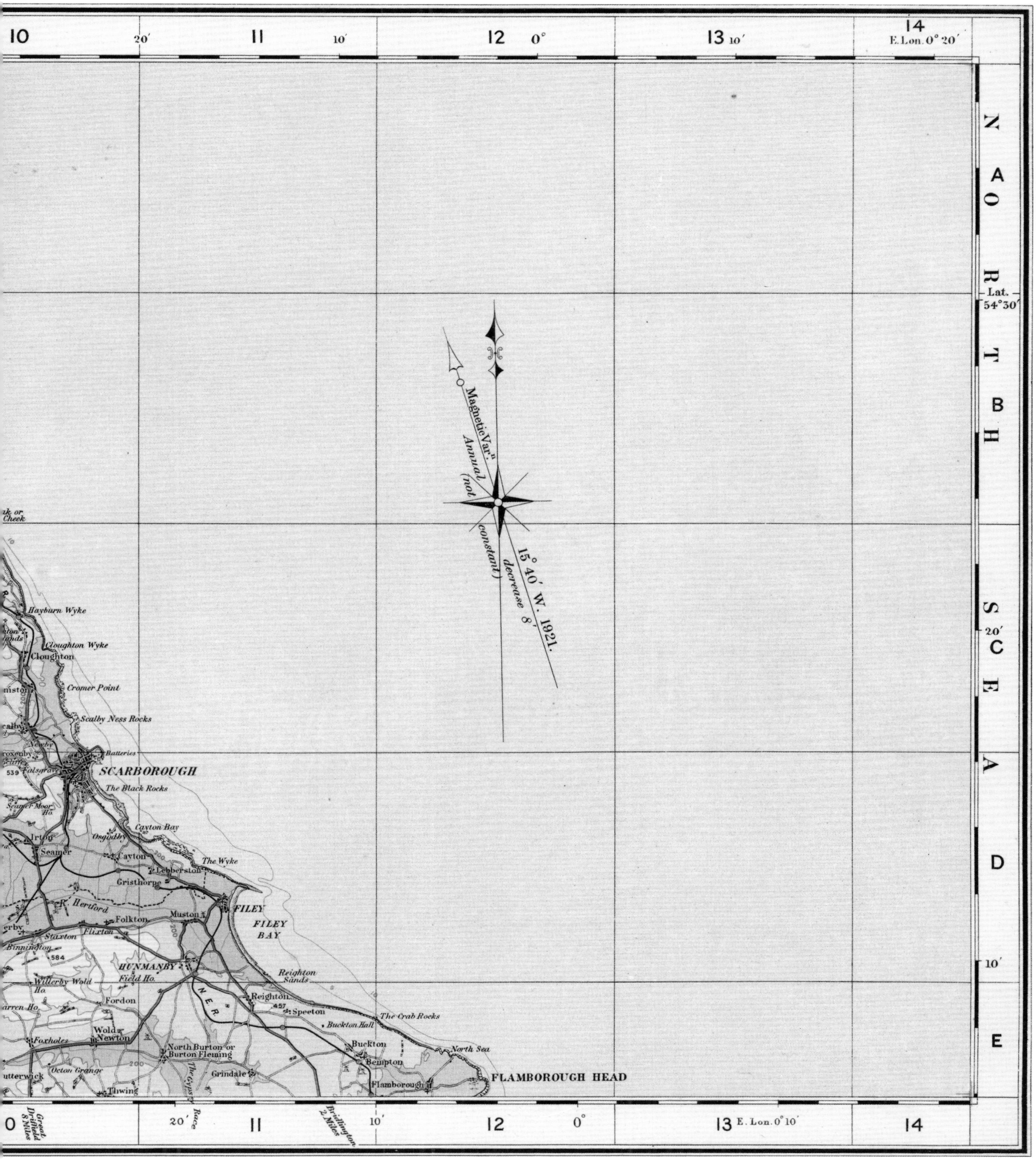

N A O R T B H S C E A D E

Lat. 54°30'

20'

10'

Magnetic Var.ⁿ Annual (not constant)

15° 40' W. 1921.

decrease 8'

Hayburn Wyke

Cloughton Wyke
Cloughton

Cromer Point

Scalby Ness Rocks

Batteries

SCARBOROUGH

The Black Rocks

Seamer Moor Ho

Cayton Bay

Irton
Seamer   Osgodby
Cayton
The Wyke
Lebberston
Gristhorpe

R. Hertford   FILEY
Folkton   Muston   FILEY BAY

Staxton   Flixton
Binnington
HUNMANBY   Reighton Sands
Willerby Wold   Field Ho.
Ho.
Fordon   Reighton
Foxholes   Wold
Newton   Speeton   The Crab Rocks
North Burton or   Buckton Hall
Burton Fleming   Buckton   North Sea
Octon Grange   Grindale   Bempton
Thwing   Flamborough   FLAMBOROUGH HEAD

①

②

1 SCARBOROUGH *1900*
This view of the harbour busy with fishing boats and coastal trading vessels, and the old houses clustered on the quays, captures the atmosphere of Scarborough in its pre-resort days. Some of this atmosphere still survives in the old town which shelters beneath the headland with its Roman signal station and ruined castle.

2 WHITBY *The Bridge 1913*
When this photograph was taken Whitby was both a working port and a resort popular with visitors to the Moors and the Yorkshire coast. The centre of the town was then, as now, the swing-bridge over the Esk and this view across the bridge looks towards Church Street and Grape Lane, where James Cook lived.

3 WHITBY *Abbey* c.*1886*
Set on a bare, windswept hill high above the town and harbour, the gaunt sandstone ruins of Whitby Abbey have always been impressive. It was here that the Synod of Whitby was held in AD664, while many centuries later the more picturesque aspects of the ruins were featured in Bram Stoker's novel *Dracula*.

③

⑥

④

⑤

4 FILEY *Sands 1901*
Set on six miles of sandy beaches, the little fishing village of Filey was a natural site for development into a resort by Victorian entrepreneurs. This view shows the fashionable Edwardian beach in its heyday, with carriages, theatrical and musical entertainments, deckchairs and parasols, and a host of elegant holiday-makers.

5 ROBIN HOOD'S TOWN *1901*
A cluster of small stone houses and steep narrow streets set below powerful cliffs has long made Robin Hood's Town into one of Yorkshire's most picturesque fishing villages, and its relative inaccessibility has protected it from the ravages of the motor car. When this view was taken most visitors came by train, enjoying the route along the cliffs that was, until its closure in the 1960s, one of England's most scenic lines.

6 SCARBOROUGH
Spa Promenade 1890
Scarborough's medicinal springs were discovered in about 1620 and the town was attracting fashionable visitors before the 18th century. Sea-bathing started in about 1730, and one of the town's claims to fame is the invention of the bathing-machine. The popularity of the waters continued through the Victorian period, prompting the construction of both the French-style spa building, completed in 1880, and the huge 1860s Grand Hotel, seen in the distance.

7 STAITHES *Bridge* c.*1886*
The precarious and huddled position enjoyed by the old fishing village of Staithes below the cliffs can be seen here. Nets are drying on the bridge, and all around are the stone cottages and terraces that gave the village its quaint appeal to the Victorians. Today the fishing boats and bridge have gone but otherwise Staithes' steep and narrow streets look much the same.

⑦

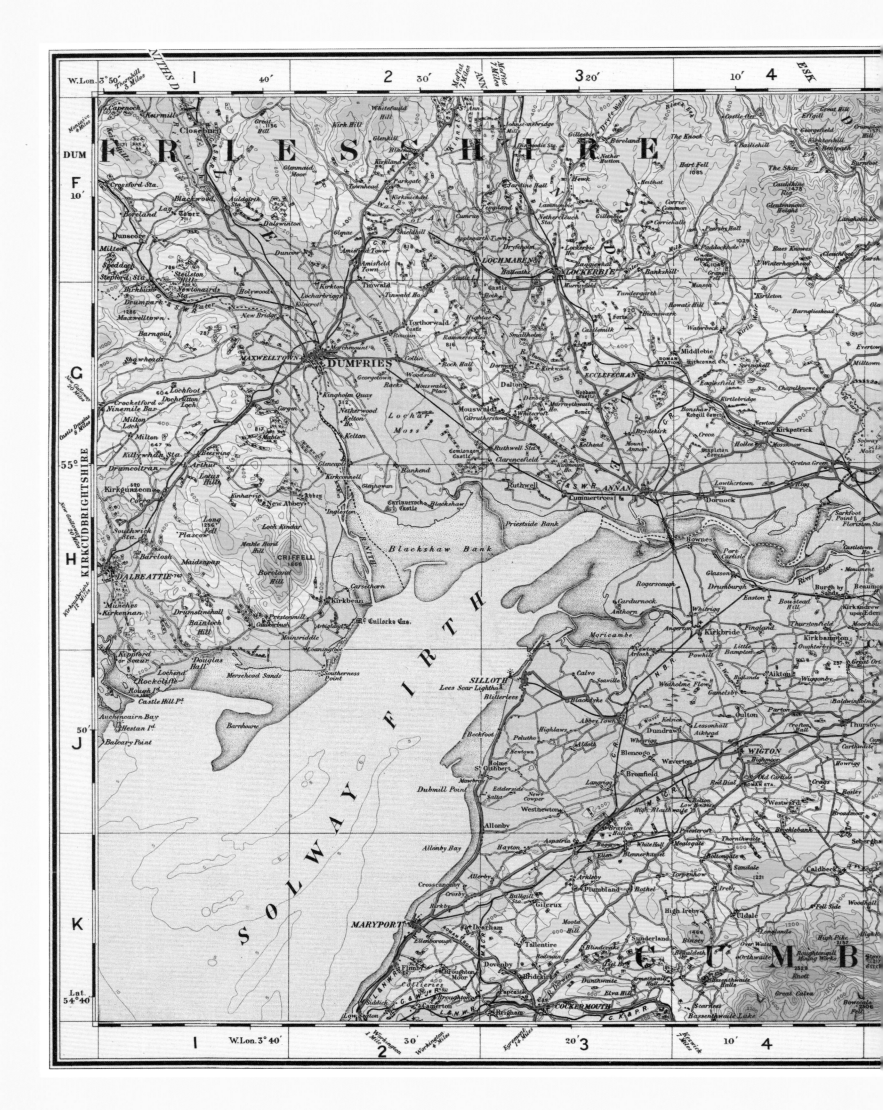

CARLISLE'S REPUTATION AS a border fortress stretching back through centuries of Anglo-Scottish strife to the Roman period was maintained in the 19th century by the addition of ranges of barracks to the old castle. In the Victorian period the military presence in Carlisle expanded considerably, with the garrison reaching a size and an importance not seen since the 16th century. Another important addition was the new Citadel, or Assize Courts. This, designed in 1810 by Robert Smirke, the architect of the British Museum, followed the pattern of Henry VIII's old citadel. Forty years later the railway station was built opposite it, and this grand Tudor-style building, designed by Sir William Tite, soon became one of Britain's busiest and most colourful stations. To be seen in its platforms were trains in the liveries of at least seven separate companies, carrying an extraordinary variety of both local and long-distance travellers. In fact, Carlisle Citadel station in the Victorian era might have given the artist W P Frith an even more exciting subject that the one he chose to paint at Paddington.

Main-line expresses on their way to and from Scotland came thick and fast, but just as interesting were the local trains. Some were on their way to Maryport – the 18th-century new town and coal harbour given a new lease of life by the railway – while others carried passengers to the large hotel at Port Carlisle where they would wait for the steam packet to Liverpool. This railway had replaced the canal cut in 1823 to link Carlisle to the Eden estuary. Others travelled to the new Solway Firth resort of Silloth, to enjoy the views of distant Scotland from this Victorian creation, or set off eastwards towards Newcastle, or southwards along the recently opened mountain route to Settle.

Victorian life in all its forms could be seen at Carlisle, but particularly notable were the large number of young couples on their way northwards to a clandestine marriage. Gretna Green was the first station across the border and so the railway played an important part in maintaining, at least until 1856, the tradition that couples wishing to marry without consent could do so in Scotland by a simple declaration in front of witnesses. After that date a minimum three-week stay in Scotland became compulsory, but the marriage could then still be celebrated without parental consent in a simple ceremony performed by the village blacksmith. In 1940 a change in the law prevented the smith from carrying out the ceremony.

①

1 COCKERMOUTH
From the Park 1906

When this photograph was taken Cockermouth was a quiet market town, serving the local agricultural community and Lake District visitors. Seen from the south, the compact town is contained by the confluence of the Derwent and Cocker rivers. In the distance are the castle ruins and the 1854 Church of All Saints', with its prominent spire. In the foreground is the railway, which opened in 1865, linking Cockermouth with Keswick, Penrith and, later, Workington – bringing new life to the town. This view still looks much the same, but the railway has been closed for some time.

2 COCKERMOUTH
Main Street 1906

Cockermouth's main street is a generous thoroughfare, lined on both sides with trees and simple Georgian buildings. Today, the street is more agreeable than in this view as the trees are now mature. In the distance is the 1875 statue of the sixth Earl of Mayo, while in the foreground is the original cast-iron clock-tower.

②

3 COCKERMOUTH
Wordsworth's House 1906
The most famous people in Cockermouth's history are the Wordsworths, and this fine house in Main Street is where the poet was born in 1770. William's father moved here in 1760 when he became steward to Sir James Lowther. Still the finest house in the town, it is now a place of pilgrimage for students and Wordsworth enthusiasts from all over the world. Apart from being painted white, the house is little-changed from when the photograph was taken. Wordsworth is also commemorated by a window in All Saints' Church.

4 COCKERMOUTH *Castle 1906*
The Romans were the first to develop Cockermouth, building a fortified settlement to the north, near Papcastle, to benefit from the strategic position offered by the river junction. In the 13th and 14th centuries the present castle was built, making use of many of the stones from the Roman settlement, and it is the ruins of this great structure that still dominate the town. This view shows the castle's commanding position.

③

④

IN THE 19TH CENTURY TWO British industries above all dominated the world, and both had their heart in County Durham. Coal-mining had been a feature of the region at least since the Middle Ages, and by the early 1600s shallow surface pits, or levels, in the Newcastle area alone were producing 200,000 tons a year – much of which was already being shipped to London and other southern ports. Output grew enormously during the 18th century, helped by modern technology in the form of steam pumps and the network of early tramways that linked the mines to the Tyne and Wear ports. By the end of the century mines had been driven 800 feet underground, and over two million tons were being shipped each year. However, it was in the Victorian period that the mines reached their peak, spreading massively throughout the region, and particularly in the triangle formed by Sunderland, Bishop Auckland and Hartlepool. By the end of the 19th century about forty million tons were being produced annually by the Durham pits, to be shipped to ports all over the world from the coal staithes at Tynemouth and South Shields, Sunderland, Seaham and elsewhere.

It was the demands of the coal industry that lead directly to the setting up of shipyards on the Tyne and Wear. In the 17th century up to 400 colliers were employed in the coal trade, and at times a hundred ships could be seen at anchor awaiting their turn at the coal wharves. Repair yards were soon set up to cater for the needs of this huge fleet and by the end of the century many of these yards had begun to build their own ships. During the 18th century small yards all along the Tyne were building these colliers, using Baltic timber and Baltic flax for the sails. In the 19th century these yards expanded massively, helped by the new technologies of iron and steam. In 1852, the first screw-driven collier, capable of carrying 650 tons of coal to London in forty eight hours, was launched and through the latter decades of the century Tyne and Wear yards built every kind of vessel for use in all parts of the world. The great names of the industry, Armstrong, Parsons, Richardson, Swan and Hunter, all rose to pre-eminence in the late 19th century, and typical of the region as a whole is the story of the yard opened in Jarrow in 1852 by Sir Charles Palmer. Employing at its peak 10,000 people, this yard built 900 ships before its closure.

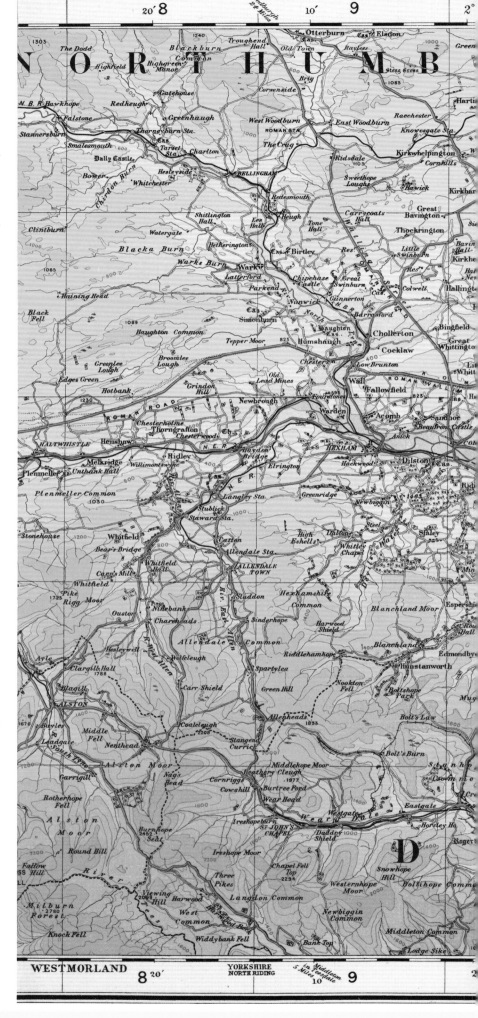

①

1 BISHOP AUCKLAND
Newgate Street 1914
Bishop Auckland's main feature, and the town's *raison d'être*, is the Bishop's Palace, the seat of the bishops of Durham for over 600 years. The entrance to the palace is from Castle Square, an extension of the market place. This view along Newgate Street shows the town's typical blend of Georgian and Victorian buildings. An interesting piece of street furniture, common in the Edwardian era, is the advertising wall-thermometer on the printers and stationers in the foreground.

2 WEST HARTLEPOOL
Church Street 1901
West Hartlepool was an entirely Victorian town, having developed from nothing to serve the dock complex that opened progressively from the 1840s. When this photograph was taken the town had become a thriving commercial community with a population of 63,000. At that time, Church Street with its trams, electric lighting, cabs and busy shops and hotels, was the centre of the town. In this century the docks have declined, but chemical and other industries have ensured West Hartlepool's continuing growth.

3 HARTLEPOOL
Lighthouse 1892
The old part of Hartlepool, whose history goes back to the foundation of the 7th-century monastery, is clustered on the narrow peninsula to the north of Hartlepool Bay. At the centre of the old town is the fine 12th-century Church of St Hilda, while on the tip of the peninsula is the lighthouse that guards the entrance to the harbour and dock complex.

②

④

③

4 BISHOP AUCKLAND
Newton Viaduct 1898
Typical of the powerful structures associated with the railway age in Britain is Newton Cap viaduct, built to carry the line from Bishop Auckland northwards towards Durham across the River Wear. In the foreground is the medieval road bridge. The railway across the viaduct was closed many years ago, and recent road schemes have greatly changed the view seen in this photograph.

5 EAST HARTLEPOOL
Elephant Rock 1886
At the end of the 19th century there were attempts to turn Hartlepool and its surroundings into a resort. A promenade with a bandstand was built, along with grand hotels, and local features of interest were used to encourage visitors. Typical was the so-called Elephant Rock, a natural formation near the sea.

6 DURHAM *Cathedral 1892*
Justifiably famous over several centuries is the classic view of Durham Cathedral rising high above its surrounding city. This view, from the north, is one that can still be enjoyed today. It is seen particularly well by visitors arriving by train.

7 DURHAM *Old Elvet 1914*
The Elvet Bridge links the cathedral city of Durham, on its rock in the Wear's horseshoe bend, with the part of the town that lies across the river to the east. Old Elvet is one of the principal streets, and this Edwardian view of it is recognisable today. The 18th-century façade of the Royal County Hotel is still a prominent feature.

⑤

⑥

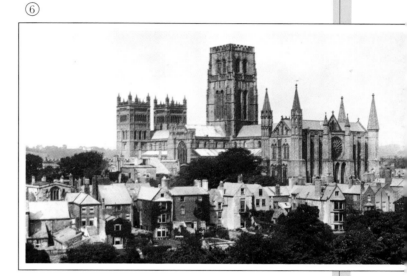

⑦

AN INTRODUCTION TO

SCOTLAND

FRANCIS FRITH had set out with a grand scheme to record all of Britain in photographs. In the end he was defeated by the scale of the task he had set himself, and many parts of Britain were never recorded by his cameras. Least successful of all, perhaps, was his coverage of Scotland where his ambitions were thwarted both by the size of the country and by the limitations of the transport network.

The comparatively inaccessible nature of Scotland at this time should not be under-estimated. Many parts of Scotland were never reached by the railway, and the lines that did struggle northwards into the Highlands were mostly completed either towards the end of Frith's life or after his death. Thus the wilder regions remained relatively remote throughout the 19th century and until the coming of the motor car, and a travelling photographer with his piles of baggage and equipment would have faced almost insuperable difficulties.

As a result, this book can only show in any detail the Lowlands, the Glasgow and Edinburgh regions, the Clyde and the Ayrshire coast, areas that received the full Frith treatment. Where Frith travelled further afield, photographs were taken of more northerly towns, for example Oban, Inveraray, Perth, Callander, Braemar, Nairn and Inver-

ness. However, in general terms most of the Highlands remained unvisited and unrecorded until well into the 20th century, and of the islands, only Skye seems to have been photographed.

Many of the photographs that do exist are unrepresentative both of the towns they show and the region as a whole, and so it seemed practical for the purposes of this book to concentrate on the areas that had been adequately covered, and which related closely to the Ordnance Survey mapping.

Further north are whole sections of map (not included in this book) with no photographs at all, underlining the point that the development of tourism in Scotland's wilder and least accessible regions is a feature of the 20th century.

Previous page
FORTH BRIDGE 1897
When this photograph was taken the Forth Bridge had only been open seven years, and it was still regarded as one of the engineering marvels of the world. The southbound train shows the scale of this massive structure, whose three great cantilevered steel spans carry the track 150 feet above the river. In the foreground can be seen one of the fleet of ferries that carried passengers and vehicles across the Forth.

OBAN ESPLANADE 1901
Little changed today is this view of Oban's handsome Victorian waterfront, always one of the most elegant of the West Highland ports. A sheltered settlement since prehistory, Oban's main period of growth was in the 19th century, development encouraged first by fishing and the Hebridean steamer services, and later by the railway, which arrived in 1880. A popular tourist resort ever since, Oban is dominated by the curious replica of the colosseum that stands above the town. Built at the instigation of a local businessman to give work to unemployed masons, and subsequently known as McCaig's folly, this structure was brand new when the photograph was taken.

② 43201 Inveraray F.F.&Co.

INVERARAY 1899
Set on the northern shore of Loch Fyne, Inveraray is still one of Scotland's most elegant small towns, having been rebuilt virtually from scratch in the late 18th century. The simple but pleasing qualities of the town and its castle were attractive to late Victorian visitors, who enjoyed the way it managed to combine sophistication and refinement with the traditional appeal of a loch-side settlement.

③

CALLANDER MAIN STREET 1899
Set in the magnificent scenery of the Trossachs, Callander became a popular late Victorian Scottish resort, thanks in part to its railway connections. The quiet main street, flanked by typical stone buildings, reflects the town's leisurely way of life at the peak of its Victorian popularity, when the visitors included notable figures such as J M Barrie.

In 1754 the royal and Ancient Club was founded in St Andrews, an event generally accepted as the start of the modern game of golf although it had in fact been played in Scotland for some 250 years before that, and Mary Queen of Scots is known to have been a golfing fanatic. St Andrews, known then as the St Andrews Golf Club, was the setting for the first British championships, held in 1857, and three years later the first British Open was held at Prestwick, in Ayrshire, on the other side of the country. Prestwick continued to stage this prestigious event each year until 1870, when St Andrews and Musselburgh joined forces with the founder club and a three-year rota was established. In 1925 it was decided that the championship had outgrown its birthplace, but the course at Prestwick remains a beloved link with the past and has associations with some of the greatest names in golfing history.

During this time golf had enjoyed a rising popularity as a competitive and leisure activity, and the opening of courses was a particular feature of resort development in late Victorian Britain. Scotland took the lead, because of its historical links with the game, and many more famous clubs were established in Ayrshire following the opening of direct and rapid railway connections from Glasgow. Among these was Troon, which boasts one of the most famous golf holes in Scotland – the short eighth known world-wide as the Postage Stamp because of its tiny green. Others were Turnberry, Irvine, Ayr and Girvan where the pleasures of the coastal scenery could be combined with a round of golf, and many of these clubs also went on to become the setting for famous international competitions and events.

The combination of fine beaches and Robert Burns associations soon brought Ayr into prominence as a resort in its own right, and development quickly spread along the coast from Girvan in the south to Saltcoats and Ardrossan in the north. The attractions of the region included the varied coastal landscape, history and a wide range of leisure activities in which golf obviously played an increasingly important part and today it is one of the country's five clearly-defined golfing coastlines.

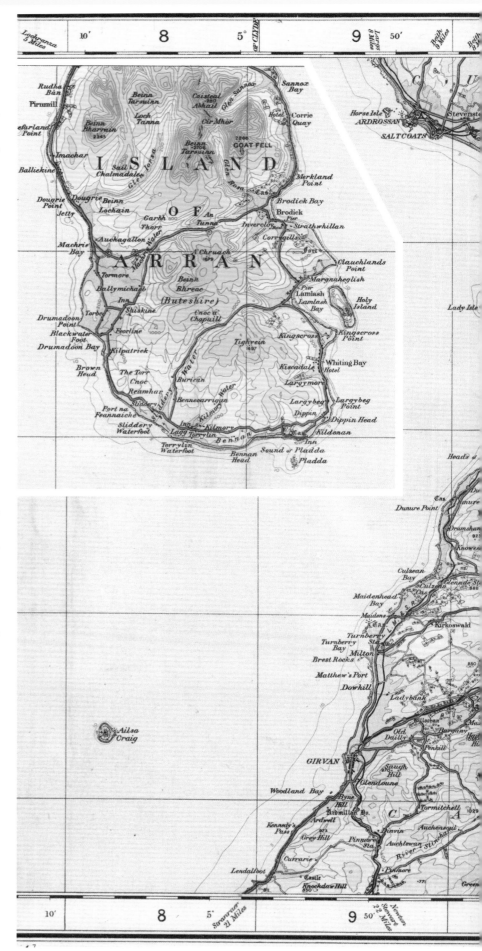

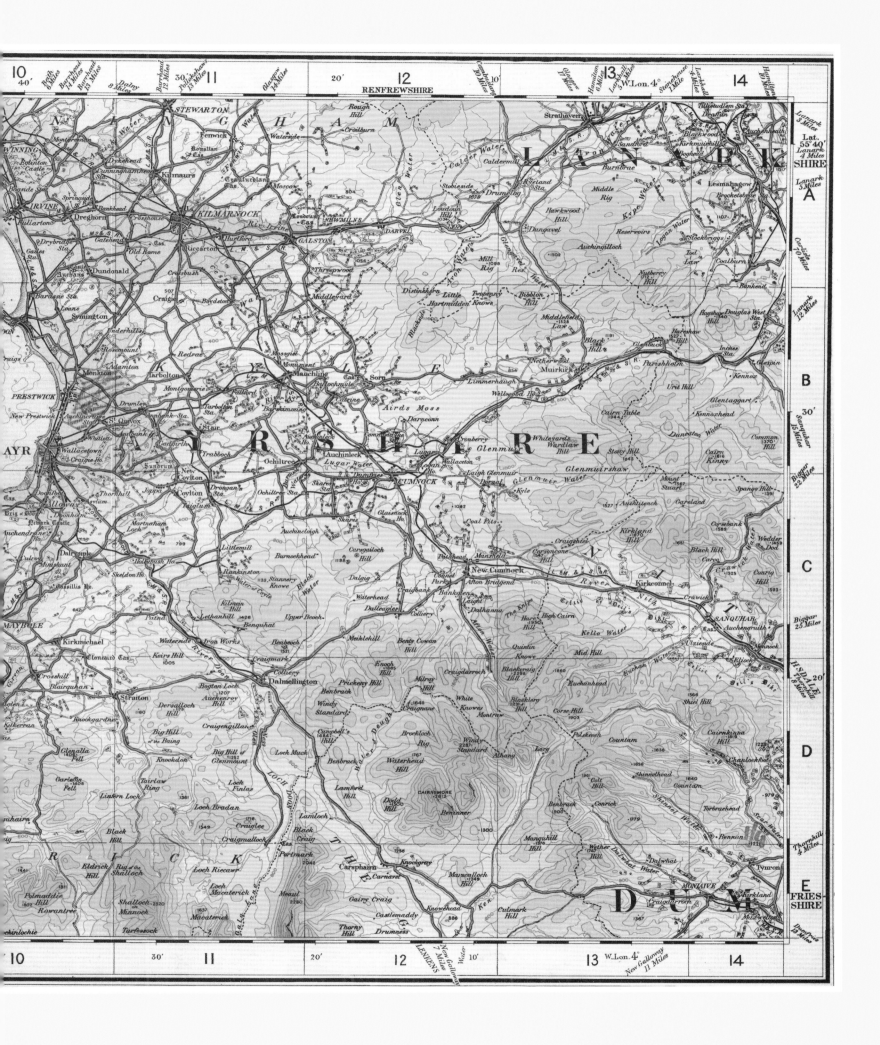

②

1 ARRAN *Castle and Loch Ranza*
Little changed today is the view of the old castle to the south of Loch Ranza, marking the spot where Robert the Bruce is reputed to have landed in 1306, but the fishing boats and the trading schooner drawn up on the beach are now a part of history.

2 ALLOWAY *Burns' Cottage 1897*
The Burns' industry was a feature of the Victorian era, when reverence for the memory of the Scottish poet began to draw visitors from all over the world. The humble cottage in which Burns was born in 1759 was already a centre of pilgrimage when this photograph was taken, as can be seen from the display of souvenir photographs by the door. Today, the cottage has been considerably smartened up and part of it now houses a Burns' museum.

3 AYR *High Street 1900*
A thriving resort town at the turn of the century, Ayr managed to combine the appeal of its fine beaches with its important place in Scottish history. The town's two heroes are commemorated in the High Street. In the distance is the Wallace Tower, erected in 1832, while in the foreground can be seen the low façade and thatched roof of the old Tam o' Shanter Inn, with its famous painting of Tam mounting his grey mare over the door. Today, this view of the High Street is still similar, but the inn is now another Burns' musueum.

4 AYR *Burns' Monument and Shell Grotto 1900*
The Burns' Monument, a rather unexpected neo-classical building, was erected in 1823 in the pleasant garden setting that it still enjoys today.

①

③

④

THE HEYDAY OF THE CLYDE and its resorts was probably in the Edwardian era but the development of the region had taken place progressively throughout the 19th century, linked directly to the emergence of the paddle steamer. The first experiments with steam-powered craft had taken place in the late 18th century and it was in 1802 that the pioneering paddle steamer, the *Charlotte Dundas*, began its short career on the Forth & Clyde Canal. In 1815 Henry Bell's *Comet* went into service on the Clyde, sailing from Glasgow to Greenock in five hours, and within five years there were forty paddle steamers at work on the river.

The numbers of ships and routes then expanded rapidly and by the 1850s there was serious competition between the various operating companies, with the steamers built increasingly for speed rather than comfort. In the 1860s this competition reached its peak with a series of races between various ships as they fought for custom. By this time, sailing on the Clyde was well established as a leisure activity, with Glasgow workers paying a shilling a head for a day out on the water. Many of the Clyde resorts – Greenock, Gourock, Hunter's Quay, Wemyss and Largs – emerged from virtually nothing in the latter part of the 19th century, but the queen of them all was undoubtedly Rothesay and today this Isle of Bute town still has a decidedly Victorian air.

Also developed at this time were select residential villages such as Strone, Kirn and Inellan where well-to-do Glasgow families built colonies of week-end and holiday homes. By the end of the century the Clyde had become one of Britain's best-known pleasure grounds for both day trips and annual holidays, and the paddle steamer was the key to this success. By this time the railway companies had joined the fray, and the emphasis had switched from speed to comfort. From the 1880s the Clyde was dominated by fleets of elegant and well-equipped vessels, operated by companies such as MacBrayne's, Williamson's, Buchanan's and the Caledonian Steam Packet Co, names famous in the annals of Clyde history, and this trade continued to grow into the Edwardian period. In 1914, for example, over forty de luxe paddle steamers were in service, linking eighty five resorts, harbours, villages, islands and other stopping points between Glasgow and the Sound of Bute, while others were operating on the enclosed waters of Loch Lomond.

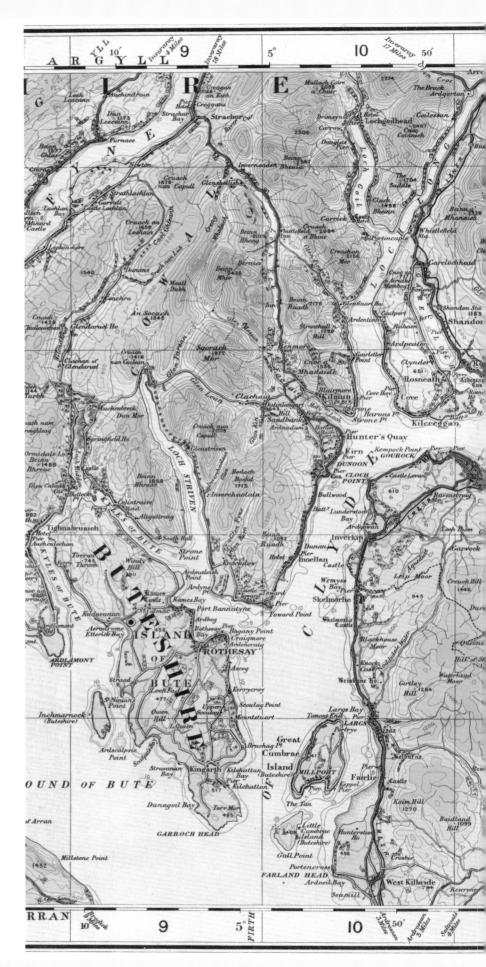

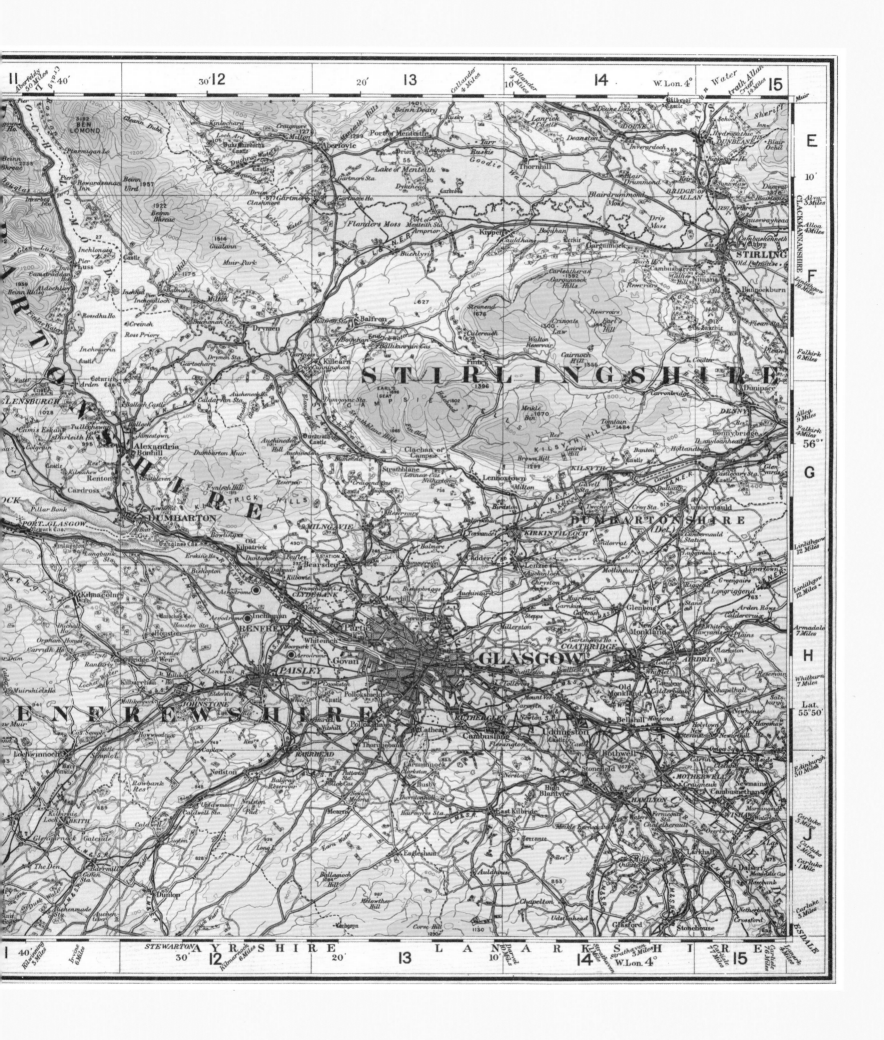

1 LOCH LOMOND *1901*
This view of the southern end of the Queen of Lochs shows the wooded islands whose appeal has changed little since they were colonised by Irish missionaries in the 5th century. Loch Lomond's popularity increased greatly in the late 19th century, thanks to the railway from Dumbarton to Balloch pier.

2 DUNOON *The Pier 1901*
In the Edwardian era Dunoon pier was a favourite calling point for Clyde steamers, with large numbers of visitors being drawn to this little resort with its castle and Burns' associations – the poet's sweetheart, Mary Campbell, having been born near by.

3 LARGS *1897*
Late Victorian Largs was still a small and pleasant family resort, with little more than a handful of streets and terraces on either side of Gogo Water. Its few hotels faced out over the beach towards Great Cumbrae. The town's rapid expansion took place from the 1920s when holiday camps and seaside entertainments turned it into the major Clydeside resort it is today.

4 ROTHESAY *1897*
Ferries still sail to Rothesay from Wemyss Bay and, although the paddle steamers in this view are long gone, Bute's principal town has maintained its Victorian atmosphere. Always the smartest of the Clyde resorts, Rothesay was essentially a late 19th-century creation and this view shows the town in its heyday.

⑥

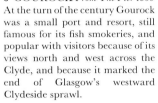

⑤

⑦

⑧

5 GLASGOW *George Square 1897*
George Square, Glasgow's heart, was laid out at the end of the 18th century, and it still retains some of the spacious elegance shown in this photograph. At the time it was taken, the buildings surrounding the square were quite new, the grand city chambers having only been completed ten years earlier. As can be seen, the square's characteristic collection of statues was already in place, with, at the centre, Sir Walter Scott.

6 GOUROCK *From The Pier 1900*
At the turn of the century Gourock was a small port and resort, still famous for its fish smokeries, and popular with visitors because of its views north and west across the Clyde, and because it marked the end of Glasgow's westward Clydeside sprawl.

7 HELENSBURGH
Princes Street 1901
This town on the north bank of the Clyde was planned as a resort in the 1780s, but in the 19th century it developed into a desirable suburb for Glasgow merchants and industrialists once the railway had made it easily accessible. This photograph shows the town's relaxed atmosphere and some of the grand buildings that adorned its streets at the turn of the century.

8 DUMBARTON *Castle 1890*
Still to be enjoyed today is this view across the Clyde towards the 17th-and 18th-century fortifications of Dumbarton Castle, set below the 240-foot basalt rock. Even in the 19th century the medieval castle was little more than a memory – the former stronghold commemorated by the Wallace Tower.

IN THE 19TH CENTURY THE
traditional rivalries between Glasgow and
Edinburgh were, if anything, more sharply defined
than they are today, with the literary and artistic
life of the two cities being a notable battle ground.
In the early 19th century Edinburgh was dominant, with its reputation as a literary city recognised throughout Europe. At its heart were two
magazines, Constable's *Edinburgh Review*, launched
in 1802, and its great rival, Blackwood's *Edinburgh
Magazine*, which first appeared in 1816.

Many literary careers were linked closely to these
publications, such as those of John Wilson, Francis
Jeffrey and John Gibson Lockhart, but standing
out above them all was the towering figure of Sir
Walter Scott. Born in the city in 1771, he lived
much of his life in Edinburgh, and his reputation as
a novelist was established there by 1815 with the
publication first of *Waverley*, and then *Guy Manner-
ing*, the first edition of which sold out in twenty four
hours. One of Scott's contemporaries was Thomas
Carlyle, who first came to Edinburgh in 1809, aged
thirteen, and stayed until 1834 when he moved to
London. By this time, Edinburgh's literary standing was waning and it was not until the latter part of
the century that the city produced a writer of
sufficient stature to inherit Scott's mantle. Robert
Louis Stevenson was born in Edinburgh in 1850
and remained there through the height of his fame
until 1887.

Although Edinburgh went on to produce other
notable figures, for example Sir Arthur Conan
Doyle and Kenneth Grahame, the emphasis had,
by then, switched to Glasgow. A group of avant-
garde painters, known colloquially as the 'Glasgow
Boys', had established the city's firm links with
European modern art movements, but it was the
architect Charles Rennie Mackintosh who was,
above all, responsible for Glasgow's reputation as
an Art Nouveau city. Born in Glasgow in 1868,
Mackintosh introduced the flowing, linear style
into Britain and explored its decorative potential
fully in his major Glasgow buildings, the School of
Art (1897–1909), the Daily Record building
(1901), the Scotland Street School, the Willow Tea
Rooms, and at Hill House near Helensburgh.

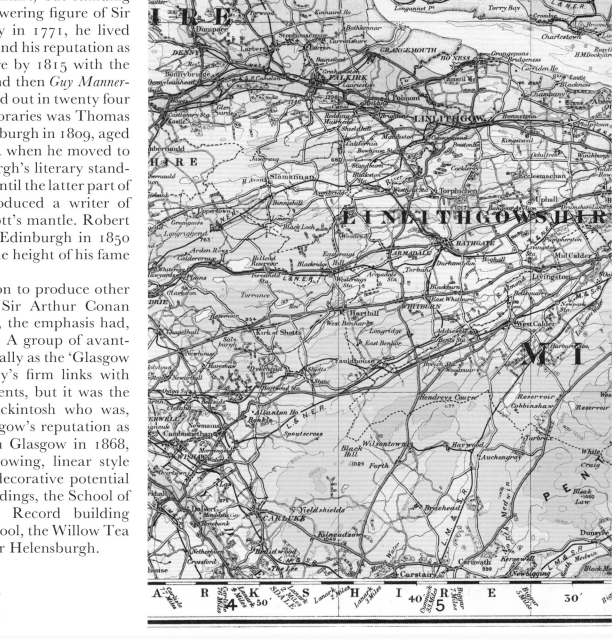

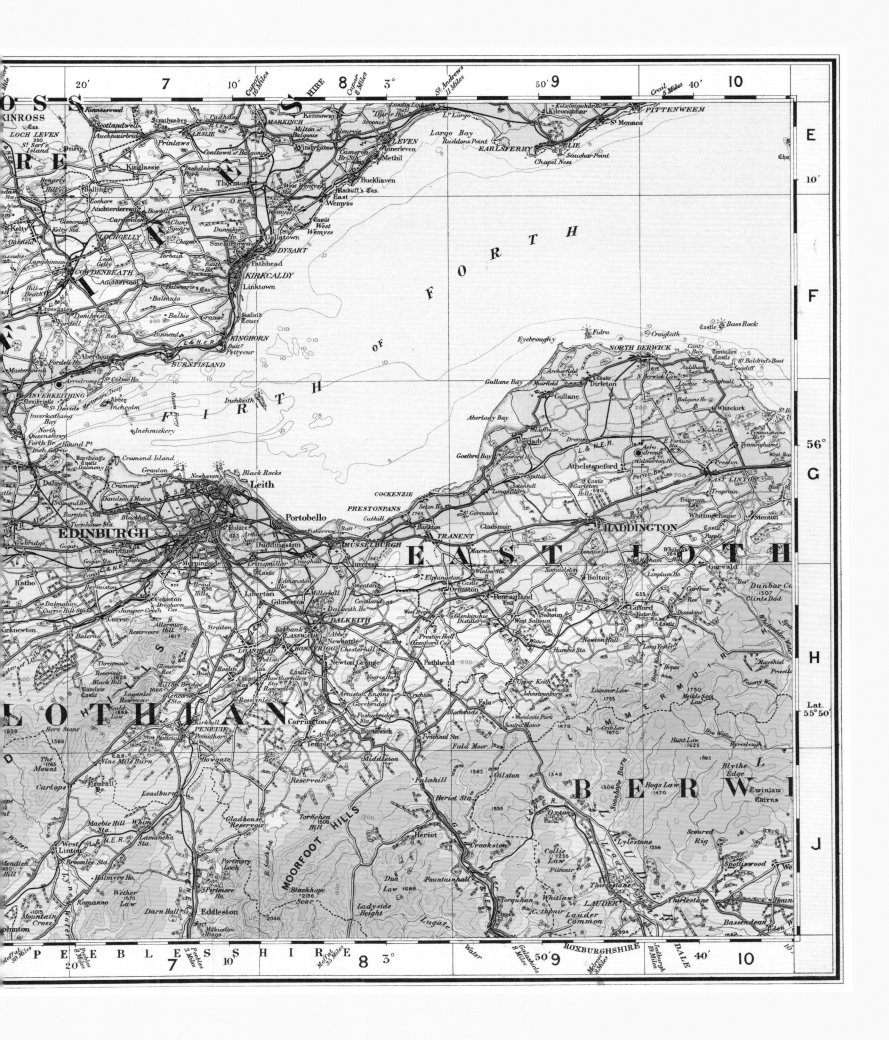

①

②

③

1 EDINBURGH
Princes Street 1897
Edinburgh's Princes Street, the city's heart since this long thorough-fare was completed in 1805, has changed little since this photograph was taken. Gone are the trams and the cobbles, but elegant shops and hotels still dominate the street whose grey façades look out towards the castle.

2 EDINBURGH
Grassmarket 1897
The old buildings of Edinburgh's Grassmarket clustered below the towering walls of the castle are still one of the pleasures of the city, although gone for ever is the delightful emptiness of the pre-car age captured in this view.

3 EDINBURGH
Castle Esplanade 1897
Edinburgh's military tattoos and Highland gatherings were as popular in the late 19th century as they are today, and these displays on the castle's esplanade were a feature of city life.

4 STIRLING *Castle and the Site of the Battle of Stirling 1899*
A castle has stood on Stirling's rock since the 11th century, and during subsequent centuries the fortification has played a major role in the history of the town that was at one time virtually the capital of Scotland. It remained a royal residence until 1603, when James VI left for England. In 1745 the town was captured by Bonnie Prince Charlie, but the castle withstood his siege.

5 STIRLING *Broad Street 1899*
The grey façades and the discrete shop fronts of Stirling's Broad Street, now a much busier road, indicate the town's rather quieter way of life at the end of the Victorian era. In the centre is the mercat cross, which had been restored and rebuilt in its present form a few years earlier, and to the left is the tolbooth clock-tower.

④

⑤

PICTURE INDEX

B

Bishopstone/Broughton

Bishopstone *Hereford. 86–87* E3
Bishopstone *Wilts. 66–67* J10
Bishopstone *Wilts. 46–47* E8
Bishopstone *Sussex 38–39* H6
Bishopstrow *42–43* C7
Bishop's Waltham *34–35* E12
Bishopsworth *42–43* B4
Bishop Thornton *142–143* F4
Bishopthorpe *142–143* G7
Bishopton *154–155* A5
Bishton *62–63* J3
Bitchfield *114–115* G2
Bittadon *26–27* A10
Bitterley *86–87* B4
Bitterne *34–35* F11
Bitteswell *90–91* A12
Bitton *42–43* A5
Bix *66–67* J13
Bixley *118–119* J12
Blaby *110–111* J12
Blackawton *22–23* H12
Black Bourton *66–67* H10
Blackburn *138–139* H13
Black Callerton *166–167* G11
Blackford *Somerset 42–43* C3
Blackford *Somerset 42–43* E5
Blackfordby *110–111* H10
Blackheath *90–91* A7
Black Heddon *166–167* G10
Blackhill *166–167* J10
Blackmore *70–71* H7
Black Notley *74–75* F8
Blacko *142–143* G1
Blackpool *138–139* H10
Blackrod *126–127* A4
Blackthorn *66–67* F12
Blacktoft *146–147* J9
Black Torrington *26–27* D9
Blackwater *50–51* D1
Blackwell *Yorks. 154–155* B4
Blackwell *Derby. 130–131* D8
Blackwell *Derby. 130–131* E11
Bladon *66–67* G11
Blaenan Ffestiniog *122–123* F11
Blaenavon *62–63* G2
Blaengwrach *58–59* E12
Blaenpenal *82–83* A10
Blaenporth *82–83* B8
Blagdon *42–43* B4
Blaina *62–63* G1
Blaisdon *62–63* G5
Blakemere *86–87* E3
Blakeney *Norfolk 118–119* F10
Blakeney *Gloucester. 62–63* H5
Blakenhall *106–107* F5
Blakesley *90–91* D12
Blandford Forum *30–31* F7
Blandford St. Mary *30–31* F7
Blankney *134–135* E2
Blaston *90–91* A14
Blatherwycke *94–95* A2
Blawith *150–151* D10
Blaxhall *98–99* C12
Blaxton *130–131* A13
Blaydon *166–167* H11
Bleadon *42–43* B3
Bleasby *110–111* E13
Bleasdale *138–139* G12
Blechingley *50–51* D4
Bleddfa *86–87* C1
Bledington *66–67* F10
Bledlow *66–67* H14
Blencogo *162–163* J3
Blendworth *34–35* F13
Bletchingdon *66–67* G12
Bletchley *70–71* E1
Bletherston *78–79* D6
Bletsoe *94–95* C2
Blewbury *66–67* J12
Blickling *118–119* G11
Blidworth *130–131* E12
Blisland *18–19* G6
Blisworth *90–91* D13
Blockley *66–67* E9
Blofield *118–119* H12
Blo Norton *98–99* B10
Bloxham *66–67* E11
Bloxholm *114–115* E2
Bloxworth *30–31* G7
Blubberhouses *142–143* F3
Blundeston *118–119* J14
Blunham *94–95* D3
Blunsdon St. Andrew *66–67* J9
Blyborough *134–135* B1
Blyford *98–99* B13
Blymhill *106–107* H6
Blyth *Northumberland 166–167* F12
Blyth *Yorks. 130–131* B12
Blythgburgh *98–99* B13
Blyton *134–135* B1
Boarhunt *34–35* F12
Boarstall *66–67* G12
Bobbington *86–87* A6
Bobbingworth *70–71* G6
Boconnoc *18–19* H7
Bocking *74–75* F8
Bocking Churchstreet *74–75* F8
Bockleton *86–87* C4
Boddington *62–63* F7
Bodedern *122–123* C8
Bodelwyddan *122–123* C13
Bodenham *86–87* D4
Bodewryd *122–123* B9
Bodfari *122–123* D14
Bodfean *102–103* F8
Bodham *118–119* F11
Bodiam *54–55* F8
Bodicote *66–67* E11
Bodmin *18–19* G6
Bodney *118–119* J8
Bodwrog *122–123* C9
Bognor *38–39* H2
Bolam *Northld. 166–167* F10
Bolam *Durham 154–155* A4
Boldon Colliery *166–167* H12
Boldre *34–35* G10
Boldron *154–155* B2
Bole *130–131* B14
Bollington *126–127* C5
Bollington *126–127* C7
Bolney *50–51* F4
Bolnhurst *94–95* C3
Bolsover *130–131* D11
Bolstone *62–63* F4
Boltby *154–155* D6
Bolton *Westmorland 150–151* A13
Bolton *Yorks. 146–147* F8
Bolton *Lancs. 126–127* A5
Bolton by Bowland *142–143* G1
Bolton-le-Sands *138–139* E12
Bolton upon Dearne *130–131* A11
Bolton Percy *142–143* G6
Bolton upon Swale *154–155* C4
Bonby *146–147* J10
Bonchurch *34–35* H12
Bondleigh *26–27* D11
Bo'ness *182–183* G5
Bonhill *178–179* G12
Boningale *106–107* J6
Bonnington *54–55* E10
Bonnybridge *182–183* G4
Bonnyrigg *182–183* H8
Bonsall *130–131* E10
Bonvilston *58–59* H14
Bookham *50–51* D3
Boothby Graffoe *134–135* E2
Boothby Pagnall *114–115* G2
Bootle *Cumberland 150–151* D9
Bootle *Lancs. 126–127* B2
Booton *118–119* G11
Boraston *86–87* C5
Borden *54–55* C9
Bordley *142–143* E2
Boreham *74–75* G8
Borehamwood *70–71* H3
Borley *98–99* E8
Boroughbridge *142–143* E5
Borrowash *110–111* G11
Borrowby *154–155* D6
Borrowdale *150–151* B10
Borthwick *182–183* H8
Borwick *150–151* E12
Bosbury *86–87* E5
Boscastle *26–27* E6
Boscombe *46–47* D9
Bosham *34–35* F14
Bosherston *58–59* inset
Bosley *126–127* D7
Bossington *46–47* D10
Boston *114–115* F4
Boston Spa *142–143* G6
Botesdale *98–99* B10
Bothamsall *130–131* D13
Bothenhampton *30–31* H4
Bothwell *178–179* J14
Botley *34–35* F12
Botolphs *38–39* H3
Bottesford *Lincs. 134–135* A1
Bottesford *Leicester. 110–111* F14
Bottisham *94–95* C6
Bottwnog *102–103* G8
Botus Fleming *22–23* H9
Boughrood *62–63* E1
Boughton *Notts. 130–131* D13
Boughton *Norfolk 118–119* J7
Boughton *Northants 90–91* C13
Boughton Aluph *54–55* D10
Boughton Malherbe *54–55* D9
Boughton Monchelsea *54–55* D8
Boulston *78–79* E5
Boultham *134–135* D1
Bourn *94–95* D4
Bourne *114–115* H3
Bournemouth *34–35* G8&9
Bournmoor *166–167* J12
Bournville *90–91* B8
Bourton *Wilts. 66–67* J9
Bourton *Dorset 42–43* E6
Bourton on Dunsmore *90–91* C11
Bourton on the Hill *66–67* F9
Bourton on the Water *66–67* F9
Boveney *50–51* B1
Bovey Tracy *22–23* F12
Bovingdon *70–71* H2
Bow *26–27* E11
Bow Brickhill *70–71* E1
Bowdon *126–127* C6
Bower Chalke *34–35* E8
Bowers Gifford *74–75* J8
Bowes *154–155* B2
Bowness *Cumberland 162–163* H4
Bowness *Westmorland 150–151* C11
Bowthorpe *118–119* H11
Box *42–43* B6
Boxford *Suffolk 98–99* E9
Boxford *Berks. 46–47* A11
Boxgrove *38–39* H1
Boxley *54–55* D8
Boxted *Suffolk 98–99* D8
Boxted *Essex 74–75* E10
Boxworth *94–95* C5
Boyieston *110–111* F9
Boynton *146–147* E11
Boynton *Suffolk 98–99* D13
Boynton *Devon. 26–27* E8
Boyton *Wilts. 46–47* D7
Bozeat *94–95* C1
Brabourne *54–55* E10
Braceborough *114–115* H2
Braceby *114–115* F2
Bracebridge *134–135* D2
Bracewell *142–143* G1
Brackenfield *130–131* E10
Brackenthwaite *150–151* A9
Brackley *66–67* E12
Bracknell *50–51* C1
Bracon Ash *118–119* J11
Bradbourne *110–111* E9
Bradden *90–91* D13
Braddock *18–19* H7
Bradenham *70–71* H1
Bradfield *Essex 74–75* F11
Bradfield *Norfolk 118–119* G12
Bradfield *Yorks. 130–131* B10
Bradfield *Berks. 46–47* A12
Bradfield Combust *98–99* C9
Bradfield on the Green *90–91* C14
Bradfield St. Clare *98–99* C9
Bradfield St. George *98–99* C9
Bradford *Northld. 166–167* G10
Bradford *Yorks. 142–143* H3
Bradford *Devon. 26–27* D9
Bradford *Somerset 30–31* E1
Bradford Abbas *30–31* F4
Bradford on Avon *42–43* B6
Bradford Peverell *30–31* G5
Brading *34–35* H12
Bradley (Lincs.) *134–135* A4
Bradley *Derby. 110–111* F9
Bradley *Stafford. 106–107* H7
Bradley *Suffolk 94–95* D7
Bradley *Hants. 46–47* D13
Bradley in the Moors *110–111* F8
Bradmore *110–111* G12
Bradninch *26–27* D13
Bradpole *30–31* G4
Bradstone *22–23* F9
Bradwell *Yorks. 130–131* C9
Bradwell *Norfolk 118–119* J14
Bradwell *Bucks 94–95* E1
Bradwell *Essex 74–75* F8
Bradwell Juxta Mare *74–75* G10
Bradworthy *26–27* D8
Brafferton *Durham 154–155* A4
Brafferton *Yorks. 142–143* E5
Brailsford *110–111* F10
Braintree *74–75* F8
Braiseworth *98–99* B11
Braithwell *130–131* B12
Bramber *38–39* G3
Bramcote *110–111* F11
Bramdean *46–47* E12
Bramerton *118–119* J12
Bramfield *Suffok 98–99* B13
Bramfield *Herts. 70–71* G4
Bramford *98–99* D11
Bramford Speke *26–27* E13
Bramhope *142–143* G4
Bramley *Yorks. 130–131* B11
Bramley *Hants. 46–47* B13
Bramley *Surrey 50–51* E2
Brampton *Cumbld. 162–163* H6
Brampton *Lincs. 134–135* C1
Brampton *Norfolk 118–119* G11
Brampton *Hunts. 94–95* B4
Brampton *Suffolk 98–99* B13
Brampton Abbotts *62–63* F5
Brampton Ash *90–91* A14
Brampton Bryan *86–87* C3
Brampton-en-le-Morthen *130–131* B11
Bramshall *110–111* G8
Bramshaw *34–35* F10
Bramshill *46–47* B13
Bramshott *50–51* F1
Bramstone *110–111* J12
Braintree *74–75* F8
Brancaster *118–119* F8
Brancepath *166–167* K11
Brandesburton *146–147* G11
Brandeston *98–99* C12
Brandiston *118–119* G11
Brandon *Suffolk 98–99* A8
Brandon Parva *118–119* J10
Branksome *34–35* H8
Branscombe *30–31* H1
Bransford *86–87* D6
Bransten *Lincs. 134–135* D2
Branston *Leicester. 110–111* G14
Bransten *Stafford. 110–111* H9
Brant Broughton *114–115* E1
Brantham *74–75* E11
Brantingham *146–147* H10
Brassington *110–111* E9
Brasted *50–51* D6
Bratoft *134–135* D5
Brattleby *134–135* C1
Bratton *42–43* C7
Bratton Clovelly *26–27* E9
Bratton Fleming *26–27* B11
Bratton Seymour *42–43* E5
Braughing *70–71* F5
Brauncewell *114–115* E2
Braunston *Rutland 114–115* J1
Braunston *90–91* C12
Braunton *26–27* B9
Brawby *158–159* D8
Brawdy *78–79* D4
Bray *50–51* B1
Braybrooke *90–91* A14
Braydon *66–67* J8
Brayton *142–143* H7
Breadsall *110–111* F10
Breadstone *62–63* H5
Brearton *142–143* F5
Breaston *110–111* G11
Breage *18–19* K3
Breamore *34–35* E9
Brean *42–43* C2
Brechfa *82–83* D10
Breckles *98–99* A9
Brecon *82–83* D14
Brede *38–39* inset
Bredenbury *86–87* D5
Bredfield *98–99* D12
Bredgar *54–55* C9
Bredhurst *54–55* C8
Bredicot *86–87* D7
Bredon *62–63* E7
Bredon's Norton *62–63* E7
Bredwardine *86–87* E2
Breedon on the Hill *110–111* G11
Breinton *62–63* E4
Bremhill *46–47* A8
Brenchley *54–55* E7
Brendon *26–27* A12
Brenkley *166–167* G11
Brent Eleigh *98–99* D9
Brentford *50–51* B3
Brent Knoll *42–43* C3
Brent Pelham *70–71* F5
Brentwood *70–71* H7
Brenzett *54–55* F10
Brereton cum Smethwick *126–127* D6
Brereton *110–111* H8
Bressingham *98–99* B10
Bretby *110–111* G10
Bretforton *90–91* E8
Bretherton *138–139* J12
Brettenham *Norfolk 98–99* A9
Brettenham *Suffolk 98–99* D9
Brewood *106–107* J7
Bricklehampton *90–91* E7
Bridekirk *162–163* K3
Bridell *78–79* C7
Bridestowe *26–27* F10
Bridford *26–27* F12
Bridge *54–55* D11
Bridge Hewick *142–143* E5
Bridgend *58–59* G13
Bridge of Allan *182–183* E4
Bridge of Weir *178–179* H12
Bridge Sollers *86–87* E3
Bridge Trafford *126–127* D3
Bridgham *98–99* A9
Bridgnorth *86–87* A5
Bridgtown *110–111* J7
Bridgwater *42–43* D2
Bridlington *146–147* E11
Bridport *30–31* G4
Bridstow *62–63* F4
Brierfield *142–143* H1
Brierley *130–131* A11
Brierley Hill *86–87* A7
Brierton *166–167* K13
Brigg *134–135* A2
Brigham *Cumberland 162–163* K3
Brigham *Yorks. 146–147* F11
Brighouse *142–143* J3
Brighstone *34–35* H11
Brighthampton *66–67* H11
Brightling *38–39* G7
Brightlingsea *74–75* G10
Brighton *38–39* H4
Brightwalton *46–47* A11
Brightwell *Suffolk 98–99* E12
Brightwell *Berks. 66–67* J12
Brightwell Baldwin *66–67* H13
Brignall *154–155* B3
Brigsley *134–135* A4
Brigstock *94–95* A1
Brill *66–67* G13
Brilley *86–87* D2
Brimfield *86–87* C4
Brimington *130–131* D11
Brimpsfield *62–63* G7
Brimpton *46–47* B12
Brimstage *126–127* C2
Brindle *138–139* J13
Bringhurst *94–95* A1
Brington *94–95* B2
Brininghamn *118–119* F10
Brinkhill *134–135* C5
Brinkley *94–95* D7
Brinklow *90–91* B11
Brinkworth *66–67* J8
Brinsley *110–111* E11
Brinsop *86–87* E3
Brinsworth *130–131* B11
Brinton *118–119* F10
Brisley *118–119* G9
Brislington *42–43* A5
Bristol *42–43* A4&5
Briston *118–119* G10
Britford *46–47* E9
Briton Ferry *58–59* F11
Britwell Salome *66–67* J13
Brixham *22–23* H13
Brixton *22–23* H10
Brixton Deverill *42–43* D7
Brixworth *90–91* C13
Brize Norton *66–67* G10
Broad Chalke *46–47* E8
Broad Clyst *26–27* E13
Broadhembury *30–31* G1
Broadhempston *22–23* G12
Broad Hinton *46–47* A8
Broadholme *134–135* C1
Broadmayne *30–31* H6
Broadstairs *54–55* C13
Broad Town *46–47* A8
Broadwas *86–87* D6
Broadway *Worcester. 66–67* E8
Broadway *Somerset 30–31* F2
Broadway *Dorset 30–31* H5
Broadwell *Gloucester. 66–67* F9
Broadwell *Oxford. 66–67* H10
Broadwindsor *30–31* G3
Broadwood Kelly *26–27* D10
Broadwoodwidger *26–27* F9
Brobury *86–87* E3
Brockdish *98–99* B11
Brockenhurst *34–35* G10
Brockhall *90–91* C13
Brockhampton *62–63* F4
Brocklesby *134–135* A3
Brockley *42–43* B3
Brockworth *62–63* G7
Brocton *110–111* H7
Brodick *174–175* *inset*
Brodsworth 130–131 A11
Brokenborough *62–63* J7
Bromborough *126–127* C2
Brome *98–99* B11
Bromeswell *98–99* D12
Bromfield *Cumberland 162–163* J3
Bromfield *Salop 86–87* B4
Bromham *Bedford. 94–95* D2
Bromham *Wilts. 46–47* B7
Bromley *50–51* C5
Brompton *Yorks. 154–155* C5
Brompton *Yorks. 158–159* D10
Brompton *Kent 54–55* C8
Brompton Ralph *42–43* D1
Brompton Regis *26–27* B13
Brompton on Swale *154–155* C4
Bromsberrow *62–63* E6
Bromsgrove *90–91* C7
Bromyard *86–87* D5
Brongwyn *82–83* C8
Bronington *106–107* F4
Bronllys *62–63* E1
Brook *Kent 54–55* E10
Brook *Isle of Wight 34–35* H11
Brooke *Rutland 114–115* J1
Brooke *Norfolk 118–119* J12
Brookland *54–55* F10
Brooksby *110–111* H13
Brookthorpe *62–63* G6
Broom *Durham 166–167* J11
Broom *Worc. 86–87* B7
Broome *98–99* A12
Broomfield *Essex 74–75* G7
Broomfield *Somerset 42–43* D2
Broomfield *Kent 54–55* D8
Broomfleet *146–147* H9
Broomhaugh *166–167* H10
Broomley *166–167* H10
Broseley *106–107* J5
Brothertoft *114–115* F4
Brotherton *142–143* J6
Brotton *158–159* A8
Brough *154–155* B1
Brough Sowerby *154–155* B1
Broughton *Yorks. 154–155* B6
Broughton *Yorks. 158–159* E8
Broughton *Lancs. 138–139* H12
Broughton *Yorks. 142–143* G2
Broughton *Lincs. 134–135* A1
Broughton *Northants. 94–95* B1

Grasmere/Hatherop

Grasmere *150–151* B11
Grassendale *126–127* C3
Grassington *142–143* F2
Grassthorpe *130–131* D14
Grateley *46–47* D10
Gratwich *110–111* G8
Graveley *Cambs. 94–95* C4
Graveley *Herts. 70–71* F4
Graveney *54–55* C10
Gravenhurst *70–71* E3
Gravesend *50–51* B7
Grayingham *134–135* B1
Grayrigg *150–151* C12
Grayshott *50–51* F1
Grays Thurrock *50–51* B7
Greasbrough *130–131* B11
Greasby *126–127* C2
Greasley *110–111* F11
Great Addington *94–95* B2
Great Alne *90–91* C9
Great Amwell *70–71* G5
Great Ashfield *98–99* C10
Great Ayton *154–155* B6
Great Baddow *74–75* H8
Great Badminton *62–63* J6
Great Bardfield *70–71* F7
Great Barford *94–95* D3
Great Barr *90–91* A8
Great Barrington *66–67* G9
Great Barton *98–99* C9
Great Bavington *166–167* G9
Great Bedwyn *46–47* B10
Great Bentley *74–75* F11
Great Billing *90–91* C14
Great Bircham *118–119* G8
Great Blakenham *98–99* D11
Great Bowden *90–91* A13
Great Braxted *74–75* G9
Great Bricett *98–99* D10
Great Brickhill *70–71* F1
Great Brington *90–91* C13
Great Bromley *74–75* F10
Great Budworth *126–127* C5
Great Burdon *154–155* A5
Great Burstead *74–75* J7
Great Busby *154–155* B6
Great Canfield *70–71* G7
Great Carlton *134–135* C5
Great Chart *54–55* E10
Great Chesterford *94–95* E6
Great Chishall *94–95* E5
Great Clacton *74–75* G11
Great Coates *134–135* A4
Great Comberton *90–91* E7
Great Cornard *98–99* E9
Great Creaton *90–91* B13
Great Cressingham *118–119* J8
Great Crosby *126–127* B2
Great Dalby *110–111* H13
Great Doddington *94–95* C1
Great Driffield *146–147* F10
Great Dunham *118–119* H9
Great Dunmow *70–71* F7
Great Easton *Rutland 94–95* A1
Great Easton *Essex 70–71* F7
Great Eccleston *138–139* G11
Great Edstone *158–159* D8
Great Ellingham *118–119* J10
Great Everdon *90–91* D12
Great Finborough *98–99* C10
Greatford *114–115* H3
Great Fransham *118–119* H9
Great Gaddesden *70–71* G2
Great Gidding *94–95* B3
Great Givendale *146–147* F9
Great Glemham *98–99* C12
Great Glen *110–111* J13
Great Gonerby *114–115* F1
Great Habton *158–159* E8
Great Hale *114–115* F3
Great Hallingbury *70–71* F6
Greatham *Durham 154–155* A6
Greatham *Hants. 46–47* D14
Greatham *Sussex 38–39* G2
Great Hanwood *106–107* J3
Great Harwood *138–139* H14
Great Haseley *66–67* H13
Great Hatfield *146–147* G11
Great Henny *98–99* E9
Great Holland *74–75* F11
Great Horkesley *74–75* E9
Great Horwood *66–67* F14
Great Houghton *Yorks. 130–131* A11
Great Houghton *Northants. 90–91* C14
Great Kelk *146–147* F11
Great Langton *154–155* C5
Great Leighs *74–75* G8
Great Limber *134–135* A3
Great Linford *94–95* E1
Great Livermere *98–99* B9
Great Longstone *130–131* D9
Great Lumley *166–167* J12
Great Malvern *86–87* E6
Great Maplestead *74–75* E8
Great Massingham *118–119* G8
Great Melton *114–115* J11
Great Milton *66–67* H13
Great Missenden *70–71* H1
Great Mitton *138–139* H14
Great Mongeham *54–55* D12
Great Musgrave *150–151* B14
Great Ness *106–107* H3
Great Oakley *Norhants 94–95* A1
Great Oakley *Essex 74–75* F11
Great Offley *70–71* F3
Great Ormside *150–151* A13
Great Ouseburn *142–143* F6
Great Oxenden *90–91* B13
Great Parndon *70–71* G5
Great Paxton *94–95* C3
Great Plumstead *118–119* H12
Great Ponton *114–115* G1
Great Raveley *94–95* B4
Great Rissington *66–67* G9
Great Rollright *66–67* F10
Great Rowsley *130–131* D10
Great Ryburgh *118–119* G9
Great Saling *74–75* F7
Great Salkeld *162–163* K6
Great Samford *70–71* E7
Great Sankey *126–127* B4
Great Saxham *98–99* C8
Great Shefford *46–47* A11
Great Smeaton *154–155* B5
Great Snoring *118–119* F9
Great Somerford *66–67* J7
Great Stambridge *74–75* J9
Great Staughton *94–95* C3
Great Steeping *134–135* D5
Great Stretton *110–111* J13
Great Strickland *150–151* A12
Great Stukeley *94–95* B4
Great Sturton *134–135* C3
Great Tey *74–75* F9
Great Tew *66–67* F11
Great Torrington *26–27* C9
Great Totham *74–75* G9
Great Wakering *74–75* J9
Great Waldingfield *98–99* D9
Great Walsingham *118–119* F9
Great Waltham *74–75* G7
Great Warley Street *70–71* J6
Great Washbourne *66–67* E8
Great Welnetham *98–99* C9
Great Wenham *98–99* E10
Great Whittington *166–167* G10
Great Wigborough *74–75* G9
Great Wilbraham *94–95* C6
Great Wishford *46–47* D8
Great Witcombe *62–63* G7
Great Witley *86–87* C6
Greatworth *90–91* E12
Great Wratting *94–95* D7
Great Wymondley *70–71* F4
Great Wyrley *110–111* J7
Great Yarmouth *118–119* J14
Great Yeldham *98–99* E8
Greenford *70–71* J3
Greenham *46–47* B11
Green Hammerton *142–143* F6
Greenhithe *50–51* B7
Greenock *178–179* G11
Greens Norton *90–91* D13
Greensted *70–71* H6
Greenwich *50–51* B5
Greet *86–87* C4
Greetham *Lincs. 134–135* D4
Greetham *Rutland. 114–115* H1
Greetland *142–143* J3
Greinton *42–43* D3
Grendon *Warwick. 110–111* J10
Grendon *Northants. 94–95* C1
Grendon Bishop *86–87* D4
Grendon Underwood *66–67* F13
Gresford *106–107* E2
Gresham *118–119* F11
Gressenhall *118–119* H9
Gressingham *138–139* E12
Gretton *94–95* A1
Grewelthorpe *154–155* E4
Greysouthern *150–151* A8
Greystoke *162–163* K5
Greywell *46–47* C13
Gribthorpe *146–147* H8
Griffithstown *62–63* H2
Grimley *86–87* C6
Grimoldby *134–135* B5
Grimsby *134–135* A4
Grimston *Leicester. 110–111* H13
Grimston *Norfolk 118–119* G7
Grindale *158–159* E11
Grindon *Durham 154–155* A5
Grindon *Stafford. 110–111* E8
Grindleton *138–139* G14
Gringley on the Hill *130–131* B13
Grindlow *130–131* C9
Grinsdale *162–163* H5
Grinshill *106–107* H4
Grinton *154–155* C2
Gristhorpe *158–159* D11
Griston *118–119* J9
Grittleton *42–43* A7
Groby *110–111* J12
Grosmont *62–63* F3
Groton *98–99* E9
Grove *Notts. 130–131* C13
Grove *Berks. 66–67* J11
Grove *Bucks. 70–71* F1
Grundisburgh *98–99* D11
Guarlford *86–87* E6
Guestling *38–39* inset
Guestwick *118–119* G10
Guilden Morden *94–95* E4
Guilden Sutton *126–127* D3
Guildford *50–51* D2
Guilsborough *90–91* B13
Guisborough *154–155* A7
Guiseley *142–143* G4
Guist *118–119* G10
Guiting Power *66–67* F8
Gullane *182–183* G9
Gulval *18–19* K2
Gumfreston *58–59* inset
Gumley *90–91* A13
Gunby *134–135* D5
Gunby *114–115* H1
Gunness *134–135* A1
Gunthorpe *110–111* F13
Gunton *118–119* J14
Gunwalloe *18–19* L3
Gurnard *34–35* G11
Gussage All Saints *34–35* F8
Gussage St. Michael *34–35* F8
Guston *54–55* E12
Gwaenysgor *122–123* C14
Gwenddwr *82–83* C14
Gwenear *18–19* K3
Gwennap *18–19* J4
Gwernesney *62–63* H3
Gwithian *18–19* J3
Gwyddelwern *122–123* F14
Gwytherin *122–123* E12
Gyffin *122–123* C12
Gyffylliog *122–123* E14

H

Habberley *106–107* J3
Habrough *146–147* J11
Hacconby *114–115* G3
Haceby *114–115* F2
Hacheston *98–99* C12
Hackford *118–119* J10
Hackforth *154–155* C4
Hackleton *90–91* D14
Hackness *158–159* C10
Hackney *70–71* J5
Hackthorn *134–135* C2
Haddenham *Cambs. 94–95* B6
Haddenham *Bucks. 66–67* G13
Haddington *134–135* D1
Haddington *182–183* G9
Haddiscoe *118–119* J13
Haddon *94–95* A3
Hadleigh *Suffolk 98–99* E10
Hadleigh *Essex 74–75* J8
Hadley *106–107* H5
Hadnall *106–107* H4
Hadlow *50–51* D7
Hadlow Down *50–51* F6
Hadstock *94–95* D6
Hadzor *86–87* C7
Hagley *86–87* B7
Hagnaby *134–135* D5
Hagworthingham *134–135* D4
Haigh *126–127* A4
Hailes *66–67* F8
Hailey *66–67* G10
Hailsham *38–39* G7
Hail Weston *94–95* C3
Hainford *118–119* H11
Hainton *134–135* C3
Haisthorpe *146–147* E11
Halam *110–111* E13
Halberton *26–27* D13
Hale *Cumberland 150–151* B8
Hale *Lancs. 126–127* C3
Hale *Cheshire 126–127* C6
Hale *Hants. 34–35* E9
Hales *118–119* J13
Halesowen *90–91* B7
Halesworth *98–99* B13
Halewood *126–127* C3
Halford *Salop 86–87* B3
Halford *Warwick. 90–91* D10
Halifax *142–143* J3
Halkin *126–127* D1
Hallaton *110–111* J14
Halling *54–55* C7
Hallington *Northld. 166–167* G9
Hallington *Lincs. 134–135* C4
Halloughton *110–111* E13
Halmore *62–63* H5
Halsall *126–127* A3
Halse *42–43* E1
Halsham *146–147* H12
Halstead *Leicester. 110–111* J13
Halstead *Essex 74–75* F8
Halstead *Kent 50–51* C6
Halstock *30–31* F4
Haltham *134–135* D4
Halton *Northld. 166–167* H10
Halton *Lancs. 138–139* F12
Halton *Cheshire 126–127* C4
Halton *Bucks. 70–71* G1
Halton East *142–143* F3
Halton Gill *154–155* E1
Halton Holgate *134–135* D5
Halton West *142–143* F1
Haltwhistle *166–167* H7
Halvergate *118–119* J13
Halwell *22–23* H12
Halwill *26–27* E9
Ham *Wilts. 46–47* B10
Ham *Surrey 50–51* C3
Ham *Kent 54–55* D12
Hamble *34–35* F11
Hambleden *Bucks. 66–67* J14
Hambledon *Surrey 50–51* E2
Hambledon *Hants. 34–35* F13
Hambleton *Lancs. 138–139* G11
Hambleton *Yorks. 142–143* H7
Hambrook *42–43* A5
Hameringham *134–135* D4
Hamerton *94–95* B3
Hamilton *178–179* J14
Hammerwich *110–111* J8
Hammoon *30–31* F6
Hampden *70–71* H1
Hampnett *66–67* G8
Hampole *130–131* A11
Hampreston *34–35* G8
Hampstead *Norfolk 118–119* F10
Hampstead *Middlesex 70–71* J4
Hampstead Norris *46–47* A12
Hampsthwaite *142–143* F4
Hampton *50–51* C3
Hampton Bishop *62–63* E4
Hampton Gay *66–67* G11
Hampton in Arden *90–91* B9
Hampton Lovett *86–87* C7
Hampton Lucy *90–91* D10
Hampton Poyle *66–67* G12
Hamsey *38–39* G5
Hamstall Ridware *110–111* H8
Hamstead Marshall *46–47* B11
Hamsterley *166–167* K11
Hanbury *Stafford. 110–111* G9
Hanbury *Worcester. 90–91* C7
Handforth *126–127* C6
Handley *126–127* E3
Handley *34–35* F8
Handsworth *Yorks. 130–131* C11
Handsworth *Warwick. 90–91* A8
Hanford *30–31* F7
Hanging Houghton *90–91* B13
Hangleton *38–39* H4
Hanham *42–43* A5
Hankerton *66–67* J7
Hankelow *106–107* F5
Hanley *106–107* F7
Hanley Castle *86–87* E6
Hanley Child *86–87* C5
Hanley William *86–87* C5
Hanlith *142–143* F1
Hanmer *106–107* F3
Hanney *66–67* J11
Hannington *Northants. 90–91* B14
Hannington *Wilts. 66–67* J9
Hannington *Hants. 46–47* B12
Hanslope *90–91* D14
Hanwell *90–91* E11
Hanworth *Norfolk 118–119* F11
Hanworth *Middlesex 50–51* C3
Happisburgh *118–119* G13
Hapsford *126–127* D3
Hapton *Lancs. 142–143* H1
Hapton *Norfolk 118–119* J11
Harberton *22–23* H12
Harbledown *54–55* D11
Harborne *90–91* A8
Harborough Magna *90–91* B11
Harbridge *34–35* F9
Harbury *90–91* C10
Harby *Lincs. 134–135* D1
Harby *Leicester. 110–111* G13
Hardenhuish *46–47* A7
Hardham *38–39* G2
Hardingham *118–119* J10
Hardingstone *90–91* D14
Hardington *42–43* C6
Hardington Mandeville *30–31* F4
Hardley *118–119* J13
Hardmead *94–95* D1
Hardwick *Lincs. 134–135* C1
Hardwick *Norfolk 98–99* A11
Hardwick *Northants. 94–95* C1
Hardwick *Cambs. 94–95* C5
Hardwick *Oxford. 66–67* F12
Hardwick *Bucks. 66–67* G14
Hardwick *Oxford. 66–67* H11
Hardwicke *62–63* G6
Hareby *134–135* D4
Harefield *70–71* J2
Harescombe *62–63* G6
Haresfield *62–63* G6
Harewood *142–143* G5
Harford *22–23* H11
Hargrave *Northants. 94–95* B2
Hargrave *Suffolk 98–99* C8
Hargham *98–99* A10
Harkstead *74–75* E11
Harlaston *110–111* H9
Harlaxton *114–115* G1
Harlech *102–103* G10
Harlesden *70–71* J4
Harleston *Norfolk 98–99* A12
Harleston *Suffolk 98–99* C10
Harlestone *90–91* C13
Harley *106–107* J4
Harlington *Beds. 70–71* F2
Harlington *Middlesex 50–51* B2
Harlow *70–71* G6
Harlow Hill *166–167* G10
Harlthorpe *146–147* H8
Harlton *94–95* D5
Harmby *154–155* D3
Harmondsworth *50–51* B2
Harmston *134–135* D2
Harnham *166–167* F10
Harnhill *66–67* H8
Haroldston St. Issells *78–79* E5
Haroldston West *78–79* E5
Harome *154–155* D7
Harpenden *70–71* G3
Harpford *30–31* H1
Harpham *146–147* F11
Harpley *118–119* G8
Harpole *90–91* C13
Harpsden *66–67* J14
Harpswell *134–135* B1
Harrietsham *54–55* D9
Harrington *Cumberland 150–151* A8
Harrington *Lincs. 134–135* D5
Harrington *Northants. 90–91* B14
Harringworth *114–115* J1
Harrogate *142–143* F5
Harrold *94–95* D1
Harrowden *94–95* B1
Harrow on the Hill *70–71* J3
Harrow Weald *70–71* J3
Harston *Leicester. 114–115* G1
Harston *Cambs. 94–95* D5
Harswell *146–147* G9
Hart *166–167* K13
Hartburn *166–67* F10
Hartest *98–99* D8
Hartfield *50–51* E6
Hartford *Cheshire 126–127* D5
Hartford *Hunts. 94–95* B4
Harthill *106–107* E4
Harthill *182–183* H5
Hartley *Northld. 166–167* G12
Hartley *Westmorland 150–151* B14
Hartley *Kent 50–51* C7
Hartley Wespall *46–47* B13
Hartington *Northld. 166–167* F10
Hartington *Derby 130–131* E9
Hartland *26–27* C8
Hartlebury *86–87* C6
Hartlepool *166–167* K14
Hartlington *142–143* F2
Hartlip *54–55* C8
Hartpury *62–63* F6
Harton *Durham 166–167* H13
Harton *Yorks. 146–147* F8
Hartshead *142–143* J4
Hartshill *90–91* A10
Hartshorne *110–111* H10
Hartwell *Northants. 90–91* D14
Hartwell *Bucks. 66–67* G14
Harvington *90–91* D8
Harwell *66–67* J11
Harwich *74–75* E12
Harwood Dale *158–159* C10
Harworth *130–131* B12
Hascombe *50–51* E2
Haselbech *90–91* B13
Haselbury Bryan *30–31* F6
Haselbury Plucknett *30–31* F4
Haseley *90–91* C9
Haselor *90–91* D9
Haselour *110–111* H9
Hasfield *62–63* F6
Hasguard *58–59* inset
Hasketon *98–99* D12
Hasland *130–131* D11
Haslemere *50–51* F1
Haslingden *142–143* J1
Haslingfield *94–95* D5
Haslington *126–127* E6
Hassall *126–127* E6
Hassingham *118–119* J12
Hassocks *38–39* G4
Hassop *130–131* D9
Hastingleigh *54–55* E10
Hastings *38–39* inset
Haswell *166–167* J13
Hatch Beauchamp *30–31* E2
Hatcliffe *134–135* A3
Hatfield *Yorks 130–131* A13
Hatfield *Hereford. 86–87* C4
Hatfield *Herts. 70–71* G4
Hatfield Broad Oak *70–71* G6
Hatfield Peverel *74–75* G8
Hatford *66–67* H10
Hatherleigh *26–27* D10
Hathern *110–111* H11
Hatherop *66–67* H9

Hucklow/Kirkoswald

Hucklow 130–131 C9
Hucknall 130–131 E11
Hucknall Torkard 110–111 E12
Huddersfield 142–143 J3
Huddington 86–87 D7
Hudswell 154–155 C3
Huggate 146–147 F9
Hughenden 70–71 H1
Hughley 106–107 J4
Hugh Town 18–19 inset
Huish Devon. 26–27 D10
Huish Wilts. 46–47 B9
Huish Champflower 26–27 B14
Huish Episcopi 42–43 E3
Hulcott 70–71 G1
Hulland 110–111 F9
Hullavington 62–63 J7
Hulme Walfield 126–127 D6
Humber 86–87 D4
Humberston 134–135 A4
Humberstone 110–111 J12
Humbleton Yorks. 146–147 H12
Humby 114–115 G2
Humshaugh 166–167 G9
Huncoat 138–139 H14
Huncote 110–111 J12
Hunderthwaite 154–155 A2
Hundleby 134–135 D5
Hundleton 58–59 inset
Hundon 98–99 D8
Hungerford 46–47 A10
Hungerton 110–111 J13
Hunmanby 158–159 D11
Hunningham 90–91 C11
Hunsdon 70–71 G5
Hunsingore 142–143 F6
Hunstanton 114–115 F7
Hunstanworth 166–167 J9
Hunsterton 106–107 F5
Hunston 98–99 C9
Hunston 38–39 H1
Hunsworth 142–143 H4
Hunter's Quay 178–179 G10
Huntingdon 94–95 B4
Huntingfield 98–99 B12
Huntington Yorks. 142–143 F7
Huntington Stafford. 110–111 H7
Huntington Hereford. 86–87 D2
Huntley 62–63 G5
Hunton Yorks. 154–155 C4
Hunton Hants. 46–47 D11
Hunton Kent 54–55 D8
Huntsham 26–27 C13
Huntshaw 26–27 C10
Huntspill 42–43 C2
Hunworth 118–119 F10
Hurley 70–71 J1
Hurn 34–35 G9
Hursley 46–47 E11
Hurst 126–127 A7
Hurstbourne Priors 46–47 C11
Hurstbourne Tarrant 46–47 C11
Hurstpierpoint 38–39 G4
Hurworth 154–155 B5
Husbands Bosworth 90–91 A13
Husborne Crawley 70–71 E2
Husthwaite 154–155 E6
Huttoft 134–135 C6
Hutton 138–139 H12
Hutton 70–71 H7
Hutton 42–43 B3
Hutton Bonville 154–155 C5
Hutton Bushel 158–159 D10
Hutton Conyers 154–155 E5
Hutton Hang 154–155 D4
Hutton Henry 166–167 K13
Hutton le Hole 158–159 C8
Hutton Lowcross 154–155 B7
Hutton Magna 154–155 B3
Hutton Roof Cumberland 162–163 K5
Hutton Roof Westmorland 150–151 D12
Hutton Rudby 154–155 B6
Hutton Sessay 154–155 E6
Hutton Wandesley 142–143 G6
Huxham 26–27 E13
Huxley 126–127 E4
Hyde 126–127 B7
Hyssington 86–87 A2
Hythe Kent) 54–55 E11
Hythe Hants. 34–35 F11

I

Ibberton 30–31 F6
Ible 130–131 E9
Ibsley 34–35 F9
Ibstock 110–111 H11
Ibstone 66–67 J14
Ickburgh 98–99 A8
Ickenham 70–71 J3
Ickford 66–67 G13
Ickleford 70–71 F3
Icklesham 38–39 inset
Ickleton 94–95 E6
Icklingham 98–99 B8
Idbury 66–67 F9
Iddesleigh 26–27 D10
Ide 26–27 E13
Ideford 22–23 F13
Iden 54–55 F9
Idlicote 90–91 E10
Idmiston 46–47 D9
Idsworth 34–35 F14
Iffley 66–67 H12
Ifield 50–51 E4
Iford 38–39 H5
Ifton 62–63 J4
Ightfield 106–107 F4
Ightham 50–51 D6
Iken 98–99 C13
Ilam 110–111 E9
Ilchester 30–31 E4
Ilford 70–71 J5
Ilfracombe 26–27 A10
Ilkeston 110–111 F11
Ilketshall St. Andrew 98–99 A13
Ilketshall St. Lawrence 98–99 A13
Ilketshall St. Margaret 98–99 A12
Ilkley 142–143 G3
Illey 90–91 B7
Illington 98–99 A9
Illogan 18–19 J3
Illston on the Hill 110–111 J13
Ilmer 66–67 H14
Ilmington 90–91 E9
Ilminster 30–31 F2
Ilsington 22–23 G12
Ilston 58–59 G10
Ilton 30–31 E3
Imber 46–47 C7
Immingham 146–147 J11
Impington 94–95 C5
Ince 126–127 C3
Ince Blundell 126–127 A2
Inchinnan 178–179 H12
Ingatestone 70–71 H7
Ingbirchworth 130–131 A9
Ingerthorpe 142–143 E4
Ingestre 110–111 G7
Ingham Lincs. 134–135 C1
Ingham Norfolk 118–119 G13
Ingham Suffolk 98–99 B8
Ingleby 110–111 G10
Ingleby Arncliffe 154–155 C6
Ingleby Greenhow 154–155 B7
Inglesham 66–67 H9
Ingleton Yorks. 150–151 E13
Ingleton Durham 154–155 A3
Ingoe 166–167 G10
Ingoldisthorpe 114–115 G7
Ingoldmells 134–135 D6
Ingoldsby 114–115 G2
Ingrave 70–71 J7
Ingworth 118–119 G11
Inkberrow 90–91 D8
Inkpen 46–47 B10
Innellan 178–179 H10
Innerleven 182–183 E8
Instow 26–27 B9
Intwood 118–119 J11
Inveresk 182–183 G8
Inverkeithing 182–183 G6
Inverkip 178–179 H10
Inwardleigh 26–27 E10
Inworth 74–75 G9
Iping 50–51 F1
Ipplepen 22–23 G12
Ippollitts 70–71 F3
Ipsden 66–67 J13
Ipstones 110–111 E8
Ipswich 98–99 D11
Irby 126–127 C2
Irby in the Marsh 134–135 D5
Irchester 94–95 C1
Ireby 150–151 E13
Irlam 126–127 B5
Irnham 114–115 G2
Iron Acton 62–63 J5
Ironbridge 106–107 J5
Irstead 118–119 H12
Irthington 162–163 H6
Irthlingborough 94–95 C1
Irton 158–159 D10
Irvine 174–175 A10
Isfield 38–39 G5
Isham 94–95 B1
Isle Abbots 30–31 E3
Isle Brewers 30–31 E3
Isleham 94–95 B7
Isles of Scilly 18–19 inset
Isleworth 50–51 B3
Isley Walton 110–111 G11
Islington 70–71 J4
Islip Northants. 94–95 B2
Islip Oxford. 66–67 G12
Itchen 34–35 F11
Itchen Abbas 46–47 D12
Itchen Stoke 46–47 D12
Itchingfield 50–51 F3
Itteringham 118–119 G11
Itton 62–63 H4
Iver 70–71 J2
Iveston 166–167 J11
Ivinghoe 70–71 G1
Ivybridge 22–23 H11
Ivychurch 54–55 F10
Iwade 54–55 C9
Iwerne Minster 30–31 F7
Iwerne Courtney or Shroton 30–31 F7
Ixworth 98–99 B9
Ixworth Thorpe 98–99 B9

J

Jacobstow 26–27 E7
Jacobstowe 26–27 E10
Jarrow 166–167 H12
Jeffreston 58–59 E6
Jevington 38–39 H6
Johnston 58–59 inset
Johnstone 178–179 H12
Jordanston 78–79 C5

K

Kaber 154–155 B1
Kea 18–19 J4
Keadby 130–131 A14
Kearsley Lancs. 126–127 A5
Kearsley Northld. 166–167 G10
Keddington 134–135 B4
Kedington 98–99 D7
Kedleston 110–111 F10
Keelby 134–135 A3
Keele 106–107 F6
Keevil 42–43 B7
Kegworth 110–111 G11
Keighley 142–143 G3
Keinton Mandeville 42–43 E4
Keisby 114–115 G2
Kelby 114–115 F2
Kelfield 142–143 G7
Kelham 130–131 E14
Kellaways 46–47 A7
Kelling 118–119 F10
Kellington 142–143 J7
Kelly 26–27 F9
Kelmarsh 90–91 B13
Kelmscott 66–67 H10
Kelsale 98–99 C13
Kelsall 126–127 D4
Kelshall 70–71 E4
Kelstern 134–135 B4
Kelston 42–43 B5
Kelty 182–183 F6
Kelvedon 74–75 F9
Kelvedon Hatch 70–71 H6
Kemberton 106–107 J5
Kemble 66–67 H8
Kemerton 62–63 E7
Kemeys Commander 62–63 H3
Kemeys Inferior 62–63 J3
Kempley 62–63 F5
Kempsey 86–87 D6
Kempsford 66–67 H9
Kempston 94–95 D2
Kempstone 118–119 H9
Kenardington 54–55 F10
Kenchester 86–87 E3
Kencott 66–67 H10
Kendal 150–151 C12
Kenderchurch 62–63 F3
Kenfig 58–59 G12
Kenilworth 90–91 B10
Kenley 106–107 J4
Kenn Devon. 26–27 F13
Kenn Somerset 42–43 B3
Kennerleigh 26–27 D12
Kennett 98–99 C7
Kenninghall 98–99 A10
Kennington 54–55 E10
Kennoway 182–183 E8
Kennythorpe 146–147 E8
Kensington 50–51 B4
Kensworth 70–71 F2
Kentchurch 62–63 F3
Kentford 98–99 C7
Kentisbeare 26–27 D14
Kentisbury 26–27 A10
Kentmere 150–151 B11
Kenton Northld. 166–167 G11
Kenton Suffolk 98–99 C11
Kenton Devon. 26–27 F13
Kenyon 126–127 B5
Kepwick 154–155 C6
Keresley 90–91 B10
Kerry 86–87 A1
Kersall 130–131 D13
Kersey 98–99 D10
Kesgrave 98–99 D11
Kessingland 98–99 A14
Keston 50–51 C5
Keswick Cumberland. 150–151 A10
Keswick Norfolk 118–119 J11
Kettering 94–95 B1
Ketteringham 118–119 J11
Kettlebaston 98–99 D9
Kettleburgh 98–99 C12
Kettlestone 118–119 G9
Kettleshulme 130–131 C7
Kettlethorpe 134–135 C1
Ketton 114–115 J2
Kew 50–51 B3
Kewstoke 42–43 B2
Kexbrough 130–130 A10
Kexby Yorks. 146–147 G8
Kexby Lincs. 134–135 C1
Keyham 110–111 J13
Keyingham 146–147 H12
Keymer 38–39 G4
Keynsham 42–43 B5
Keysoe 94–95 C2
Keyston 94–95 B2
Keyworth 110–111 G12
Kidbrooke 50–51 B5
Kidderminster 86–87 B6
Kiddington 66–67 F11
Kidlington 66–67 G11
Kidmore End 46–47 A13
Kidsgrove 106–107 E6
Kidwelly 58–59 E9
Kilbarchan 178–179 H12
Kilbirnie 178–179 J11
Kilbourne 110–111 F11
Kilburn 154–155 D6
Kilby 90–91 A12
Kilconquhar 182–183 E9
Kilcreggan 178–179 G10
Kildale 154–155 B7
Kildwick 142–143 G2
Kilgwrrwg 62–63 H4
Kilham Yorks. 146–147 E10
Kilkhampton 26–27 D8
Killamarsh 130–131 C11
Killearn 178–179 F13
Killerby 154–155 A4
Killinghall 142–143 F4
Killington 150–151 D13
Kilmacolm 178–179 H11
Kilmarnock 174–175 A11
Kilmaurs 174–175 A11
Kilmersdon 42–43 C5
Kilmeston 46–47 E12
Kilmington Wilts. 42–43 D6
Kilmington Devon. 30–31 G2
Kilmun 178–179 G10
Kilnsea 146–147 J13
Kilnwick 146–147 G10
Kilnwick Percy 146–147 G9
Kilpeck 62–63 F3
Kilpin 146–147 H8
Kilsby 90–91 B12
Kilsyth 178–179 G14
Kilton 158–159 A8
Kilve 42–43 C1
Kilverstone 98–99 A9
Kilvington 110–111 F14
Kilwinning 174–175 A10
Kilworth Beauchamp 90–91 A13
Kilworth Harcourt 90–91 A13
Kimberley Notts. 110–111 F11
Kimberley Norfolk 118–119 J10
Kimble 70–71 H1
Kimblesworth 166–167 J12
Kimbolton Hereford. 86–87 C4
Kimbolton Hunts. 94–95 C3
Kimmeridge 30–31 H7
Kimpton Herts. 70–71 G3
Kimpton Hants. 46–47 C10
Kincardine Fife 182–183 F5
Kineton 90–91 D10
Kingarth 178–179 J9
Kingerby 134–135 B2
Kingham 66–67 F10
Kinghorn 182–183 F7
Kinglassie 182–183 E7
Kingsbridge 22–23 J11
King's Bromley 110–111 H9
Kingsbury 90–91 A9
Kingsbury Episcopi 30–31 E3
King's Caple 62–63 F4
Kingsclere 46–47 B12
King's Cliffe 114–115 J2
Kingscote 62–63 H6
Kingsdon 42–43 E4
Kingsdown Kent 50–51 C6
Kingsdown Kent 54–55 D9
Kingsey 66–67 G13
Kingskerswell 22–23 G12
Kingsland 86–87 C3
King's Langley 70–71 H2
Kingsley Cheshire 126–127 C4
Kingsley Staffs. 110–111 F8
Kingsley Hants. 46–47 D14
King's Lynn 114–115 H7
King's Meaburn 150–151 A13
King's Newnham 90–91 B11
Kingsnorth 54–55 E10
King's Norton 110–111 J13
King's Nympton 26–27 C11
King's Pyon 86–87 D3
King's Ripton 94–95 B4
King's Somborne 46–47 D11
King's Stanley 62–63 H6
King's Sutton 66–67 E12
Kingsteignton 22–23 G12
Kingsterndale 130–131 D8
Kingsthorpe 90–91 C13
Kingston Staffs. 110–111 G8
Kingston Camb. 94–95 D5
Kingston Somerset 42–43 E2
Kingston Kent 54–55 D11
Kingston Devon. 22–23 J11
Kingston I. of Wight 34–35 H11
Kingston Bagpuize 66–67 H11
Kingston by Sea 38–39 H4
Kingston Deverill 42–43 D6
Kingstone Heref. 66–67 E3
Kingstone Somerset 30–31 F3
Kingston Lisle 66–67 J10
Kingston near Lewes 38–39 H5
Kingston Russell 30–31 H5
Kingston Seymour 42–43 B3
Kingston upon Hull 146–147 H11
Kingston upon Soar 110–111 G11
Kingston upon Thames 50–51 C3
King's Walden 70–71 F3
Kingswear 22–23 H13
Kingswinford 86–87 A7
Kingswood Glouc. 62–63 J6
Kingswood Glouc. 42–43 A5
Kingswood Surrey 50–51 D4
King's Worthy 46–47 D12
Kington Heref. 86–87 D2
Kington Worc. 90–91 D8
Kington Langley 42–43 A7
Kington Magna 30–31 E6
Kington St. Michael 42–43 A7
Kingweston 42–43 D4
Kinlet 86–87 B5
Kinnerley 106–107 H2
Kinnersley Salop. 106–107 H5
Kinnersley Heref. 86–87 D3
Kinnerton 126–127 E2
Kinoulton 110–111 G13
Kinross 182–183 E6
Kinsham 86–87 C3
Kinson 34–35 G8
Kintbury 46–47 B11
Kinver 86–87 B6
Kinwarton 90–91 D8
Kiplin 154–155 C4
Kippax 142–143 H5
Kippen 178–179 F13
Kirby 154–155 B6
Kirby Bedon 118–119 J12
Kirby Bellars 110–111 H13
Kirby Cane 98–99 A12
Kirby Grindalythe 146–147 E9
Kirby Hill Yorks. 154–155 B3
Kirby Hill Yorks. 142–143 E5
Kirby Knowle 154–155 D6
Kirby-le-Soken 74–75 F11
Kirby Misperton 158–159 D8
Kirby Moorside 158–159 D8
Kirby Sigston 154–155 C5
Kirby Underdale 146–147 F8
Kirby Wiske 154–155 D5
Kirdford 50–51 F2
Kirkandrews upon Eden 162–163 H5
Kirkbean 162–163 H2
Kirk Bramwith 130–131 A12
Kirkbride 162–163 H4
Kirkburton 130–131 A9
Kirkby 126–127 B3
Kirkby cum Osgodby 134–135 B2
Kirkby Fleetham 154–155 C4
Kirkby Green 134–135 E2
Kirkby in Ashfield 130–131 E11
Kirkby la Thorpe 114–115 F3
Kirkby Lonsdale 150–151 D13
Kirkby Malham 142–143 F1
Kirkby Mallory 110–111 J11
Kirkby Malzcard 154–155 E4
Kirkby Muxloe 110–111 J12
Kirkby on Bain 134–135 D4
Kirkby Overblow 142–143 G5
Kirkby Stephen 150–151 B14
Kirkby Thore 150–151 A13
Kirkby Underwood 114–115 G2
Kirkcaldy 182–183 F7
Kirkconnel 174–175 C13
Kirk Deighton 142–143 G5
Kirk Ella 146–147 H10
Kirkgunzeon 162–163 H1
Kirk Hallam 110–111 F11
Kirkham Lancs. 138–139 H11
Kirkham Yorks. 146–147 E8
Kirk Hammerton 142–143 F6
Kirkhampton 162–163 H4
Kirkharle 166–167 F10
Kirk Haugh 162–163 J7
Kirkheaton Northld. 166–167 G10
Kirkheaton Yorks. 142–143 J4
Kirkintilloch 178–179 G14
Kirk Ireton 110–111 E10
Kirk Langley 110–111 F10
Kirkleatham 154–155 A7
Kirk Leavington 154–155 B6
Kirklington 130–131 E13
Kirkliston 182–183 G6
Kirk Merrington 166–167 K12
Kirkmichael Ayr 174–175 C10
Kirknewton 182–183 H6
Kirk of Shotts 182–183 H4
Kirkoswald Ayr 174–175 D9
Kirkoswald 162–163 K6

Llanberis/Lydiate

Llanberis *122-123* E10
Llanbeulan *122-123* D8
Llanbister *86-87* B1
Llanblethian *58-59* H13
Llanboidy *82-83* D7
Llanbradach *62-63* J1
Llanbrynmair *102-103* J12
Llanbyther *82-83* B10
Llancarfan *58-59* H14
Llancillo *62-63* F3
Llancynfelyn *102-103* K11
Llandaff *42-43* A1
Llandawke *58-59* E8
Llanddaniel-Fâb *122-123* D9
Llanddarog *82-83* E10
Llanddeiniol *102-103* M10
Llanddeiniolen *122-123* D10
Llandderfel *102-103* F13
Llanddetty *62-63* G1
Llanddensant *Anglesey 122-123* C8
Llanddensant *Carnar. 82-83* D12
Llanddew *82-83* C14
Llanddewi *58-59* G9
Llanddewi-Aberarth Upper *82-83* A9
Llanddewi-fâch *86-87* E1
Llanddewi 'r Cwm *82-83* B14
Llanddewi Velfrey *78-79* E7
Llanddewi-Ystradenny *86-87* C1
Llanddoget *122-123* D12
Llanddona *122-123* C10
Llanddulas *122-123* C13
Llanddyfnan *122-123* C9
Llandecwyn *102-103* F10
Llandefaelog-fach *82-83* C14
Llandefalle *62-63* E1
Llandefeilog *82-83* E9
Llandegai *122-123* D10
Llandegfan *122-123* D10
Llandegla *106-107* E1
Llandegley *86-87* C1
Llandegwning *102-103* G8
Llandegyeth *62-63* H3
Llandeilo-graban *86-87* E1
Llandeilor-Fan *82-83* C13
Llandloy *78-79* D4
Llandenny *62-63* H3
Llandevenny *62-63* J3
Llandilo *82-83* D10
Llandinabo *62-63* F4
Llandinam *102-103* K14
Llandogo *62-63* H4
Llandovery *82-83* C12
Llandow *58-59* H13
Llandowror *82-83* E8
Llandrillo *102-103* F14
Llandrillo-yn-Rhos *122-123* C12
Llandrindod Wells *82-83* A14
Llandrinio *106-107* H2
Llandrygarn *122-123* C8
Llandudno *122-123* C12
Llandulas *82-83* C12
Llandwrog *122-123* E9
Llandybie *82-83* E10
Llandyfodwg *58-59* G13
Llandyfriog *82-83* C8
Llandyfrydog *122-123* C9
Llandygwdd *82-83* C7
Llandysillio *106-107* H2
Llandyssil *86-87* A1
Llandyssilio-gogo *82-83* A8
Llandyssul *82-83* C9
Llanedeyrn *42-43* A2
Llanedwen *122-123* D9
Llanedy *58-59* E10
Llanegryn *102-103* J10
Llanegwad *82-83* D10
Llaneilian *122-123* B9
Llanelen *62-63* G2
Llanelian-yn-Rhos *122-123* C12
Llanelidan *106-107* E1
Llanelieu *62-63* E1
Llanelltyd *102-103* H11
Llanelly *Carmar. 58-59* F10
Llanelly *Brecknock. 62-63* G2
Llanelwedd *82-83* B14
Llanenddwyn *102-103* H10
Llanengan *102-103* G8
Llanerch Aeron *82-83* A9
Llanerchymedd *122-123* C9
Llanerfyl *102-103* J14
Llanfabon *62-63* J1
Llanfachraeth *122-123* C8
Llanfachreth *102-103* H11
Llanfaelog *122-123* D8
Llanfaes *122-123* C10
Llanfaethlu *122-123* C8
Llanfaglan *122-123* E9
Llanfair *102-103* G10
Llanfair-ar-y-bryn *82-83* C12
Llanfair Caereinion *106-107* J1
Llanfair-Clydogau *82-83* B10
Llanfairfechan *122-123* D11
Llanfair-is-gaer *122-123* D10
Llanfair-mathafarncithaf *122-123* C9
Llanfair-Nant-Gwyn *78-79* C7
Llanfair Nant-y-Gôf *78-79* C5
Llanfair-Orllwyn *82-83* C8
Llanfair-pwllgwyngyll *122-123* D10
Llanfair Talhaiarn *122-123* D13
Llanfair-y-Cwmwd *122-123* D9
Llanfairynghornwy *122-123* B8
Llanfair-yn-neubwll *122-123* C8
Llanfallteg West *78-79* D7
Llanfaredd *82-83* B14
Llanfechan *106-107* H1
Llanfechell *122-123* B8
Llanferres *126-127* E1
Llanfflewyn *122-123* B8
Llanfigael *122-123* C8
Llanfigan *62-63* F1
Llanfihangel Aberbythych *82-83* D10
Llanfihangel Abercowin *82-83* E8
Llanfihangel-ar-arth *82-83* C9
Llanfihangel Bachellaeth *102-103* G8
Llanfihangel-Bryn-Pabuan *82-83* A13
Llanfihangel Cilfargen *82-83* D10
Llanfihangel Esgeifiog *122-123* D9
Llanfihangel-Glyn-Myfyr *122-123* F13
Llanfihangel-helygen *82-83* A14
Llanfihangel-Nant-Bran *82-83* C13
Llanfihangel-Nant-Melan *86-87* D1
Llanfihangel Penbedw *78-79* C7
Llanfihangel Rhos-y-corn *82-83* C10
Llanfihangel Rhydithon *86-87* C1
Llanfihangel Tal-y-llyn *62-63* F1
Llanfihangel-Tre'r-Beirdd *122-123* C9
Llanfihangel-ty'n-Sylwy *122-123* C10
Llanfihangel-yng-Ngwynfa *102-103* H14
Llanfihangel-yn-nhowyn *122-123* C8
Llanfihangel-y-Pennant *102-103* J11
Llanfihangel-Ystrad *82-83* B10
Llanfillo *62-63* F1
Llanfoist *62-63* G2
Llanfor *102-103* G13
Llanfrothen *102-103* F10
Llanfrynach *82-83* D14
Llanfwrog *122-123* C8
Llanfyllin *106-107* H1
Llanfynydd *82-83* D10
Llanfyrnach *82-83* D7
Llangadfan *102-103* J13
Llangadock *82-83* D11
Llangadwaladr *122-123* D8
Llangaffo *122-123* D9
Llangam *82-83* E9
Llangan *58-59* H13
Llanganten *82-83* B13
Llangar *122-123* F14
Llangarren *62-63* F4
Llangasty Tal-y-llyn *62-63* F1
Llangathen *82-83* D10
Llangattock *62-63* G1
Llangattock-lingoed *62-63* G3
Llangattock nigh Usk *62-63* G2
Llangattock-Vibon-Avel *62-63* G3
Llangedwyn *106-107* G1
Llangefni *122-123* C9
Llangeinor *58-59* G13
Llangeinwen *122-123* D9
Llangeitho *82-83* A10
Llangeler *82-83* C8
Llangelynin *Carnarvon. 122-123* D11
Llangelynin *Merioneth. 102-103* J10
Llangendeirne *82-83* E9
Llangennech *58-59* F10
Llangennith *58-59* G9
Llangenny *62-63* G2
Llangerniew *122-123* D12
Llangeview *62-63* H3
Llangian *102-103* G8
Llangibby *62-63* H3
Llangiwg *58-59* E11
Llanglydwen *78-79* D7
Llangoed *122-123* C10
Llangoedmor *78-79* B7
Llangollen *106-107* F1
Llangolman *78-79* D6
Llangorse *62-63* F1
Llangoven *62-63* H3
Llangower *102-103* G13
Llangranog *82-83* B8
Llangristiolus *122-123* D9
Llangstone *62-63* J3
Llangua *62-63* F3
Llangunllo *86-87* C1
Llangunnor *82-83* D9
Llangurig *102-103* L13
Llangwm *Denbigh. 122-123* F13
Llangwm *Pembroke. 58-59* inset
Llangwm-isaf *62-63* H3
Llangwnadl *102-103* inset
Llangwstenin *122-123* C12
Llangwyfan *Anglesey 122-123* D8
Llangwyfan *Denbigh. 126-127* D1
Llangwyllog *122-123* C9
Llangwyryfon *102-103* M10
Llangybi *Carnarvon. 102-103* F9
Llangybi *Cardigan. 82-83* B10
Llangynhafal *126-127* D1
Llangynidr *62-63* G1
Llangyniew *106-107* J1
Llangynin *82-83* E8
Llangynllo *82-83* C8
Llangynog *Montg. 102-103* G14
Llangynog *Brecknock. 82-83* B14
Llanhamlach *62-63* F1
Llanharan *58-59* G13
Llanharry *58-59* G13
Llanhennock *62-63* J3
Llanhilleth *62-63* H2
Llanhowell *78-79* D4
Llanidloes *102-103* L13
Llaniestyn *102-103* G8
Llanigon *62-63* E1
Llanilar *102-103* L10
Llanilid *58-59* G13
Llanina *82-83* A9
Llanishen *Monmouth. 62-63* H4
Llanishen *Glamorgan. 42-43* A1
Llanllawddog *82-83* D9
Llanllawer *78-79* C5
Llanllechid *122-123* D10
Llanlleonfel *82-83* B13
Llanllowell *62-63* H3
Llanllwchaiarn *86-87* A1
Llanllwni *82-83* C9
Llanllyfni *122-123* E9
Llanllugan *102-103* J14
Llanmadog *58-59* F9
Llanmartin *62-63* J3
Llanmaes *58-59* H13
Llanmerewig *86-87* A1
Llanmihangel *58-59* H13
Llannefydd *122-123* D13
Llannon *58-59* E10
Llannor *102-103* G8
Llanover *62-63* G2
Llanpumsaint *82-83* D9
Llanreithan *78-79* D5
Llanrhaiadr-ym-Mochnant *106-107* G1
Llanrhwydrys *122-123* B8
Llanrhychwyn *122-123* E11
Llanrhyddlad *122-123* B8
Llanrhystyd *82-83* A10
Llanrian *78-79* D4
Llanrothel *62-63* G4
Llanrug *122-123* D10
Llanrwst *122-123* E12
Llansadurnen *58-59* E8
Llansadwrn *Anglesey 122-123* C10
Llansadwrn *Carmarthen. 82-83* C11
Llansannan *122-123* D13
Llansannor *58-59* H13
Llansaintfraed *62-63* G3
Llansaintfraed in Elvel *86-87* D1
Llansantffraid *82-83* A10
Llansantffraid Cwmdeuddwr *82-83* A13
Llansantffraid-Glan-Conway *122-123* C12
Llansantffraid Glyn Ceiriog *106-107* F1
Llansantffread *62-63* F1
Llansawel *82-83* C10
Llansilin *106-107* G1
Llansoy *62-63* H3
Llanspyddid *82-83* D14
Llanstadwell *58-59* inset
Llanstephan *Radnor. 86-87* E1
Llanstephan *Carmarthen. 58-59* E8
Llanthewy-Rytherch *62-63* G3
Llanthewy Skirrid *62-63* G2
Llanthewy Vach *62-63* H2
Llantilio-Crossenny *62-63* G3
Llantilio-pertholey *62-63* G2
Llantood *78-79* C7
Llantrisant *Anglesey 122-123* C8
Llantrisant *Glamorgan. 58-59* G14
Llantrissent *62-63* H3
Llantrithyd *58-59* H14
Llantwit Fardre *62-63* J1
Llantwit-Major *58-59* H13
Llantysilio *106-107* F1
Llanuwchllyn *102-103* G12
Llanvaches *62-63* J3
Llanvair-Discoed *62-63* J3
Llanvair Kilgedin *62-63* G3
Llanvair Waterdine *86-87* B2
Llanvapley *62-63* G3
Llanverwys *82-83* B11
Llanvetherine *62-63* G3
Llanveynoe *62-63* F2
Llanvihangel Crucorney *62-63* F2
Llanvihangel Llantarnam *62-63* J2
Llanvihangel near Roggiett *62-63* J3
Llanvihangel nigh Usk *62-63* G3
Llanvihangel Pontymoil *62-63* H2
Llanvihangel-tor-y-mynydd *62-63* H3
Llanvihangel-ystern-Llewern *62-63* G3
Llanwarne *62-63* F4
Llanwddyn *102-103* H13
Llanwenllwyfo *122-123* B9
Llanwenog *82-83* B9
Llanwern *62-63* J3
Llanwinio *82-83* D8
Llanwnda *Carnarvon. 122-123* E9
Llanwnda *Pembroke. 78-79* C5
Llanwnen *82-83* B10
Llanwnog *102-103* K14
Llanwonna *58-59* F14
Llanwrda *82-83* C11
Llanwrin *102-103* J12
Llanwrthwl *82-83* A13
Llanwrtyd *82-83* B12
Llanwrtyd Wells *82-83* B12
Llanwyddelan *102-103* J14
Llanyblodwel *106-107* H2
Llanycefn *78-79* D6
Llanychaer *78-79* C6
Llanychaiarn *102-103* L10
Llanychan *126-127* E1
Llanycil *102-103* G13
Llanymawddwy *102-103* H12
Llanymynech *106-107* H2
Llanynghenedl *122-123* C8
Llanynis *82-83* B13
Llanyre *82-83* A14
Llanystumdwy *102-103* F9
Llan-y-wern *62-63* F1
Llawhaden *78-79* E6
Llechcynfarwydd *122-123* C8
Llechryd *82-83* C7
Llowes *86-87* E1
Llysfaen *122-123* C12
Llyswen *62-63* E1
Llysworney *58-59* H13
Llys-y-fran *78-79* D6
Loanhead *182-183* H8
Lochgelly *182-183* F7
Lochgoilhead *178-179* E10
Lochmaben *162-163* F2
Lochwinnoch *178-179* J11
Lockerbie *162-163* F3
Lockerley *46-47* E10
Locking *42-43* B3
Lockinge *66-67* J11
Lockington *Yorks. 146-147* G10
Lockington *Leicester. 110-111* G11
Lockton *158-159* C9
Loddington *Leicester. 110-111* J14
Loddington *Northants. 90-91* B14
Loddiswell *22-23* J11
Loddon *118-119* J12
Lode *94-95* C6
Loders *30-31* G4
Lodsworth *50-51* F1
Loftus *158-159* A8
Lolworth *94-95* C5
London { *70-71* J4&5
London { *50-51* B345
London Colney *70-71* H3
Londonthorpe *114-115* F1
Long Ashton *42-43* A4
Long Bennington *114-115* F1
Longbenton *166-167* G12
Longborough *66-67* F9
Long Bredy *30-31* H4
Longbridge Deverill *42-43* D7
Long Buckby *90-91* C12
Long Burton *30-31* F5
Long Chawson *110-111* G13
Long Compton *66-67* E10
Longcot *66-67* J10
Long Crendon *66-67* G13
Long Crichel *34-35* F8
Long Ditton *50-51* C3
Longdon *Stafford. 110-111* H8
Longdon *Worcester. 62-63* E6
Longdon upon Tern *106-107* H5
Long Drax *146-147* H7
Long Eaton *110-111* G11
Longfield *50-51* C7
Longford *Derby. 110-111* F9
Longford *Shropshire 106-107* H5
Longford *Gloucester. 62-63* F6
Longham *118-119* H9
Longhirst *166-167* F11
Longhope *62-63* G5
Long Ichington *90-91* C11
Long Lawford *90-91* B11
Long Load *30-31* E4
Long Melford *98-99* D9
Long Marston *Yorks. 142-143* F6
Long Marston *Gloucester. 90-91* D9
Long Marton *150-151* A13
Long Newnton *62-63* J7
Long Newton *154-155* A5
Longney *62-63* G6
Longnor *Staffs. 130-131* D8
Longnor *Shropshire 106-107* J4
Long Parish *46-47* C11
Long Preston *142-143* F1
Longridge *138-139* H13
Long Riston *146-147* G11
Longsdon *106-107* E7
Long Stanton *94-95* C5
Longstock *46-47* D10
Long Stowe *94-95* D4
Long Sutton *Lincs. 114-115* G5
Long Sutton *Hants. 46-47* C13
Long Sutton *Somerset 42-43* E4
Longton *Lancs. 138-139* J12
Longton *Staffs. 106-107* F7
Longtown *Cumbld. 162-163* G5
Longtown *Hereford. 62-63* F2
Long Whatton *110-111* G11
Longwitton *166-167* F10
Longworth *66-67* H11
Loose *54-55* D8
Lopen *30-31* F3
Loppington *106-107* G3
Lostock Gralam *126-127* C5
Lostwithiel *18-19* H7
Lothersdale *142-143* G2
Loughborough *110-111* H12
Loughor *58-59* F10
Loughton *Shropshire 86-87* B5
Loughton *Bucks. 70-71* E1
Loughton *Essex 70-71* H5
Lound *Notts. 130-131* C13
Lound *Suffolk 118-119* J14
Louth *134-135* B4
Loversall *130-131* B12
Loveston *58-59* inset
Lovington *42-43* D5
Low Catton *146-147* F8
Low Coniscliffe *154-155* B4
Lowdham *110-111* F13
Low Dinsdale *154-155* B5
Lower Beeding *50-51* F4
Lower Boddington *90-91* D11
Lower Bullingham *62-63* E4
Lower Cam *62-63* H6
Lower Dunsforth *142-143* E6
Lower Halstow *54-55* C9
Lower Hardres *54-55* D11
Lower Heyford *66-67* F12
Lower Lemington *66-67* E9
Lower Penn *86-87* A7
Lower Sapey *86-87* C5
Lower Shuckburgh *90-91* C11
Lower Slaughter *66-67* F9
Lower Swell *66-67* F9
Lower Winchendon *66-67* G13
Lower Withington *126-127* D6
Lowesby *110-111* J13
Lowestoft *98-99* A14
Loweswater *150-151* A9
Lowick *Lancashire 150-151* D10
Lowick *Northants. 94-95* B2
Lowthorpe *146-147* F11
Lowton *126-127* B5
Loxbeare *26-27* C13
Loxhore *26-27* B10
Loxley *90-91* D10
Loxton *42-43* C3
Lubenham *90-91* A13
Luccombe *26-27* A13
Luckington *62-63* J6
Lucton *86-87* C3
Ludborough *134-135* B4
Ludchurch *58-59* inset
Luddenham *54-55* C10
Luddesdown *50-51* C7
Luddington *Lincs. 146-147* J9
Luddington *Warwick. 90-91* D9
Ludford *86-87* B4
Ludford Magna *134-135* B3
Ludford Parva *134-135* B3
Ludgershall *Bucks. 66-67* G13
Ludgershall *Wilts. 46-47* C10
Ludgvan *18-19* K2
Ludham *118-119* H13
Ludlow *86-87* B4
Luffincott *26-27* E8
Lufton *30-31* F4
Lugwardine *86-87* E4
Lullingstone *50-51* C6
Lullington *Derby. 110-111* H9
Lullington *Somerset 42-43* C6
Lullington *38-39* H6
Lulsley *86-87* D6
Lund *146-147* G10
Lunt *126-127* A2
Luppitt *30-31* F1
Lupton *150-151* D12
Lurgashall *50-51* F1
Lusby *134-135* D4
Luss *178-179* F11
Lustleigh *26-27* F12
Luston *86-87* C4
Lutley *86-87* B7
Lutlington *38-39* H6
Luton *70-71* F3
Lutterworth *90-91* A12
Lutton *Lincoln. 114-115* G5
Lutton *Northants. 94-95* A3
Luxborough *26-27* B13
Luxulian *18-19* H6
Lydbury North *86-87* A3
Lydd *38-39* inset
Lydden *54-55* E12
Lydeard St. Lawrence *42-43* D1
Lydford *26-27* F10
Lydham *86-87* A2
Lydiard Millicent *66-67* J8
Lydiard Tregoze *66-67* J8
Lydiate *126-127* A3

Widworthy/Zenner

Widworthy 30–31 G2
Wield 46–47 D13
Wigan 126–127 A4
Wiggenhall St. Germans 114–115 H6
Wiggenhall St. Mary Magdalen 114–115 H6
Wiggenhall St. Mary the Virgin 114–115 H6
Wiggenhall St. Peter 114–115 H7
Wigginton Yorks. 142–143 F7
Wigginton Stafford. 110–111 J9
Wigginton Oxford. 66–67 E11
Wigginton Herts. 70–71 G1
Wigglesworth 142–143 F1
Wiggonholt 38–39 G2
Wighill 142–143 G6
Wighton 118–119 F9
Wigmore 86–87 C3
Wigsley 134–135 D1
Wigston Magna 110–111 J12
Wigston Parva 90–91 A11
Wigtoft 114–115 F4
Wigton 162–163 J4
Wike 142–143 G5
Wilbarston 90–91 A14
Wilberfoss 146–147 G8
Wilburton 94–95 B6
Wilby Norfolk 98–99 A10
Wilby Northants. 94–95 C1
Wilby Suffolk 98–99 B11
Wilcot 46–47 B9
Wilcote 66–67 G11
Wilcrick 62–63 J3
Wildboarclough 130–131 D7
Wilden 94–95 D3
Wildsworth 130–131 B14
Wilksby 134–135 D4
Willand 26–27 D14
Willaston 126–127 C2
Willaston 106–107 E5
Willen 94–95 E1
Willenhall Stafford. 110–111 J7
Willenhall Warwick. 90–91 B10
Willerby 158–159 D10
Willerby 146–147 H10
Willersey 90–91 E8
Willesborough 54–55 E10
Willesden 70–71 J3
Willesley 110–111 H10
Willersley 86–87 D2
Willey Shrop. 106–107 J5
Willey Warwick. 90–91 A11
Willian 70–71 F4
Willingale Doe 70–71 G7
Willingale Spain 70–71 G7
Willingden 38–39 H7
Willingham Lincs. 134–135 C1
Willingham Cambs. 94–95 B5
Willington Northld. 166–167 G12
Willington Durham 166–167 K11
Willington Derby. 110–111 G10
Willington Beds. 94–95 D3
Willisham 98–99 D10
Willitoft 146–147 H8
Williton 42–43 D1
Willoughby 90–91 C12
Willoughby on the Wolds 110–111 G12
Willoughby Waterless 90–91 A12
Willoughton 134–135 B1
Wilmington Kent 50–51 C6
Wilmington Sussex 38–39 H6
Wilmslow 126–127 C6
Wilnecote 110–111 J9
Wilpshire 138–139 H13
Wilsden 142–143 H3
Wilsford Lincs. 114–115 F2
Wilsford Wilts. 46–47 B8
Wilsford Wilts. 46–47 D9
Wilshampstead 94–95 E2
Wilsthorpe 114–115 H3
Wilton Yorks. 154–155 A7
Wilton Yorks. 158–159 D9
Wilton Wilts. 46–47 D8
Wimbish 70–71 E6
Wimbledon 50–51 C4
Wimblington 94–95 A5
Wimborne Minster 34–35 G8
Wimborne St. Giles 34–35 F8
Wimbotsham 114–115 J7
Wincanton 42–43 E5
Winceby 134–135 D4
Wincham 126–127 C5
Winchcomb 66–67 F8
Winchelsea 38–39 inset
Winchester 46–47 D11
Winchfield 46–47 C14
Wincle 126–127 D7
Windermere 150–151 C11
Windley 110–111 F10
Windlesham 50–51 C1
Windrush 66–67 G9
Windsor 50–51 B2
Windygates 182–183 E8
Winestead 146–147 J12
Winfarthing 98–99 A10
Winford 42–43 B4
Winforton 86–87 D2
Winfrith Newburgh 30–31 H6
Wing Rutland. 114–115 J1
Wing Bucks. 70–71 F1
Wingate 166–167 K13
Wingerworth 130–131 D10
Wingfield 98–99 B11
Wingham 54–55 D12
Wingrave 70–71 G1
Winkburn 130–131 E13
Winkfield Wilts. 42–43 B6
Winkfield Berks. 50–51 C1
Winkleigh 26–27 D11
Winksley 154–155 E4
Winlaton 166–167 H11
Winmarleigh 138–139 G12
Winnington 126–127 D5
Winscombe 42–43 B3
Winsford Cheshire 126–127 D5
Winsford Somerset 26–27 B13
Winsham 30–31 F3
Winslade 46–47 C13
Winsley 42–43 B6
Winslow 66–67 F14
Winson 66–67 G8
Winster 130–131 E9
Winston Durham 154–155 A3
Winston Suffolk 98–99 C11
Winstone 66–67 G7
Winterborne Abbas 30–31 H5
Winterborne Came 30–31 H5
Winterborne Clenston 30–31 G6
Winterborne Herringstone 30–31 H5
Winterborne Houghton 30–31 G6
Winterborne Monkton 30–31 H5
Winterborne Kingston 30–31 G7
Winterborne St. Martin 30–31 H5
Winterborne Steepleton 30–31 H5
Winterborne Stickland 30–31 F6
Winterborne Tomson 30–31 G7
Winterborne Whitchurch 30–31 G6
Winterborne Zelstone 30–31 G7
Winterbourne Glouc. 42–43 A5
Winterbourne Berks. 46–47 A11
Winterbourne Bassett 46–47 A8
Winterbourne Dauntsey 46–47 D9
Winterbourne Earls 46–47 D9
Winterbourne Gunner 46–47 D9
Winterbourne Monkton 46–47 A8
Winterbourne Stoke 46–47 D8
Winteringham 146–147 J9
Wintersett 146–147 J5
Winterslow 46–47 D9
Winterton Lincs. 146–147 J9
Winterton Norfolk 118–119 H13
Winthorpe Notts. 130–131 E14
Winthorpe Lincs. 134–135 D6
Winton 150–151 B14
Wintringham 158–159 E9
Winwick Lancs. 126–127 B4
Winwick Northants. 90–91 B12
Winwick Hunts. 94–95 B3
Wirksworth 110–111 E10
Wirswall 106–107 F4
Wisbech 114–115 H5
Wisbech St. Mary 114–115 J5
Wisborough Green 50–51 F2
Wiseton 130–131 B13
Wishaw Warwick. 90–91 A9
Wishaw Lanark. 182–183 J4
Wisley 50–51 D2
Wispington 134–135 D3
Wissett 98–99 B12
Wistanstow 86–87 A3
Wistaston 106–107 E5
Wiston Pembroke 78–79 E6
Wiston Sussex 38–39 G3
Wistow Yorks. 142–143 H7
Wistow Leicester. 90–91 A13
Wistow Hunts. 94–95 B4
Wiswell 138–139 H14
Witcham 94–95 B5
Witchford 94–95 B6
Witchampton 34–35 F8
Witchingham 118–119 H10
Witham 74–75 G8
Witham Friary 42–43 D6
Witham on the Hill 114–115 H2
Withcall 134–135 C4
Withcote 110–111 J14
Witheridge 26–27 D12
Witherley 110–111 J10
Withernsea 146–147 H13
Withernwick 146–147 G11
Withersfield 94–95 D7
Witherslack 150–151 D11
Withington Shrop. 106–107 H4
Withington Hereford. 86–87 E4
Withington Glouc. 66–67 G8
Withiel 18–19 G6
Withiel Florey 26–27 B13
Withnell 138–139 J13
Withybrook 90–91 A11
Withycombe 26–27 A14
Withycombe Raleigh 26–27 F14
Withyham 50–51 E6
Withypool 26–27 B12
Witley 50–51 E2
Witnesham 98–99 D11
Witney 66–67 G10
Wittenham 66–67 H12
Wittering 114–115 J2
Wittersham 54–55 F9
Witton 118–119 G12
Witton 118–119 H12
Witton Gilbert 166–167 J11
Witton le Wear 166–167 K11
Wiveliscombe 42–43 E1
Wivelsfield 38–39 G5
Wivenhoe 74–75 F10
Wiveton 118–119 F10
Wix 74–75 F11
Wixford 90–91 D8
Wixoe 98–99 E7
Woburn 70–71 E1
Woburn Sands 70–71 E1
Woking 50–51 D2
Wokingham 46–47 A14
Woldingham 50–51 D5
Wold Newton Yorks. 158–159 E10
Wold Newton Lincs. 134–135 B4
Wolfhampcote 90–91 C12
Wolferlow 90–91 C5
Wolferton 114–115 G7
Wolford 66–67 E10
Wollaston Shrop. 106–107 H2
Wollaston Worcester. 86–87 A7
Wollaston Northants. 94–95 C1
Wolsingham 166–167 K10
Wolstanton 106–107 F6
Wolston 90–91 B11
Wolvercot 66–67 G11
Wolverhampton 106–107 J7
Wolverley 86–87 B6
Wolverton Warwick. 90–91 C9
Wolverton Bucks. 90–91 E14
Wolverton Hants. 46–47 B12
Wolves Newton 62–63 H3
Wolvey 90–91 A11
Wolviston 154–155 A6
Wombleton 158–159 D7
Wombourn 86–87 A7
Wombridge 106–107 H5
Wombwell 130–131 A11
Womenswold 54–55 D12
Womersley 142–143 J6
Wonastow 62–63 G4
Wonersh 50–51 E2
Wonston 46–47 D11
Wooburn 70–71 J1
Woodbastwick 118–119 H12
Woodborough Notts. 110–111 F12
Woodborough Wilts. 46–47 B9
Woodbridge 98–99 D12
Woodbury 26–27 F14
Woodchester 62–63 H6
Woodcote 106–107 H6
Woodcott 46–47 C11
Woodchurch Cheshire 126–127 C2
Woodchurch Kent 54–55 E9
Wood Dalling 118–119 G10
Woodditton 94–95 C7
Woodeaton 66–67 G12
Woodend 90–91 D12
Wood Enderby 134–135 D4
Woodford Cheshire 126–127 C7
Woodford Northants. 94–95 B2
Woodford Essex 70–71 J5
Woodford Wilts. 46–47 D9
Woodford Bridge 70–71 J5
Woodford Halse 90–91 D12
Wood Green 70–71 J4
Woodgreen 34–35 E9
Woodhall 134–135 D4
Woodhall Spa 134–135 D3
Woodham 154–155 A4
Woodham Ferrers 74–75 H8
Woodham Mortimer 74–75 H8
Woodham Walter 74–75 G8
Woodhorn 166–167 F12
Woodhouse 110–111 H12
Woodhurst 94–95 B4
Woodland Durham 154–155 A3
Woodland Devon. 22–23 G12
Woodlands 34–35 F8
Woodleigh 22–23 J11
Woodmancote Glouc. 66–67 F7
Woodmancote Sussex 38–39 G4
Woodmancott 46–47 C12
Woodmansterne 50–51 D4
Woodnesborough 54–55 D12
Woodnewton 94–95 A2
Wood Norton 118–119 G10
Woodplumpton 138–139 H12
Woodrising 118–119 J10
Woodsetts 130–131 C12
Woodsford 30–31 H6
Woodstock 66–67 G11
Woodthorpe 110–111 H12
Woodton 98–99 A12
Woodville 110–111 H10
Wood Walton 94–95 B4
Wookey 42–43 C4
Wool 30–31 H7
Woolacombe 26–27 A9
Woolaston 62–63 H4
Woolaton 110–111 F12
Woolavington 42–43 D3
Woolbeding 50–51 F1
Wooldale 130–131 A9
Woolfardisworthy 26–27 C8
Woolfardisworthy 26–27 D12
Woolhampton 46–47 B12
Woolhope 62–63 E5
Woolland 30–31 F6
Woolley 142–143 J5
Woolley 94–95 B3
Woolley 42–43 B6
Woolpit 98–99 C9
Woolstaston 106–107 J3
Woolsthorpe 114–115 G1
Woolston 34–35 F11
Woolstone Bucks. 94–95 E1
Woolstone Gloucester. 66–67 F7
Woolstone Berks. 66–67 J10
Woolverstone 98–99 E11
Woolverton 42–43 C6
Woolwich 50–51 B5
Woore 106–107 F5
Wootton Lincs. 146–147 J11
Wootton Stafford. 110–111 F8
Wootton Northants. 90–91 D14
Wootton Beds. 94–95 D2
Wootton Berks. 66–67 H11
Wootton Oxford. 66–67 F11
Wootton Kent 54–55 E11
Wootton Bassett 66–67 J8
Wootton Courtney 26–27 A13
Wootton Fitzpaine 30–31 G3
Wootton Glanville 30–31 F5
Wootton Rivers 46–47 B9
Wootton St. Lawrence 46–47 C12
Wootton Wawen 90–91 C9
Worcester 90–91 D6
Wordwell 98–99 B8
Wordsley 86–87 A7
Worfield 86–87 A6
Workington 150–151 A8
Worksop 130–131 C12
Worlaby 146–147 J10
Worlaby 134–135 C4
Worle 42–43 B3
Worleston 126–127 E5
Worlingham 98–99 A13
Worlington 94–95 B7
Worlingworth 98–99 C11
Wormbridge 62–63 F3
Wormegay 114–115 H7
Wormhill 130–131 D8
Wormingford 74–75 E9
Worminghall 66–67 G13
Wormington 66–67 E8
Wormleighton 90–91 D11
Wormley 70–71 H5
Wormshill 54–55 D9
Wormsley 86–87 D3
Worplesdon 50–51 D2
Worsall 154–155 B5
Worsborough 130–131 A10
Worsley 126–127 A6
Worstead 118–119 G12
Worston 138–139 G14
Worth Sussex 50–51 E4
Worth Kent 54–55 D12
Wortham 98–99 B10
Worthen 106–107 J2
Worthenbury 106–107 F3
Worthing 118–119 H10
Worthing 38–39 H3
Worthington 110–111 H11
Worth Matravers 34–35 J8
Worting 46–47 C12
Wortley 130–131 B10
Worton 46–47 B8
Wortwell 98–99 A12
Wothorpe 114–115 J2
Wotton 50–51 D3
Wotton under Edge 62–63 J6
Wotton Underwood 66–67 G13
Woughton on the Green 70–71 E1
Wouldham 54–55 C8
Wrabness 74–75 E11
Wragby 134–135 C3
Wramplingham 118–119 J10
Wrangle 114–115 E5
Wrawby 134–135 A2
Wraxall Somerset 42–43 A4
Wraxall Dorset 30–31 G4
Wreay 162–163 J5
Wrelton 158–159 D8
Wreningham 118–119 J11
Wrentham 98–99 A13
Wressell 146–147 H8
Wrestlingworth 94–95 D4
Wretton 114–115 J7
Wrexham 106–107 E2
Wribbenhall 86–87 B6
Wrightington 138–139 J12
Wrington 42–43 B4
Writhlington 42–43 C5
Writtle 70–71 G7
Wrockwardine 106–107 H5
Wrockwardine Wood 106–107 H5
Wroot 130–131 A13
Wrotham 50–51 D7
Wroughton 46–47 A9
Wroxall Warwick. 90–91 C9
Wroxall Isle of Wight 34–35 H12
Wroxeter 106–107 J4
Wroxham 118–119 H12
Wroxton 90–91 E11
Wyberton 114–115 F4
Wybunbury 106–107 E5
Wyck Rissington 66–67 F9
Wyddial 70–71 E5
Wye 54–55 E10
Wykeham 158–159 D10
Wyken 90–91 B10
Wyke Regis 30–31 J5
Wylam 166–167 H10
Wylye 46–47 D8
Wymeswold 110–111 G12
Wymington 94–95 C2
Wymondham Leicester. 114–115 H1
Wymondham Norfolk 118–119 J10
Wynford Eagle 30–31 G4
Wyrardisbury 50–51 B2
Wyre Piddle 90–91 D7
Wysall 110–111 G12
Wythall 90–91 B8
Wytham 66–67 G11
Wyton Yorks. 146–147 H11
Wyton Hunts. 94–95 B4
Wyverstone 98–99 C10

Y

Yafforth 154–155 C5
Yalding 54–55 D7
Yanworth 66–67 G8
Yapton 38–39 H2
Yarburgh 134–135 B4
Yarcombe 30–31 F2
Yardley 90–91 A9
Yardley Gobion 90–91 E14
Yardley Hastings 94–95 D1
Yarkhill 86–87 E5
Yarlington 42–43 E5
Yarm 154–155 B5
Yarmouth I. of Wight 34–35 H10
Yarnscombe 26–27 C10
Yarnton 66–67 G11
Yarpole 86–87 C3
Yarwell 114–115 J2
Yate 62–63 J5
Yatesbury 46–47 A8
Yattendon 46–47 A12
Yatton Hereford. 62–63 F5
Yatton Somerset 42–43 B3
Yatton Keynell 42–43 A7
Yaverland 34–35 H13
Yaxham 118–119 H10
Yaxley Suffolk 98–99 B11
Yaxley Huntingdon. 94–95 A3
Yazor 86–87 D3
Yeadon 142–143 G4
Yealand Conyers 150–151 E12
Yealand Redmayne 150–151 E12
Yealmpton 22–23 H10
Yearsley 154–155 E7
Yeaveley 110–111 F9
Yedingham 158–159 D9
Yelden 94–95 C2
Yelford 66–67 H10
Yelling 94–95 C4
Yelvertoft 90–91 B12
Yelverton Norfolk 118–119 J12
Yelverton Devon. 22–23 G10
Yeovil 30–31 F4
Yeovilton 30–31 E4
Yerbeston 58–59 E6
Yetminster 30–31 F5
Yiewsley 70–71 J2
Yokefleet 146–147 J9
York 142–143 F7
Yorkley 62–63 G5
Youlgreave 130–131 D9
Youlton 142–143 F6
Yoxall 110–111 H9
Yoxford 98–99 C13
Ysceifiog 126–127 D1
Ysgubor-y-coed 102–103 K11
Ysptty-Ifan 122–123 F12
Yspytty-Ystwyth 102–103 M11
Ystrad-Dyfodwg 58–59 F13
Ystradfellte 82–83 E13
Ystradgynlais 58–59 E12
Ystrad-Meurig 82–83 A11
Ystradowen 58–59 H13

Z

Zeal Monachorum 26–27 D11
Zeals 42–43 D6
Zennor 18–19 K1